Thread

by
Alicia Brady
with
Debbie Bell

RHIZOME
PUBLISHING

Pueblo, Colorado

Thread
Copyright © 2012 by Alicia Brady
Published by Rhizome Publishing

Cover design by Mathias Valdez of LastLeaf Printing
lastleafprinting.com

Cover photo by Ed Flores

RHIZOME PUBLISHING
Rhizome Publishing, LLC
120 S Union
Pueblo, Colorado 81003

facebook.com/rhizomepublishing
rhizomepublishing.com
On Twitter: @rhizomepub

Press inquiries: *publicity@rhizomepub.com*

Printed in the United States of America
First Printing: September 2012

ISBN 13: 978-1-61943-009-9

For those who prayed, believed, fought, and had mighty faith. You gave me the courage to persevere! Thank you.

May you see that the good can outweigh the bad... if we allow it to.

Blessings

Alicia

I would like to express my gratitude to the many people who walked with me through this journey. There are too many people to list them all, but please know that I am thankful for each and every one of you. I would like to say a special thank you to:

- The University of Arizona faculty, especially the School of Dance, for standing by me and helping me graduate from the school of my dreams.

- The community of Tucson, including the Ronald McDonald House, for your many acts of kindness and comfort for my family and myself.

- The community of Cañon City, Colorado and the wonderful people of the Evangelical Free Church for rallying around my family and me as we struggled through this ordeal.

- To all of my dance family, now all over the world, for helping me regain my passion and reason for dancing.

- To all my doctors for doing "your job" even when the odds were stacked against me. Thank you for fighting for me.

- To the hundreds of prayer warriors, all over the world. Sorry we woke you up in the middle of the night so many times.

- To those in prison ministry and the ones we minister to, for bringing healing to my soul.

- To my close friends, you know who you are, for being there for me as I cried, complained, hurt and healed. I love you all.

- To Jonathan and Debbie for taking this journey of writing with me. Thank you for sharing your gifts, I couldn't have done it without you.

- To my family for loving me and supporting me in some very dark, difficult days. It is your unconditional love that carried me through.

- To my Dad and Mom, your gracious and thankful hearts helped me see the light at the end of the tunnel. Words cannot express what you have done for me. I am proud to be your daughter.

- To my Lord and Savior, Jesus Christ, for not only saving me, but for sparing my life. I am who I am because of this experience, and now, I wouldn't change it for anything.

Prologue

"You intended to harm me, but God intended it for good to accomplish what is now being done." -Gen. 50:20

by Dena Brady

Every parent dreads receiving a life-altering phone call in the middle of the night. My parents received that call at 3 a.m. Sunday, October 12, 2008, dragging them from deep sleep.

My mom remembers it this way:

I was a little disoriented as I stumbled into the living room to answer. I figured it was probably a prank call. Who else calls at 3 a.m.? I picked up the phone and answered, and a man on the other end asked if I was Deanna Braddy. He didn't even know my name, more confirmation it was a prank call. I told him I was Dena Brady, and then waited for a string of foul words or offensive comments. Instead, I listened as a very calm voice identified itself as David from University Medical Center in Tucson, Arizona.

My first thought was Alicia had been in a car accident. I began shaking and my entire world narrowed to the distant voice on the other end of the line. Nothing could prepare me for what I heard next. The very calm voice said, "Alicia wanted me to call you."

I thought, "That's good, right? I mean, obviously, she's alive and she's conscious. It can't be too bad, can it?" Then he told me there had been an accident… and my daughter had been shot. Time stood still before I dimly heard a voice screaming and vaguely wondered who it was. Then I realized it was me.

My screams of, "Oh, my God! Oh, my God! Oh, my God! What happened?" awoke my husband, Randy, and he came running from the bedroom. I couldn't answer him because I, usually the calm one, was hysterical. I collapsed into a chair and tried to make sense of what Chaplin David was saying. He didn't know any details about the shooting, but that Alicia was conscious and he would try to get a phone to her so we could talk to her before she went into surgery. He hung up with the promise to call back in just a couple of minutes.

Randy was frantic, yelling at me, "What's going on? What happened?"

Through sobs I answered, "Our daughter. Alicia's been shot." His feet shot out from underneath him as he crumpled into another chair, saying, "Oh, no! Oh, no!"

Our hands found each other's and we grasped tightly, praying she would be okay, waiting for the phone to ring. After an eternity, it did. On the other end, David handed the phone to Alicia. Randy picked up an extension, so we both got to hear her. I will never forget her first words: "Hi, Mommy." To this day they are the most comforting words ever spoken to me. I was under the false impression that if she was conscious and could talk, then she must not be badly hurt. Without the string of miracles that followed, those would have been the last two words I ever heard from her.

I don't remember what else we said, but I know she told us she was doing okay and they were taking her into surgery. We told her we loved her and would be there as soon as we could get there – but it's a long way from Cañon City, Colorado, to Tucson, Arizona. We said goodbye through frantic tears, not knowing if we would ever see our precious child alive again.

Chapter One

What lies behind us and what lies before us are small matters compared to what lies within us –Ralph Waldo Emerson

I WAS BORN AND RAISED IN CAÑON City, a small town nestled among the foothills in the center of Colorado. The population of Cañon is a little over fifteen-thousand with ninety-three percent Caucasian. I lived a very sheltered life and always felt safe and secure. We left our cars and homes unlocked, never fearing violence. It was as though we lived in a bubble; everyone knew each other and reached out a helping hand when needed.

As a sixth generation Coloradoan I, along with my family, cherished the beautiful Rocky Mountains and the many enjoyable outdoor activities. Some of my best memories with my family are of camping, hiking, skiing, horseback riding, and swimming in lakes. My parents, Randy and Dena, taught me what was important while growing up. They placed value on the things we needed, not the things we wanted – on the things that brought us joy, not the things society said we needed to have. My parents are such hard, honest workers. They work and live their lives with integrity. We never had new cars, a huge house, or went on big shopping sprees. We never needed those things.

I was blessed with three siblings. My two older brothers Sean and Chris, and younger sister Kendra and I were a part of each others' lives. Yeah, we did not always get along. I would say it was most likely the boys' fault, and they would say the opposite, but we loved each other, and would do anything for one another. As we grew up we supported one another and learned to appreciate how blessed we were. The four of us were happy and believed we were complete, but another blessing came our way when I was a junior in high school.

The day before my Junior Prom, my parents received a telephone call about a newborn cousin whose parents were unable to care for her. My mom asked my dad if our family could take her in. My dad simply said yes, and our church rallied around us. Mom made one phone call and her friends held a baby shower for her the very next day. We received everything we needed. One phone call and we were ready for baby Emma. My parents already had children who were almost grown – we were 21, 18, 17, and 15 years old. They were about to be empty nesters, yet they took in a newborn baby. Of course, Emma has been the biggest blessing to all of us! We adopted her six months later, and now I can't imagine life without her.

I was also lucky enough to grow up knowing all of my cousins, aunts, uncles, grandparents, and even some of my second cousins, great-uncles, great-aunts, and great-grandparents. One of my favorite memories with my cousins on my dad's side was "grandkid night." All eleven of us would go to my grandparents' house and have a big supper. Then we would watch movies, play games and the older kids would read to the younger ones. We piled into beds and in sleeping bags on the floor for the night. The next morning, my grandma would make a giant breakfast: bacon, sausage, eggs, hash browns, toast, biscuits and gravy, pancakes, and anything else we wanted. I am a bacon lover, so she would make sure there was an entire pound, just for me. Family time was cherished.

I had a serious competitive streak as a child. My thirst for competition was as natural as drawing breath. I remember playing dodge ball – the game that so many kids grew up hating – with an intensity that surprised even my teacher, Mrs. Hanenberg. When most girls were trying to hide in the back, I was the one running up to the line and grabbing the balls, chucking them at the other kids. In fourth grade, we did a fitness test where we would take turns holding a chin-up position on a bar. I waited until the other girls had given it their best shot, and then I would take my turn last and hold it one second longer, even if my skinny little arms felt like they were about to give out! I loved the idea of challenging myself.

Not only was I competitive, but I was very strong willed as a child. This is not surprising because I come from a long line of strong willed women, just ask any of the men in my family. Although my strong personality challenged my parents, it was the thing made me try something over and over again until I got it perfect. That character trait grew into a tenacity that would later keep me alive.

My parents tried hard to find appropriate avenues to channel my youthful passion. They enrolled me in a local gymnastics studio, and I simply loved it! It seemed as though I had found my calling; however, an injury forced an early retirement.

Next my mom started looking for a dance studio that suited my personality. She quickly learned the difference between a "competition" studio and a "concert" studio. Competition studios focus more on tricks (leaps and turns) and can cost thousands of dollars in costume and competition fees. Concert studios focus more on technique and performance quality, adapting to all various styles of dance. There are both types for a reason, and some fit into one type better than the other, but I was fortunate to end up in a concert studio!

My teacher, Zetta Alderman, put me in a beginners' combination class to start. In just a matter of weeks, she asked me to jump to ballet and jazz – she wanted me in the Christmas show. When the time came for me to actually take the class, I was terrified. This was a new feeling for me – nothing scared me! But I just didn't want to go. So Zetta bribed me... with a piece of chewing gum. Wrigley's Big Red. That stick of gum changed my life.

That simple beginning was the start of my life's work. At the end of dance class, mom would almost have to pull me out of the studio because I wanted to stay. I always wanted to go back for more because dancing was such a joy! It was my passion. I can't even say exactly when I fell in love with it – it just happened, and I knew that it was my life's ambition.

Although dance kept me very busy, I valued the time I spent with my friends. They kept me grounded and, many times, pointed out to me there were other things in the world besides dance. On the weekends we would hang out together at Sonic, cruise Main Street (which is something my parents and grandparents used to do), watch movies at friends' houses, or just sit around and talk. I know, lame. But that's what you do in a small town that has one bowling alley and one theater. The company of great friends kept us all out of trouble and high school was an unforgettable time. I was also involved in many extra-curricular activities, including National Honor Society, the dance team and the vocal music department.

Sunday mornings were spent in church from the time I was a baby, clear through high school. I was raised in faith – the thread of Christianity woven intricately into the brilliant tapestry of my life. We went to the Evangelical Free Church every Sunday and regularly attended Sunday School, joined Awanas and lived a conservative life. God was a part of everyday conversations and I was surrounded by people of faith. It was what I knew.

I believe I was born to dance. It was a gift that I acknowledged and cherished from my youth. My childhood gave me all the tools I would need to fulfill my dream. Looking back, I realize my family supported my every move. I knew what I wanted to do at an early age and was fortunate enough to have the family support and the personal drive to meet the challenges. I now believe God prepared me for the biggest ordeal of all, a stray bullet that found its way to me.

Chapter 2

*There is a way that seems right to a man, but in the end it
leads to death. Proverbs 14:12*

an interview with Dez Freemore

I HAD A FUN, EXCITING CHILDHOOD, PRETTY much like every
other kid in the neighborhood. As a young child my mom, sister,
brother, and I lived with my grandmother and grandfather. My
sister is two years older than me and my brother is three years
younger. All of us have different dads. My aunt lived with us too,
with her kids. Looking back, it was pretty crowded in that little
house, but that stuff don't matter as a kid.

My mother is everything to me and so most of my friends consider me a "momma's boy." She was the main person that raised
me to be the man I am today. She always took good care of me
and gave me everything I needed. She worked hard, sometimes
at two or three jobs, to make enough money for us to survive.
She also gave me a lot of the freedom I wanted as a teenager. She
knew it was important for me to just be who I was, make my own
decisions, and make my own way in the world. We are very close,
"best friends", and I feel comfortable telling her anything. Well,
most anything; I still remember in the back of my head that she
my mother.

I don't know my real father. I mean, I know who he is, but not as a person. He wasn't ready to be saddled with a kid when I came along, so he's never been a part of my life. That don't bug me none because I had other great men in my life who showed me how to be a man. My grandfather was the first man in my life. We lived with him when I was little and he did as much as he could to help raise me. I remember having lots of fun with him and he always had time to do things with me. I learned things like religion, hard work, how to fix things around the house or on cars. I am the first grandson so we have a very close bond.

I have a stepfather who also helped mold me into a man but is very different from my grandfather. He educated me on the things you need to survive in this world. Things like sports, how to fight, becoming a leader and not a follower. He showed me how to get money when I needed it and always protect yourself and family by any means. He taught me that family is most important and you step up and don't let no one trash your family. My stepdad sold crack, smoke weed and drink alcohol, but he would always tell me to never do the stuff. Of course, I was just like every other kid in the neighborhood and did it anyway. I was 11 the first time I smoke weed. My stepfather and I did a lot of stuff together and have a very close relationship. He is locked up in prison right now, but I still keep in touch and write him as much as I can.

Going to school was mandatory in my house. My mom knew that an education was important. She never got one and that's why she has to work so hard; she wants better for me. My mom never forced me to get straight A's but I couldn't get lower than a D. As long as I passed, she was pretty cool. Being late for school or not going wasn't allowed because I was expected to do my best. My mother also kept me in sports: soccer, basketball and football. She knew I needed stuff to do besides just hang. I got pretty good at that stuff and gained my respect from the neighborhood.

I was pretty much "born" into the gang because my stepfather is deeply involved in the gang activity going on. He is a leader in the community so everyone just accepted me in. It is my right. Even though other people around consider us gangbangers, we didn't really look at it like that. It was just the guys we knew that lived in the same neighborhood. Because I was living in the neighborhood since day one, I wasn't "jumped in" to the gang or didn't have to deal with any type of initiation. I witness initiations of people who moved into the neighborhood and wanted to be a part, but I didn't have to do it myself.

We had a lot of fun times together; summer was the best. We would get into a lot of stuff like go to the neighborhood pool, chase girls, get into fights, play ball, or did whatever we wanted. I had to check in every day but didn't have a curfew, so stayed out as late as I wanted.

At school, my neighborhood was represented by just a few of us. Most of the other minority students from lower living were in a rival gang, from a different neighborhood. We would talk crap to each other or mind our own business if we would run into each other during passing periods or at lunch. Sometimes we get into a fight here and there when the other gang would talk crap or put us to the test to see how tough we were. Not a big deal, it was just the way we did. I learned to use my fists and gained a lot of respect cause I was good at it.

My stepfather taught me two very important things at a young age. One was to go with your gut feeling and trust no one. Never. I didn't trust any of the other members that I grew up with or that I knew as I got older. The person you think is your friend today may stab you in the back tomorrow. I just learned how to hold my own as a person. There were a few members that was well respected that I was cool with. Even with them I only give or show my trust to a certain point. The other thing he taught me was that if you're gonna do something, do it by yourself. If you in it with others and the heat comes, they get scared and give it up, you pay the price. Either that or they decide you owe them to keep their mouths shut. If you alone, you don't have to worry about anyone snitching or having their hands out.

I have been around guns all my life. I understand at a young age the good and bad of having a gun. I didn't own a weapon when I was young or as a teenager, but I knew where and how to get one if I felt I needed it. I have guns now but not for gangbanging, more for to protect myself and my family. My stepdad taught me how to handle a gun, not to use on people, but to have if I needed it. Now I carry a revolver wherever I go. You never know what the other person might have or what they might do. I know that if I pull it out, I better be ready to use it.

I been shot at or heard shots so many times I can't count them. It happens at homes, parking lots, the parks, in my neighborhood. Being shot at is a wild experience because you never know when the shooter will stop and you don't know where the bullets are going. I just remember getting out of the way, hitting the ground, running away. Sometimes I thought about running to my strap (gun) so I can bust (shoot) back or make sure anyone I am with didn't get hit. I've had some close calls but I am really blessed that I am still alive.

I actually got shot when I was a teenager. We was all hanging out in the neighborhood, playing ball, chasing girls, etc. Two old school cars drive by and the gangsters in the cars was yelling out their neighborhood and throwing up their sign. So of course we began to yell out our set and throw up our signs as well. They did their thang and we did our thang and then they left. Well, a few minutes later we see the same two cars come back and some of us were throwing up our set. I really didn't pay no mind until I started hearing shots come from the cars. My first response was to RUN. My friend and I was running and then I just hit the ground. My friend yelled, "Get up!" I got back up and was running again because I was really pumped up, but something very hot was cooking inside my leg. My leg went dead and I just went back down, holding it. I will never forget the feeling, my leg was numb, but I could feel burning. There was also blood coming out. That's when I realized I was hit. It was just a bullet from a .22 and it didn't do much damage. I had it taken out at the hospital and was back to normal in a couple of days.

Some of my gang weren't so lucky that night. Gangbanging is just the way life is and you kinda get used to fighting, shootings and stabbings. You never get used to watching your friends die and you know that you gotta go back out there and make it right. Not the easiest life, but the one I know and know how to survive in.

I never shot anyone but I have been in a lot of fights. I started fighting as a teen and got better and better at it. I never tried to hurt someone until they died, but wanted to knock them out or make them quit. I always set my mind to bomb first because the other person wanted to hurt me. If I was fighting in front of my peers I would really try to knock the person out. I'm fighting to gain more respect and build up my status in everyone eyes that was watching. The more I fought, the better I got at it, and the more respect I have. Street fighting is not like a boxing ring. There are no rules and no referee. You better know your stuff.

When people see a gang, it is viewed as a problem or a negative thing. That just not so. Some neighborhoods have positive things like parties or sports. They try to support the local kids and make a difference for them and their families. You see gangs every day in America, so what's the deal. Colleges have gangs. The sororities and fraternities wear colors; have secret handshakes, initiations and hand signs. Course the largest gang in America is the police. They have the power to do whatever they want. Police have guns, wear colors, earn stripes, and talk in code. They also retaliate when one of their members dies in the line of duty. They just like any other gang. A gang is just something that you was born and raised around or you were new to the neighborhood and are learning how to adapt. It isn't "bad," it's just another way of living.

Chapter Three

One is born to be a dancer. No one teacher can work miracles, nor will years of training make a good dancer of an untalented pupil. One may be able to acquire a certain technical facility, but no one can acquire an exceptional talent. I have never prided myself on having an unusually gifted pupil. A Pavlova is no one's pupil but God's– George Balanchine

STARTING COLLEGE WAS A WHOLE NEW LIFE for me, one I'd been dreaming about for years. I could only hope the actual experience would live up to the picture I had painted in my mind.

That picture began to form when I was just in third grade. Other dancers from my studio were performing in a concert at the Arizona Jazz Dance Showcase at the University of Arizona in Tucson. Students ranged in age from 12 through college. I was only nine years old, but I was dancing in a piece at the concert to replace a girl who had broken her foot. That meant I also was allowed to attend the workshops and Master Classes taught by university professors and famous guest choreographers. My mom was there with me.

"It was truly amazing to watch Alicia," mom said. "Here were students 12 years old through college, and right in the middle of them was this tiny nine-year-old girl!"

Obviously, I didn't have the same level of technique that some of the others had, but I worked so hard to get all of the choreography just right, and kept up with all the other older kids as best as I could.

"I remember sitting there crying as I watched her," mom said. "It was hard to believe that remarkable child was mine."

On my end, I was simply enveloped by the world of dance. It folded its alluring arms around me and whispered to every fiber of my being. For the first time, the world of dance opened up to me and I saw what I could do with it. I knew then and there I wanted to attend the University of Arizona as a dance major to become a professional dancer. Some of the same professors I learned from when I was nine years old would later on become my college professors and play a major role in my life.

In July of 2006, just a couple of months after high school graduation, my mom and both my sisters went with me to the University of Arizona for freshman orientation. Kendra babysat Emma at the hotel, while mom and I sat through different sessions about college life. I vaguely remember one of them was on safety. Mom took it much more seriously than I did.

"They talked about never walking around campus on your own after dark; always have a buddy with you," mom remembers. "The university even had an on-campus transportation system. You could call for someone to pick you up between the hours of 6 and 11 p.m. and take you back to your dorm. They called it Safe Ride. I felt good about that, because I knew Alicia would have late hours due to rehearsals."

I, on the other hand, didn't pay much attention. Rarely did I use Safe Ride. I did not see the point. I was too excited to be on campus at the very university that represented my dancing future. I was so naïve. Late at night, I walked places by myself or with other girls and never thought anything of it, like any college girl does. I was completely unaware of the danger. What could happen to me? At that age you think you are invincible. You can ask anyone around that age, and they all think the same way. Sure, I had been told, but I didn't really pay attention. I was lucky, because nothing ever happened to me on campus. It wasn't even that the campus was that unsafe; I was a young woman. That in itself made it unsafe.

August finally arrived and, with it, the chance for me to attend college! My parents drove me to Tucson and helped move me into the dorms. It was hard to drive away from my childhood home, my beloved siblings, and my warm little community, but the UofA awaited me almost eight hundred miles away.

When we got there, I realized my dorm, Manzanita Mohave, housed a lot of the fine arts students including about ninety percent of the other dancers. I soon met my roommate, who was from Canada and seemed like a very sweet girl. She ended up being a great friend, and easy to live with. This was a huge relief, because we have all heard the horror stories about college roommates, or any roommate for that matter. Our room was small, just like any dorm, but I had so much stuff! I've never been a light packer, and my mom and dad thought we would never get it all into my room. It took us a couple of days, but we finally packed it all in there.

The time had arrived to say goodbye to my parents. Of course I was excited to be a "big girl" and live away on my own, but it was hard to let go of that final hug and watch them drive away. I was so happy about the changes in my life, but I knew both my parents had mixed emotions about me leaving. I was their first girl, and their first child to leave the state for college.

I knew they were proud and thrilled for me. They didn't invest all that time and money because they didn't believe in me. They didn't drive me eight hundred miles to a school where they thought I wouldn't be able to thrive and be that best that I could be, and come closer to reaching my dreams, but that still doesn't make it any easier to let your little girl go. Here I was, at the school of my dreams, beginning the next chapter of my life. They knew I would do remarkably well, because they saw to it I had all the skills to meet my goals.

Even as a little girl in elementary school, I started to learn how to be a leader and how to prioritize. My mom even joked with my kindergarten teacher that if she ever had a really bad day, I could run the class for her. I seemed to love my early schoolwork and I was very organized, even in first grade. I used to come home from school, pull papers out of my backpack and say, "Mommy, here are the things you need to read." I did my best to keep those grades up even in elementary school, made sure to make straight A's, and that was with piano lessons, band, student council, Awana, soccer, and of course dance. At that time, I was dancing four days a week for about three hours each day. Maybe some of my ambition had to do with my mom teaching at my elementary school or me being a "goodie goodie," but most of all I just worked hard at everything I did.

In middle school I was in band and student council and played volleyball, basketball and ran track. I worked hard to stay strong in academics, and stayed involved with other student activities like student council. I know we all look back now and think, "Elementary and middle school? Not hard." But when you are a 13 or 14 year old... it IS hard!

Then came high school. High school is a stressful time in any teenager's life for many different reasons. Some of my classes included an incredible amount of work, but I always managed to get my assignments finished on time if not before. I made certain to always meet my deadlines and never used my schedule as an excuse. I never turned in a late paper, although sometimes it was close!

During my junior year of high school I spent my lunch time in the school library with my friend Sarah Ary. We packed our lunches to eat while we did our homework. I remember taking a chemistry class that year. I knew I wouldn't have the time to get any of it done later, so I had to do it at lunch. She is still one of my closest friends. We look back and talk about how disciplined we were for seventeen year olds. No one else was eating their lunch in the library with us!

I managed to keep up academically while also being involved in many extra-curricular activities, including National Honor Society. Of course, one of my favorite curricular activities was the Cañon City High School Dance Team, where I danced all four years. It was one of the few ways I was able to stay involved because my busy schedule didn't allow time for much else. Because I had been dancing for so long, I did a lot of the choreography for the team and taught the other girls several days a week. My sophomore, junior and senior years, I was captain of the team – our sponsor thought I had a lot to add to the mix, so she made it work with my in and out schedule.

I also participated in the school's vocal music department throughout high school. Our director, Todd Albrecht, allowed Kim Gair and I to help choreograph songs, teach the choreography and clean up the pieces for performances. It took a lot of outside time to prepare, and we met with "Mr. A" during lunch and sometimes on weekends. The different choirs had a very demanding performance schedule throughout the year, including fundraisers and a three-day competition trip. Mr. A and I developed a very special relationship, which became very evident by all the help he gave me later on.

Throughout the years, I understood that I was making sacrifices for my dance. I missed a lot through my high school years, but I still did my level best to have a life outside of dance. I attended Homecoming dances, football games, spring dances, Prom, basketball games and more. I had friends from all different circles in high school. I would like to believe I was well accepted and liked by other students. I did my best to keep a cheerful nature at school.

My mom wears her heart on her sleeve and I knew she was heartbroken. She kissed me goodbye and walked away, knowing that she was forever leaving the little girl she had known for the last nineteen years. I was now a young woman, branching out on my own. Our relationship was forever changed. It was a good change, progressive, as it should be. But still… I know my mom felt intense sorrow.

Fortunately, my parents picked up my enthusiasm and shared the excitement with me. I called home almost every evening, usually walking home after rehearsals – alone, after dark – to share my day. I talked of juggling classes, homework, rehearsals, shows, social life and more. Of course, I did become homesick. Nothing in Tucson was familiar to me. Everything was new, which was also the exciting part. Sometimes I'd call home crying because I wanted to be there if even for a few days. But I lived 800 miles away, and it wasn't possible.

So I did my best to move along with my new life. I established who I was in the new environment, and immersed myself in dance and with that came some new, lifelong friends. As a freshman I bonded with all of the other dancers there, because we had most of our classes together whether they were dance or academic. As dancers, we connect with one another in a distinct and unique way that is different from the average person. We were all there as dancers. We are all artists. Despite what some may think, and what social media has now turned it into, we don't dance to be sexual or even to stay in shape. We dance for the sake of movement. It is a form of art, a form of expression. There is something incredibly special about dancing and moving with the people that you care about and love.

College life is different for dancers. Unlike growing up and going to school during the day, and then heading to dance at night, I spent all of my day dancing! I was dancing for my degree. How many people can say they get to wake up and do what they love every day? I did.

A typical day for me would start with a modern dance class. The first year of college is a huge change for anyone. I loved this modern class because this time together allowed us not only to grow as dancers and movers, but as people and friends. We were experiencing the same life changes, and we were so blessed to be with each other. This was the time when "the class" became "our class." This was the time when we grew as movers and as humans. I believe it has to do with not only the physical aspect of dance, but the openly emotional element, too. When we dance, we hold nothing back – our movement expresses pain, sadness, trauma, happiness, joy, shame, and so much more. Every UofA dance major is dedicated and serious about their dance training, and we knew to hold nothing back even if that means exposing the deepest part of us. Like the great modern dancer Martha Graham famously said, "Movement never lies."

After modern class I would go to an academic. After that I would head back to the dance building for ballet, and then back to another academic. Around 3:30 we would have rehearsals. These were the rehearsals we would have, to learn the choreography for all of our shows. A typical day for a dancer at the UofA would be from 9 in the morning to 7 at night – or longer. But we knew that it was a privilege to be there, not a right. We all soaked in as much information and knowledge as we could.

I was used to a crazy schedule. In high school we got out at 2:45 each afternoon, and I immediately went to dance team from 2:50 to 3:30. We were picked up at the high school at 3:30 for the hour-and-a-half drive to Colorado Springs. Dance started at 5, and we usually pulled up just as class began. We danced until 9 and then hopped back in the car to head home, arriving at 10:30. I usually took a nap on the way up and then did homework in the car as we drove home. In the darkness, I wore a headlamp so I could see my studies. Kim and I called them our homework headlamps!

I was always exhausted by the time we arrived home, but I had learned at an early age that in the cutthroat world of dance, there would always be someone better than me. There would always be another white, brown-hair, brown-eyed girl fighting for the same spot that I was. So, I did everything I could to be my best. I knew I couldn't be better than everyone, so I did my best to be the best that I could be. Driving an hour and a half each way, and doing homework in the car were just part of it.

After getting home at 10:30 I'd jump in the shower, finish any homework I had left and then, finally, get in bed. I'd be up at 6 the next morning to do it all over again. But don't let my busy schedule fool you; I was like any other teenager in the morning. Grumpy! I was not a happy camper getting my butt out of bed in the morning, but I still got up. I rarely woke up with a smile on my face. Most of the time I woke up to my dad making coffee a lot louder than the average person – humming, singing, trying to play to the piano, or doing all of this at the same time. Seriously. Ask any of my siblings. Who knows why he needed his vocal cords warmed up in the early morning!

During concert preparation, I had to be at the studio seven days a week, adding four to six hours of dancing on Saturday and another five hours on Sunday. Not many parents would do what mine did; they always believed in me and never questioned my desire and determination. Day after day, week after week, month after month and year after year I continued this grueling schedule. But it was my choice, so I never complained. Instead, I worked proactively to fit every piece of my life together.

Dance spilled over into every aspect of my life – eating right, staying healthy, keeping in top shape. Clearly, I was created with a strong will and was able to use that to my advantage. I had spent years and years in training to make my body as resilient and strong as possible. I now believe God was preparing me for what was to come. Not yet knowing the full picture, I was willing to make sacrifices for my life's dream of dancing and traveling the world.

And now, I was in my element! Every moment, I was surrounded by people who had worked for this opportunity their entire lives – just like I had. I had found my second family in this tightly-knit dance program. The University of Arizona School of Dance is ranked number three in the nation. It is known for its well rounded program in ballet, modern, and jazz. There are only twenty-five to thirty dance majors accepted into the program every year. Our freshman year most of us did not have our cars; we all lived on campus and ended up spending nearly every waking moment together. Our class was very rare, because that closeness has carried through the years. Our closeness played a huge role in what would come later and how it affected everyone. Even today, we are all there for each other and always will be.

Blair Jimison, another freshman dancer, captured our spirit perfectly:

"As time progressed, our small group of out-of-towners in pink ballet tights became a family," Blair said. "We loved to dance, we loved the Tucson sun and, most importantly, we loved each other. As we watched the other classes, above us and below, fight over coveted roles when it came to casting, our family collective shared in each other's successes – and pain."

My freshman year I found some of the best friends I have ever had, two in particular. Moira Docherty roomed right across the hall from me and Sarah Turturro was a floor above us. The three of us ended up sharing an off-campus apartment starting our sophomore year.

My first impression of Moira was that she was a snob, but I came to realize I was a bit jealous because she is tall, thin, blonde and absolutely gorgeous! What I thought was aloofness and conceit turned out to be her natural shyness. We now laugh at how wrong first impressions are, because I've told her many times what I first thought of her. We started spending time together and, although it took us awhile to open up to one another, I quickly saw she was one of the kindest and most thoughtful people I had ever met. By the time we left school for Thanksgiving break that first semester, I already considered her to be one of my best friends.

We spent all of our time together, not only dancing or hanging out and watching movies or going out, but just sitting and talking to each other for hours about anything and everything. There are very few people that I have ever had that kind of connection with. I looked forward to every moment we got to spend together. As that new-friend shyness faded, we slowly peeled one another back layer by layer; we got to know each other on several levels. We shared everything from the deepest parts of our personalities to the most fun, light-hearted levels. I had the best times of my life with that girl!

Most dancers will tell you we are a different breed. We are. We have to find friends that are the right fit for us. Just like a dance shoe there is always one that will make us most comfortable, the one that will bring out the best in us or make us be our best. And that is Moira for me. I think the reason why our friendship was able to last through everything was because of the foundation we built in the beginning. That foundation was built on trust.

And then there was Sarah. I met her in class one day, where we briefly said "Hi" to each other. The first time we really spoke was one night at dinner – yes, all us dancers ate every meal together, too. I remember sitting right across from her and again thinking how shy she was. I guess I attract shy people, which is funny because I do not consider myself a shy person. We slowly started hanging out together.

There are very few people who can make me laugh like Sarah can. Just as with Moira, Sarah and I also connected right away. Some of the best memories I have are walking with Sarah on campus and laughing about who knows what; I just remember laughing. There was a little store on campus called the U-Mart, where we always went together after rehearsal to get these amazing cookies. The same Asian guy was working every day at that time, so he got to know us. One day I came in and Sarah wasn't with me, so he asked in his cute accent, "Where your tweeeen at?" Of course he knew we weren't really twins, but it shows how much time we spent together.

One night the three of us decided to hang out together, and from then on we were inseparable. I spent every moment I had with those two girls. Our trio was complete and undividable.

Almost from the beginning of our freshman year, all the other dancers knew to include all three of us because we were always together. Instead of saying, "What are you doing tonight, Alicia?" it became, "What are SarahAliciaMoira doing tonight?" Just like that, all one word, in that order.

The threads of our lives intertwined to become as one. We were a part of a very rare group who stayed roommates throughout all of college. Our friendship was built on hours, days, and weeks of getting to know each other. We didn't just go out and party. We were bonded together in a way that could not be broken, even after circumstances literally tore us apart. It is not a coincidence that this was the only school I had applied to and that these were the girls who became my best friends. They are also strong Christians, and I know the Lord pulled our lives together so we would be a source to each other when the time would come to lift each other up and keep each other strong.

Overall, my freshman year went pretty much as expected. I was in several shows and, although my family couldn't attend any of them, I was able to send them the performances on DVD. Toward the end of the year, something went wrong with my body. Again.

Thread

Throughout my childhood, I wasn't necessarily prone to injuries, but they seemed to come my way just because of my level of activity. When I was four, I was climbing on a wall of bricks and fell and hit my forehead. It happened so fast I didn't have time to put my hands out to catch myself. I got up, walked to my mom, and passed out at her feet. Later she told me that she had been talking about how dramatic her kids were. She scooped me up in her arms and saw a golf ball-sized hematoma right between my eyes, scaring her to death. It took six full weeks for all that blood to dissipate; a long time for my mom to endure the stares of others who assumed that she did something to me. Only those who knew me well understood I was responsible for my own injuries.

Right after that I started preschool. My daycare provider noticed how tired I seemed to be, but my parents assumed it was just taking me awhile to adjust to my new school schedule. After a few weeks, they realized it was more than a different schedule – something was wrong. I would seem fine and then suddenly collapse and claim to be unable to even walk. Other days I complained about my tummy seriously hurting. It took three months, two or three trips to the emergency room and several doctor visits to discover that I had mono, at age five. It was another three to four months before I really began to feel like myself again. My energy and enthusiasm for life slowly returned.

I had started gymnastics classes around age four. About a year later I was practicing somersaults on the balance beam. My coach stepped back and told me to try it on my own. I did a successful somersault but then fell off the beam, breaking my left arm in the process. I remember landing on it twisting behind my back and hearing it snap; then, it bounced back into place.

Always trying to be in command, even as a five year old, I started yelling at everyone, telling them what to do. I told them to call my parents, like they might not have thought of it themselves. Turned out my arm was dislocated and my elbow was fractured – a piece of the bone had completely broken off . It ended up being a huge injury, and my first introduction to serious bodily damage.

That injury introduced me to the operating room, where my

elbow was pinned back together. My arm was in a cast for awhile, and when it finally came off, I had no use of my left hand. I couldn't grasp or lift things; all the small muscles in the palm of my hand atrophied and it became flat, with curved fingers. One day I asked my mom, "Mommy, what does handicapped mean?" She didn't say it, but her heart broke as she thought, *It's what you are now.*

Eventually, I had to undergo another surgery to reroute the nerve. About eight months after the accident, I had full use of my hand again – it was weaker than my right hand, but at least it worked. I spent years working to regain what I lost. My broken elbow forced an early retirement from gymnastics.

My next physical hurdle was a very odd one. I was in fourth grade and one Sunday right before Christmas complained that my foot hurt and was tingling. Within a few hours, I couldn't even walk. The next day, I went to my pediatrician, who sent me to an orthopedic doctor. They ran several tests – blood work, x-rays, bone scan, Doppler study. He had no idea what had caused it, but all the soft tissue in my foot and ankle had been affected. Regardless of the cause, I needed rehabilitation and started therapy several days a week. It took about five weeks before I could walk again, and the doctor finally decided it had been a spider bite although no one ever saw an entrance puncture. Of course, my dancing routine was seriously affected and I had to work very hard to get back to where I was before it happened.

I was hitting my stride as a dancer but was slowed again when I was fourteen and fell during class; my footing came out from underneath me as I was doing an *sauté arabesque*. I landed hard on the front of my body, but managed to jerk my head up so I didn't hit my face, which whipped my neck back. As a dancer you know you are going to fall, because things go wrong like in anything else. Sometimes your mind and body don't connect the way you want, but you usually get right back up and things are just fine. This time was very different. At first, I thought I was okay, but I soon realized something had gone awfully wrong. I had suffered a brain-stem trauma.

I couldn't walk without help. My body trembled uncontrollably, and my brain was in a fog. My dance teacher tried to get my mom to agree to let me dance in the concert that was about a week after that injury. Mom kept saying I was not capable of dancing, but the instructor didn't really believe her – until we went to watch the concert. Mom had to help me walk into the auditorium and even help me sit in a chair. I couldn't get up without assistance, and my eyes had a distant, glassy stare. My teacher and other students in the dance company were stunned. It took so much time and therapy, but I eventually rehabilitated my body once again.

I seemed to be back in a position I knew all too well. We spent much of that summer going to doctors, trying to figure out why my left hip was hurting all the time. I was in constant, severe pain. Finally, that August, we found a surgeon who was convinced I had a labral tear even though the MRI tests hadn't shown anything. The labrum, a type of cartilage, surrounds the socket in our ball-and-socket joints. It helps provide stability to the joint as well as flexibility and motion – all things a dancer needs.

Sadly, it was already time to start school for my sophomore year, so I went back to Tucson in August and then flew home for a weekend in mid-September. I came home on a Thursday, had surgery Friday, and then flew back to Arizona on Sunday. I did have a significant tear in the labrum, and the surgeon cleaned out a lot of shredded cartilage. I was in awful pain as I hobbled around on crutches, but I was determined not to miss school and get back to dance as soon as possible. Once again, I was down but not out.

In addition to the physical pain and hard rehabilitation work, this injury made life very difficult because we had moved to an off-campus apartment several miles away from school. I didn't have my car there, so friends drove me to school most of the time. I had to use public transportation a couple of times, which was an adventure in itself. Tucson public transportation. Scary!

I didn't get to dance a lot my sophomore year, but that time was memorable for a couple of other reasons. When we moved into the apartment we were able to meet some new friends, which opened up a whole new world for us. Being a girl in the dance world, I was around gay men all the time – that's just how it was. I love all those boys, but sometimes you just need something different and a bit more masculine to look at. We were excited to meet some new people at the apartment complex, and to take a step outside of our little bubble. We still weren't the partiers of the complex, but we were having fun.

Money was very tight when I was at college, but whose wasn't. I worked part time in the dance office as part of the school's work-study program, and I was fortunate that my parents were paying my rent. My job took care of paying for food, toiletries, entertainment, clothing and everything else. But it didn't matter, because all three of us were in the same situation. We spent our time in our apartment or the dance building. There wasn't much need for new clothes, except dance clothes, so most of our extra money went toward a nice night out to dinner or our favorite frozen yogurt place.

Recovery from hip surgery took even longer than I expected. I started dancing some in spring semester, but I was certainly not back where I wanted to be. I really had no idea how long it would take me to get back. I returned home for the summer, worked at a local restaurant and danced in Colorado Springs. I spent time with my family and friends. Kendra had just graduated high school and we spent lots of time together with our mom doing our favorite thing, watching "chick flicks." The summer flew by and once again August rolled around.

Time to go back to Tucson. I was starting to move again, but wasn't where I needed to be. I went ahead and signed myself up for the upper-level dance classes. I definitely was not ready for that, but I knew I could do it. I am the type of person that just has to make myself go for it or else it will never get done. My hip was healed, I was in great physical shape, and I was headed toward being in great dance shape. Being in great physical/running shape is completely different than being in great dance shape.

Two months later, in October, our season of dance performances began in earnest. I was excited for the Jazz Dance Showcase, which I had missed the year before because of my injury. I was ready to dance on the Stevie Eller Stage and to dance in the piece choreographed by the dance professor I had admired since I was just nine years old, Susan Quinn Williams, who would soon play a huge part in my life. It was such a dream come true to be there. I was so proud, because I knew what a privilege it was to be in my shoes. This was the show that I had come and watched over and over since the age of nine. It was my chance to get to be that college student up on stage that so many little girls looked up to.

To say I always loved to perform is perhaps an understatement. Family photographs show an all-American group nicely posed, sitting still with lovely smiles on their faces. Well, except for me – I always had one leg lifted up over my head, my arms spread wide with an over the top smile or some other whimsical pose. Splits were second nature. Picture after picture shows my natural enthusiasm for performance. I simply loved the camera! And videos were even better. My life-long friend Emily Hoerner and I spent hours in the back yard with the video camera, making home movies. Then we would go back inside and settle the entire family in for a night of videos, an event that became a cherished family pastime for many years. At least our parents enjoyed it, not so much our older brothers!

Emily and I also loved to make "pointe shoes" out of plastic cups and dance around the kitchen when we were in first or second grade. You can't get a pair of point shoes until your feet are properly developed, and your technique is strong enough. We had such wild imaginations at that age! We put tissues in the bottom of the plastic cups and then stuffed our feet down inside. We stood on the tips of our toes and danced around the room before we fell to the floor, laughing at ourselves. Who said Dixie cups were for drinking? My favorite was when I made my brothers be my ballet partner. I was a little bossy, and they indulged their little sister. It didn't matter if we had an audience; we were dancing for the sake of dancing.

I couldn't imagine my life being any different, but God had other plans.

The night of October 11, 2008, began much as many other

nights of my college career. The School of Dance had a show called "Five." Liz Callaway, the original singing voice of the Disney character "Anastasia," was a special guest performer. We were all on a high, just from being in her presence. She knew how to light up a stage! It was a wonderful experience and a beautiful performance, and we were ready to celebrate. Some of the dancers planned a cast party and we were going to that later. SarahAliciaMoira also had been invited to hang out with some of our other friends who were UofA athletes, so we chose to go there first. Needless to say, we knew the athletes were not only level headed and honestly sweet people, but most of the guys were really gorgeous to look at.

We didn't really know where we were going so we took a cab. We had planned to meet up at a friend of a friend's house, so we trusted that we would be safe. We had no idea it was in a notoriously bad part of Tucson, or we wouldn't have gone to begin with.

As we were getting out of the cab, I remember the cab driver asking, "Are you sure you girls want to stay here? This is a bad part of town."

We all three quickly looked at each other and then dismissed her warning, paid, and hopped out, giving her our thanks.

Not having paid much attention to what was going on outside when we first pulled up, we were quickly made aware that there were a large amount of people there, almost to the point where we didn't know where to go or where to look for our other friends. We were very confused and a little shocked, because we had no idea that there were going to be so many people there. We thought we were meeting up with a few friends. This was far from a few friends. Moira tried to contact the person who had invited us to come over. She called and called and called but never got a hold of him, so we decided to go inside to see if we could find him. When we entered the house, right away unsteady anxiety began to run through my body and slowly started to turn into paranoia. It became apparent that the feeling was mutual because the moment we walked in, we all stood a little closer to each other. We walked a little further through the house to the kitchen to see if we could find him. We stopped and stood there for maybe three minutes. It felt like a thousand eyes were piercing us. All three of us looked at each other and decided to go back outside. When we headed out I glanced back over my shoulder at some of the people, and I didn't recognize a single face in the house.

We immediately ran into some other friends outside, so we stood on the sidewalk enjoying the warm Tucson night and trying to decide where to go and what to do. We were a perfect picture of college friends having fun as we moseyed across to the other side of the street.

SarahAliciaMoira were there with our friends Nilo and Ryan, as well as Jake and Danielle, whom I had just been introduced to that night. Jake decided that he was going to drive and I trusted him because my other friends knew him and trusted him. We girls continued to chat and were completely unaware of what was beginning to go on around us. Suddenly, the guys started shoving us into the car, trying to make us go faster. We didn't think anything of it and got in.

ﷺ

I don't know why I remember some things with perfect clarity, but I know where we were all sitting. Of course, it was SarahAliciaMoira in the very back. I was sitting on the passenger side, and Moira was to my left. Next to her was Sarah. Right after I got in I realized the front passenger seat was open. No one sat there because we were shoved in so quickly. I saw that front seat open and thought about jumping out quickly and hopping into the open seat. That's when one of the guys said, "Let's get out of here, it looks like somebody has a bat."

It wasn't a bat. It was a shotgun.

It all happened so very quickly, in less than a minute. Jake had already started the car; it was parked on the right side of the road. We all looked through our left windows toward where the guys had pointed at the gun. I saw nothing. Then I heard one really loud POP, like a firecracker in the distance. But up close it sounded like a rock had hit the car.

Then, an unfamiliar heat washed over me from head to toe, as my body was surrounded and sucked into a tunnel. My ears rang loudly, but I could not hear. My entire body throbbed, but was numb from shock. Then Sarah started screaming. Her screams brought back my hearing and feeling. A strange smell came into the car, and the right side of my abdomen started to burn. I cupped my hand over the spot that was ablaze and my hand raised as my abdomen puffed and swelled like a balloon in mere seconds. Then something warm began to seep between my fingers. I pulled my hand back and brought it up to my face. I saw something dark. Then I recognized the smell of gunpowder and the sight of blood.

I realized I had been shot.

Chapter Four

It is chaos that initiates the sagacity of being human.
– Blair Jimison

Eyewitness statements in the police report from that horrifying night are typical for a gang-related incident. Everyone has a different story, because they are all trying to hide something. As my life hung by a thread, two football players explained events leading up to the shooting in their own words.

"Johnson stated that as they arrived there were around 20 people standing outside the house," the report reads. "He described the scene as being lots of people and cars. He walked inside and found an additional 40 or more people inside the house."

"Johnson noticed that there were Pima Community College students, UofA students, and Tucson locals at the house. There were a lot of different people who continued to come in and out, but he didn't pay too much attention to them. He noticed four people who walk into the house, and in his words stated, 'Being from L.A., it was obvious that they were gang related.' When he saw these four gang members, he had a feeling that there was going to be trouble. He heard someone inside the house state 'Blood gang,' and the gang members he noticed were dressed in all blue, and were throwing up gang signs in return. Then he heard someone from inside holler 'Swoop Woop.' The term 'Swoop Woop' is a gang slang meaning that the Blood gang member is calling out the other gang members. Johnson stated that one of 'Crip' members got offended, and began throwing out gang signs and claiming 'Crips.'

"Jeremy, who was one of the residents of the house, approached the gang members and persuaded them to leave. He told them that the police had been called, and that there were too many people at the house. According to Johnson, the gang members left without causing a problem."

Another football player remembers the night's events this way:

"Once Roberts heard the gang slurs inside the house he decided that he should leave and he walked out to the back yard. He jumped the wall and walked to the front yard where he met another teammate. As they were standing in the front yard he heard another male voice stating, 'Don't do it... don't do it.' He turned around and saw a Hispanic male holding a shotgun in his hand. There was another Hispanic male behind him holding a handgun and they were standing next to a white Lincoln town car. Once he saw the males with the guns he walked over to the other side of the house.

"Across the street a few of the 'Crip' gang members were hanging around a blue Cadillac."

This is where the police think they were shooting the AK-47. Some of the other gang members say they saw the Crips with the AK-47, but no one ever said they clearly saw one particular person shoot the gun.

"After the shots were fired everyone ran down the street with everyone else to try and get into their cars or inside the house. Then the Hispanic male holding the handgun fired 6-7 shots into the air, and Roberts and more people started running as the shots were being fired."

"After he had taken cover behind a car, he saw the blue Cadillac across the street drive over an electrical box and take off down the street. Then all the lights on the streets went out, and more shots were fired into the air."

And before the air cleared, I was already fading. Every breath I took was becoming weaker. Two opposite worlds had collided, and I was paying the price.

When something so powerful pierces your body there are no words, no analogy to describe the feeling, the pain, and the fear that strikes you. Think of the worst pain possible, and then multiply it by a million. Unless you have been shot before, you can't begin to understand it. My world narrowed to the gaping wound in my right side. My roommate and I had both been shot, but fortunately Sarah's wound was superficial, and thank the Lord no one else in the car had been hit.

The instant the bullet struck the car, all the occupants of the car suffered a blow to mind and body, causing distinct individual reactions. Trauma affects people differently – some can continue to talk, move, think, feel, etc. For others, the trauma is so profound that it takes complete control. My body went into shock from the severe physical wound, while my friends' went into shock from the deafening noise; it intensified as they watched me bleed.

I removed my hand from my abdomen and saw blood. I said, "I think I've been shot."

Sarah looked at me and started screaming, while Moira looked at me and shut down into complete silence. It's funny how our personality traits reflected our reactions – Sarah leans a bit toward the dramatic, Moira is more quiet, and I fall somewhere in between.

Eventually, I realized Sarah initially started screaming because a bullet had skidded along the top of her leg. Her leg was bleeding and felt like it was on fire. She couldn't tell if the bullet had skimmed her or if it was embedded somewhere in her thigh. Moira was sitting between the two of us and, although we can laugh about this now, frantically tried to figure out who to help first.

She didn't know what to do, because Sarah was screaming, "They are going to have to cut off my leg!"

Should Moira help the friend to her left, who was going to have to have her leg amputated? Or should she help the friend to her right, who had blood pouring out her side? Danielle leaped into action to help me, so Moira turned to apply pressure to Sarah's leg. My world slowed as I continued to hold my hand over my wound. Every heartbeat was an eternity. What happened in five seconds felt like five minutes. I looked into the eyes of my two best friends as they sat to my left. Sarah stopped screaming, and no one said a word. I saw the fear in their eyes, and they saw the fear in mine. We all knew what was happening. I was dying. I looked and then turned my head straight; an act that felt like it took a lifetime. My right hand stayed on my side, and I had nothing to hold with my left. Nilo, who was sitting right in front of me, had a little bit of a 'fro hairdo going at the time; as the excruciating pain began to get even stronger I grabbed onto his hair. I felt bad later, but that's all my hand could find to grasp onto.

Danielle, whom I had just met, looked at me in the seat behind her. She saw that I was bleeding and jumped into action. I think she reacted the way she did because she didn't have any connection with me – we had no shared history. Although she was scared to death – she was watching someone slowing dying before her – it was easier for her to focus on the mechanics than it was for Sarah and Moira.

Danielle's mom is a nurse, and she remembered hearing her talk about applying pressure to a wound. Although Danielle never thought she would be in a situation quite like this, she hopped over the seat and sat, as best she could, right in front of me. She looked me straight in the eye and started talking to me. She put her hand over mine and applied as much pressure as she could.

"What's your name?" Danielle asked me. She knew, because we had just met earlier that night, but she was trying to keep me awake and involved.

"My name is Alicia," I said.

"What do you do at school?" she asked.

"I dance," I said.

Danielle kept asking me questions to keep me alert. She made me look her directly in the eye and kept me talking to her. I was so uncomfortable, but deathly afraid to move at all. I thought I had been paralyzed, because I couldn't feel my legs. I asked Danielle if I could move or if she could help me change positions.

"No," she said. She was cool under fire. "Sit still."

I listened. I did try to wiggle my toes and realized that I actually could. I was so grateful in that one second that I knew I could still use my legs. The shock that had besieged my body had literally numbed them.

The boys in the car called 911. Luckily we already were pulling away from the curb, because the scene quickly turned to chaos. Jake thought he would pull over once we were out of the neighborhood and help put pressure on my wound, maybe try to help me get more comfortable while waiting for emergency medical services to reach us. Before he stopped, Danielle asked Jake to turn the light on so she could see me better. Danielle saw the blood just pouring from my body.

"You can't stop, Jake," she said. "You have to keep going."

You know how people say when you are about to die, your life flashes before your eyes? Well, it does. Right then I started seeing my life and the things I had missed. I thought of friends I hadn't seen in awhile, family members, my precious baby sister. I wondered why I hadn't found time to return phone calls. I asked myself if I told Mom and Dad I loved them the last time I talked to them. I should have done this, or I should have done that. I saw the look on Danielle's face and I thought, *Wow. I am going to die.*

Then I looked at her and said, "I don't want to die."

Even as I said it, I realized what I really meant was, *I don't want to die like this. Not like this.*

Danielle said in a confident, reassuring voice, "You're not going to die. Look at you. You're awake and talking to me." She did not tell me she was terrified that, indeed, it was likely that I would die. I discovered that much later.

I thought, *You're right. I am awake and still able to talk.*

Jake continued to drive. He flew past the closest hospital along the way. With two gunshot victims in his car he still had the presence of mind to make a critical decision. He knew that the University Medical Center in Tucson was nearby. As a world-class athlete – a decathlete, to be exact – Jake had been to UMC many times and knew it has one of the best trauma centers in the country. He knew exactly where to go. That decision, a decision others would not have made, played a major role in saving my life.

The first stop light we found was red, so of course he stopped. I

39

looked at Danielle.

"He can't stop," I told her. "If he stops at the lights, I am going to die."

All the girls in the car heard me. They all started yelling at Jake to drive faster. He immediately looked both ways. I remember we all looked with him. We looked to the left, and then when we looked right, we saw a police officer at the light. Then Jake ran the red light, driving right past the officer. When I first saw the police car, part of me was thinking, *Maybe he can turn on his lights and escort us, maybe help us get there faster.* But I don't think he even saw us.

Jake took off at over 80 miles per hour and ran every red light. Right then I said my first prayer of the night.

"Lord, please don't let us get hit by a car now," I prayed fervently.

What is typically a 20- or 25-minute drive turned into 10 minutes for us. The entire time, Danielle was applying so much pressure to my side her hand went numb. Even though she no longer had feeling in that hand, she continued to push while talking to me. Danielle's voice kept me awake. I never passed out. But, I also think that my lifetime of dancing had something to do with my resilience. It took all the endurance that I had built during my entire existence to make it alive to that emergency center. I had to tell myself to breathe, to take in as much oxygen as I possibly could.

Just breathe through the pain, I thought. But by the time we got to the hospital, I was in so much pain I could barely take a breath. My body was folded over on itself, but I was still awake. I'd lost so much blood; I couldn't hold my head up any longer. I remembered feeling the blood trickling down my abdomen when I was first shot, but it had gradually become thicker and heavier as it flooded away. My body was shutting down as more and more blood spilled out. It felt like it was clumping up inside of me, then rising to the surface before falling out. And then the process would repeat again and again. Each time a glob of blood dropped out, my body sank lower and lower.

Because the boys had called 911, ER nurses were waiting for us when we pulled up to the emergency room entrance. I thanked the Lord for placing Jake in exactly that place at that time. I needed to have him there. He was trained to think and act quickly under pressure, so he got us to the hospital incredibly fast. We all said we were glad he was driving that night. No one else could have done that.

Those who were able, jumped out of the car, and the hospital workers pulled Sarah out. Sarah yelled, "Help her, help Alicia! Please!" The nurse who was trying to get me out couldn't really see how much I was bleeding. Because everyone else had hurried out of the car, I think he assumed my wounds weren't so bad.

"Hop out," he said while looking at me.

"I can't move," I whispered. So he reached in and grabbed underneath both arms and dragged me out of the car. Sarah remembers watching him pull me out like a rag doll, nearly lifeless, as a trail of blood followed, and put me in a wheelchair, which made me angry because it hurt and I still couldn't sit upright. He immediately saw the blood and realized my skin had gone a deathly shade of gray. The nurse flew into panic mode, and he took off running with me.

"Get the hell out of my way!" he shouted over and over again, as he ran down the hallway with me.

When I saw his face and understood his reaction, I thought, *OK, this is it. I really am going to die.* At that moment, I tried to prepare myself. I didn't know how to do that. The thought of my heart suddenly stopping shook me, so I told myself to remain calm and told myself it was OK. *People die. You won't hurt anymore.* It was strange. Crazy. You can't prepare yourself to die – at least, not like this. Not at 21 years old.

The nurses got me into the ER and threw me onto the exam table. The second I hit that table I recognized the smell, the feel, the whiteness and the acoustics of the room as the place where people are incapacitated; the place where people die. I left my body.

My out-of-body experience was exactly like the stories so many others have told. I simply was no longer attached to my body; I was watching myself from above. It was surreal – there was no way that was me. How could I look down at myself? Thankfully it only lasted a couple of seconds, and as the doctors flew to my side, I was me again.

The first thing they did was cut everything off of me. Shirt, pants, undies, bra, shoes, everything. I later came to realize this

41

moment was symbolic of what my life would become. In that instant, everything was stripped from me – soon, even my name would no longer be mine. I felt branded when they put that hospital gown on me; my old identity disappeared.

Hospital personnel quickly worked to stabilize me by starting an intravenous line and putting an oxygen mask over my face. They told me to breathe. While they frantically worked, a police officer came over to me and started asking me questions about the shooting.

Are you kidding me? I thought. *I'm trying to BREATHE! I am half dead right now and you are trying to ask me questions?* I simply couldn't answer him and one of the doctors stepped in and told him he would have to ask his questions later. The officer stepped back and waited to collect all of the evidence that was blood stained and had bullet fragments. Even in my condition, I was very upset because he took all of my clothes. Even then, I thought, *Can you please save those jeans and that bra for me? Those are my favorites.* I knew they were only doing what they had to, but it still disturbed me.

I found out later the officer was already at the hospital taking reports from another shooting that had happened that night. Sadly, mine was one of seven different shootings that took place that night in Tucson. Including Sarah and me, there had been 11 gunshot victims that night – and those were just the wounded that had been brought to the University Medical Center.

As the officer stepped back, the doctor came close and started to ask me questions.

"What's your name? Age? Do you drink? Smoke? Do drugs? Have any tattoos? Are you associated with a gang? Do you have a boyfriend that is associated with a gang? Do you know anybody who is associated with a gang?" she asked.

I was just thinking to myself, *No, no, no, no, no, no, NO!* All that came out was one quiet no.

I thought to myself, *Do you know who you are talking to?* I understood the questions were protocol and they were required by law to ask. But I thought, *Can you SEE me? Do I look like someone who is in a gang?* I was wearing my skinny jeans with a little tank top and cute high heels. The front of my hair was pulled back in a little pouf. I just kept thinking, *Really? Really?* Besides my appearance, there were other factors that should have told them I wasn't a gang member. I wasn't cursing at them. I had a best friend in the other room crying her eyes out and refusing to talk, because they wouldn't let our other friend come in to be with her.

I repeat: I understand it was protocol, but wow! I couldn't believe they were asking me these questions. I thought, *If only you knew me. If only you knew my family and my friends, you wouldn't be asking me these questions.*

They eventually asked me if I knew what happened.

"I don't know," I managed to say. Every word took more energy than I had. "Someone shot me."

I was stabilized very quickly and began to believe I would live at least through the night. I hit a natural high. It was strange; I wasn't happy, but I finally thought I would make it through this. I had never passed out and was still alive in my new safe zone, the hospital. I had just been through the worst half-hour of my life, which I thought then would be the worst moment I would ever live. Again, life held a few more surprises.

Before I went into surgery, one of the doctors found my little pink phone. I asked them to call my parents in Colorado and my professor Susan Quinn, who had always told her students to call day or night if necessary. I had all the right numbers in my phone, so Chaplain Dave made the calls. He eventually played such a big part in all our lives. Dave came in to see me almost every time he was working at UMC to chat, pray and just visit.

He called my parents that night and asked me if I wanted to talk to them. Of course, I said yes. Although the bleeding had stopped, my body still was growing weaker every second. I knew it would take everything I had to be as reassuring for them as I possibly could be. I knew that they were going to be devastated, beyond that I didn't know what their reaction might be, but at least I could talk to them to ease their minds as much as possible.

"Hi, Mommy," I said when we all were on the phone, including my dad. Mom asked what happened and I said, "I don't know, someone shot me." That's really the only part of the conversation I remember.

Susan received the next call.

Susan Quinn. The first time I met Susan I was nine years old. I was taking a master class from her at the UofA Jazz Dance Showcase. It was the first year I attended. I remember being terrified of her! As I grew up dancing Susan would come to teach at my dance studio at least once a year. I would also see her every year when I went to Jazz Dance showcase in Arizona. Basically, I just saw and took from her consistently from 9 years old until college. As I matured as a person and as a dancer I grew to love her. Not only was I captivated with her style of dance and choreography, but I learned to appreciate her gregarious personality and big heart! Susan was not only my long time dance teacher and now professor. She was my mentor and friend. I knew her well, and trusted that she would be by my side to help in any way that she could.

"Who? Alicia?" she asked when Chaplain Dave gave her the news. "The Alicia I have known since she was nine years old?" Indeed, one and the same. She called some of the dancers who were together that night, and they all came to the hospital to begin the long wait.

اللّٰه

So many different things were happening, all at the same time. While I was being stabilized, Sarah was in another ER room just across the hall from me. Officers asked her questions and took pictures of her and her leg. They would not allow Moira into the ER to see her, although Sarah kept asking for her. Sarah finally said she wouldn't answer any more questions until they allowed Moira to be with her! Finally, staff allowed Moira into the ER to be with Sarah.

About this time, I started to ask if they could put me under anesthesia or at least give me pain meds. The answer was always "no." I was in an incredible amount of pain, and although time was flying by, it still took about two hours before I was ready for the operating room. They needed information on where I was hit and the damage that my body sustained before they could operate.

They had to run several tests – x-rays, CAT scans, yada, yada, yada – to know what needed to be done. The doctors lifted me onto another bed to wheel me out for those tests, and when they picked me up, they said, "Wow! You're so light!" I never said it out loud, but the dancer inside me smiled and thought, *Thank you!*

As they took me out for testing, I rolled right past Sarah and Moira. They both looked at me and cried, "Alicia! Alicia!" Sarah reached out for me, but of course she wasn't allowed to get up or get close to me. Sarah remembers me trying to wave my blood stained hand and give her a smile. I found out later she had a dreadful time in that emergency room, because she was so close she could hear everything my doctors were saying. However, directly giving her information was against patient privacy laws. No one would tell her anything.

Finally, I was ready for surgery. To my surprise, they had me sign a consent form. I was so weak by then I could barely lift my arm, so one of the doctors held my arm while I tried to scribble my name. Doctor Peter Rhee came in and told me they found the entrance wound but no exit injury. The x-ray showed bullet fragments, so it was possible the bullet was still inside my body.

Doctor Rhee, chief trauma surgeon, said the bullet had struck my liver. As a dancer, I know the biomechanics of my body well, but was not fully aware of the vital functions of the liver. I thought, *You can still live with just part of your liver?*

The liver aids in a wide range of things from helping detoxify the body to aid in digestion. It is required for survival, and there is no alternative for it. The only good news was the liver is the only organ in the body that regenerates itself.

It finally was time for surgery. Moira exited Sarah's room and came over to me as I was being wheeled to surgery. The orderly pushing my bed stopped, so she could talk to me. My dear friend took my hand and said, "I am so sorry, Alicia. I am so sorry this happened to you." For the first time that night, I saw her start to cry. "This shouldn't have happened," she said.

I remember thinking to myself, *Be strong, Alicia. Be strong, because I need the people around me to be strong for me.* At that moment I thought everything would be fine after a single surgery. I told Moira, "It's OK. It's OK." Then they took me back for what would be a six-hour surgery.

News of my shooting was spreading like wildfire. Friends and dancers gathered in the waiting room. Fortunately, Susan was there, too. Because I had given hospital staff Susan's name, they gave her information they would give no one else – not even Moira, who was with me when I came in. Susan was able to pass information along to everyone.

The night wore on. More dancers came to visit. Sarah, Moira, Danielle, Jake, Nilo, Susan and others stayed all night long. After the six-hour surgery, Doctor Rhee came out and spoke with Susan. All in the waiting room were hoping to hear the news. I was alive.

Dr. Rhee said, "I took out the ascending colon, part of the liver, the floating ribs. Well, I should have taken everything out, but then she wouldn't be here. It's not the bullet that does the damage, it's the blast."

He explained a bullet ripples like a rock being dropped into a lake – the immediate damage is compounded by the shockwaves that distress the entire body.

The shooting appeared to be gang related, so the hospital was not allowed to give out my real name. They gave me an alias according to the standard protocol. A random word is chosen; a word that means nothing at all. This is for the patient's protection, because often in such shootings, gang members will come back and try to 'finish the job'. Even though I had not been the target, the events of the night were still unclear, so the hospital staff were doing their job and being very careful. I went by this name during my entire stay at the hospital.

The alias they selected for me was **Thread, I.M.**

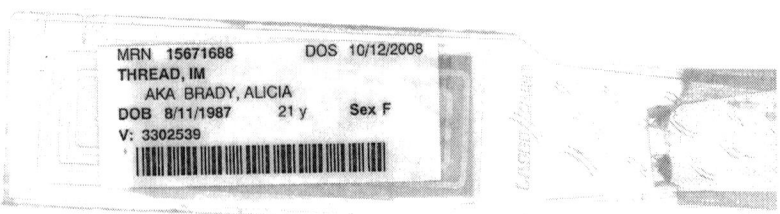

MRN 15671688   DOS 10/12/2008
THREAD, IM
     AKA BRADY, ALICIA
DOB 8/11/1987   21 y   Sex F
V: 3302539

Chapter Five

I was pushed back and about to fall, but the Lord helped me.
The Lord is my strength and my defense; he has become my
salvation. I will not die but live, and proclaim what the Lord
has done. –Psalm 118:13, 14, 17

I AWOKE FROM SURGERY STILL UNABLE TO move my body. I was fully awake but paralyzed from the anesthesia and other drugs being pumped into me. The first thing I clearly remember was hearing Susan's voice as she stepped into my room.

"Oh, Alicia! Oh, Alicia… I think she's trying to wake up! Are you trying? Are you trying to wake up?" she asked. Susan's dancers know her personality is straightforward and crazy, but full of passion and love for everyone. She continued to talk – to me, to the nurses, to everyone listening to her. "Oh, yup, yup, she is moving her toe. She is trying to wake up!" The funny thing is that I was trying to move my toe! It was about 9 a.m. Sunday morning.

I managed to open my eyes and think, *Is this real? Reality? Am I dreaming? Is this a trick of my imagination?* It was only the first of hundreds of times throughout my entire hospital stay that I would wake with a deep gasp, hoping I would emerge from the hell that encased me. Trauma like this doesn't just damage physically, it tortures every part of your life. It digs in and finds its way into every nook and cranny. To survive, you try to make yourself believe that reality is fictitious. Your mind is an incredibly powerful force, and it can easily play tricks on you. Even today, I sometimes wonder if I am living in a dream, because what I went through was so illusory.

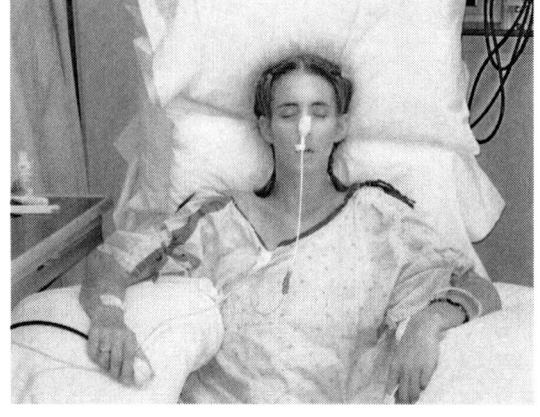

In my case, reality truly set in when my parents walked into my hospital room. They tried to comfort me while I tried to do the same for them by giving them a smile. It probably came out as more of a grimace, because I didn't have much to give. My body had already deteriorated in a short amount of time. They both gave me a kiss on the cheek, and when I couldn't return the kiss, I began to realize how helpless I really was. They couldn't hug me or really touch anything but my hand or my face. I was wounded too badly to be touched anywhere else.

My parents arrived at the hospital less than an hour after my surgery was finished. This was no surprise because that is who my parents are. They stood by my side in everything that I did; they were used to traveling. Most of that traveling came as a sacrifice on their part to benefit me.

ﺠ

When I started middle school, my teacher Zetta relocated her studio, Colorado Jazz Dance Company, to Colorado Springs – the far, north side, which was about an hour and a half drive each way. At that time, there were several of us girls going to her class, so we all shared rides and my parents only had to drive maybe once a week. In the beginning, I was there three or four days a week. Over the next couple of years, it was five days a week, but the month before any concert, it grew to seven days a week.

By the time I entered high school, Kimberly Gair and I were the only two Cañon City dancers still making the drive to Colorado Springs, so we had just two families who each drove us two or three times a week. We were both perfectly capable of driving ourselves, but neither of our parents thought it would be safe for us to be on the road for an hour and a half each way after such a full and tiring day. We were in dance classes a steady five days a week by now.

I don't know too many parents who would do what mine did. They did it day after day, week after week, and year after year. There they were already by my side.

ﷺ

My life had already changed drastically, and the worst was still to come. Just a few hours ago, I was an independent, 21-year-old woman dancing at a top school, and now I could barely lift a finger. My life literally had been pulled out from underneath me. You know the saying that life can change within the blink of an eye? In my case, it was as fast as a speeding bullet. (Where is Superman when you need him?!)

Many people came to the hospital to see me that first day. I couldn't carry a conversation, but my parents were very grateful. They came to Tucson in fear and terror. Their perception of the city and its residents was not a pleasant one. My parents' entire world had been flipped upside down, and nothing could change that – but when all my friends and dance family showed up, their attitudes changed. A steady stream of people came through the doors... other dancers, instructors, friends of friends, and even Jake and Danielle, whom I hadn't known before that night. My parents were overwhelmed by everyone, their compassion and love for me as well as for them. My visitors helped my mom and dad see that this place wasn't all corrupt, that the good can outweigh the bad.

Although the situation itself was grim, we did manage to be lighthearted and laugh whenever we could. Early on in the hospital my dancing was mistaken for another kind of dancing.

When anyone asked what I did, I said I was a dancer. At first, I got some nasty looks. Once, my dance professor Susan was in the room with me. She quickly stepped in and said, "Hey, she isn't an exotic dancer, okay! She is a classically-trained dancer. She does ballet, modern, jazz..." It took a while for my entire medical team to understand.

Everyone who knows me understands my humor leans toward the sarcastic side; something I picked up from my dad. Even while I was in the hospital I would still punch jokes to lighten the mood, at least when I could talk. This situation in itself was not humorous, it was sad, dramatic and overall, heartbreaking. Close friends came to see me, yet had no idea what to say, and I understood. What do you say? "So, Alicia, how does it feel to get shot?" Anyway, when people heard the news they expected the worst, but it had just been a day or two. At that point, I hadn't lost any weight and all my wounds were covered. My skin was yellowish gray, my abdomen was swollen, and I had IVs, a catheter and a drain tube. Although it is shocking to see anyone in a hospital bed, I didn't look too bad compared to what was to come. I looked good enough that my visitors were unable to truly comprehend how gravely wounded I was.

The main difference in my life at that point was that I simply couldn't move. I barely had the energy to lift a finger. If I wanted a drink of water, someone had to help me. So I tried to make conversation. I told my friends how the doctors had told me I was really light, and how they took my favorite pair of jeans. I kept telling the girls, "Hey, have you seen some of the doctors around here? Some of them are really cute. I'll keep an eye out for you!" I did everything I could to lighten the mood. It was the only sense of control I had. I could control what I said and how I reacted to all of this, and that was about it. I needed to keep a smile on my face for as long as I could. Even if the humor came only once a day, once a week, and even though laughing, smiling, and talking were extremely painful, it was the little bit of Alicia that was left.

Later that first day, detectives from the Tucson Police Department paid me a visit to take my statement. I remember them coming to my side and holding a tape recorder up to my face. They asked me questions that took all the energy I had to answer. It was even harder to think. The nurses had told them to make it quick, and they did – but I still remember telling myself, *Now, Alicia, don't fall asleep on them.*

Another reason the TPD came was to find out how to contact my family. They had no idea the Randy and Dena in my room were my parents.

The detectives kept saying things along the lines of, "We are trying to contact Alicia's family now."

Mom was thinking, *Do you mean her grandparents or something?* Then finally she said, "We are her parents!"

The detectives were stunned my family not only already knew I had been shot, but were by my side. They asked how my parents found out, so mom explained the chaplain had called them. If I had been unconscious when I got to the ER, no one would have known who to call. My parents still wouldn't have been aware of what had happened.

للّٰه

I was on highly-addictive painkillers, (Dilaudid, which is seven times stronger than morphine, and OxyContin, which is synthetic heroin), but the main concern was to keep me alive. In order to do that, I had to be able to move. And, in order to move, I had to control my pain. If I didn't move, I would be prone to infections, pneumonia and other illnesses. I already was so frail, my chances of fighting off disease had dropped dramatically. So the pain meds were necessary, and I would deal with coming off of them later. I was on a PCA pump (patient-controlled analgesia), which meant I could give myself medication at specific intervals. Trust me, every time that button lit up to signify the availability of another dose of meds, I pushed it. The drugs would go into my IV and straight to my veins, providing me whatever temporary relief I could find. I often needed help pushing that button, but I would not let it out of my sight – I wouldn't even let it out of my hand! Visitors could hold my hand, but the button was always there. It became a joke, because I was always asking, "Where's my button?" It is in every hospital picture with me.

I was so appreciative of all of my visitors! But there were a couple of small things that were making me crazy! I know everyone was just trying to comfort me, but so many people were rubbing or stroking my face. I just couldn't stand it. I couldn't say much at first, and had a hard time speaking up for myself, so I asked my mom to tell everyone else to quit touching my face. And my hair! It was so greasy from people running their hands through it. In the end I wouldn't get a normal shower for over 41 days. I hadn't washed my face since the night of the accident, and I obviously hadn't washed my hair. So my mom got the message across, and people finally stopped. Now, I have a new phobia about people touching my face. I just don't like it. Maybe it reminds me too much of that time and place.

I finally got into a face-cleansing regiment, and as time went on, my daily visitors began to help. Every morning and night I had someone wash and lotion my face. Most of the time, my mom, Susan or one of my grandmothers did it for me. I even had my dad try to do it a few times. Of course I bossed everyone around and told them they were doing it wrong, but I was thankful to have someone helping me wash up. It was really important for me, because it was one of the few things that made me feel like a girl. When you are in a hospital, gender goes out the door. Everyone is treated the same – just because I am a girl, didn't mean I was going to get extra pampering. Fortunately, I did have incredible nurses who took some extra time with me. They shaved my legs and underarms for me. I even had one CNA who braided my hair once or twice a week.

Nurses and CNA's truly are overlooked. I'm not saying it doesn't take heart to be a doctor, but it is impossible to be a nurse and not care. Because I was in the hospital for so long, I saw most of them multiple times. My parents and I all developed relationships with them. They were so kind, friendly, and personal – I think a lot of that had to do with my parents' attitudes. Mom and Dad knew everyone was working to save their little girl, one day at a time. I would like to think that most of the time, I had a good attitude toward them, too. We were always undoubtedly admiring of them and the care they offered. Much of the time their care meant discomfort for me, but they were using their healing hands on me. They didn't put me in this situation, yet they helped me. One of them told us they don't get thanked a lot, which shocked me. She said most of the time they received complaints. The care that I received at University Medical Center was outstanding! I am convinced that if I had been at any other hospital, I would not be alive today. My parents and I will be forever thankful. They literally saved my life.

The doctors are there to save lives. Their jobs are much different than the nurses, who have the time to focus on the patients' comfort and get to personally know each patient. The nurses would have four to five patients each day, and in ICU it was one-on-one care. In comparison, the surgeons – especially in the trauma unit – have double, triple the patients to provide care for in a single day. Not all, but a lot of the doctors' bedside manners were not as gentle as the nurses, and they would probably be the first ones to tell you that. They have a job to do. They get in and get it done. At first, they told me if everything went smoothly, I would be hospitalized for four or five days. That didn't happen.

Hospital patients have no sense of time. Doctors make their rounds at five o'clock in the morning. Others are in and out at all hours of the day and night cleaning your room, changing dressings, drawing blood or taking vital statistics. Because my liver was damaged, I was unable to eat. I just couldn't. The first week I was hospitalized, I took in around 1,200 calories total. It was also hard for me to drink anything, so naturally I was dehydrated. That meant phlebotomists couldn't just come in, take my blood, and go. It was come in, poke, poke, poke a little more, maybe draw a bit of blood, so poke again, and finally leave. I was already miserable. All the poking made my existence ten times worse.

Another daily ritual was the 3:00 a.m. x-ray of my lungs. Naturally, my medical team was concerned about pneumonia due to the fact that I was lying in bed much of the time. All the ribs on my right side were shattered, so it was a nightmare to have someone come in my room, move my body to the appropriate position, put a hard board underneath me, and then tell me to take a deep breath and hold it. Taking shallow breaths was difficult; taking a deep breath was excruciating, and holding it, near impossible. Yet, as awful as those x-rays were, the worst part of my day was wound care.

Taking care of my wounds was a job the doctors and nurses did on a daily basis. Although I could have, I chose not to look at my wounds. The shooting happened in October; it wasn't until five months later, in March, that I first looked at them. I just couldn't do it. In the beginning, my entrance wound was a little bigger than the size of a quarter, and my exit wound was a bit larger than a nickel. As things got worse, so did my open wounds. Some of the residents who came into the room and saw my wounds for the first time couldn't help but show their shock. It was alarming to see a young woman with gaping holes in her body. During my first surgery I was cut from just beneath my sternum all the way to my pubic bone. This midline incision was closed with 32 staples.

علم

Painful doesn't even begin to describe the daily wound care regimen. I had never heard of packing wounds before, but quickly found out it was the best way to keep the wounds clean and allow the body heal from the inside out. Just thinking about it is still terrifying. The nurse would come into my room, wash her hands, use sanitizer and then put on gloves. She would set out the supplies: Kerlix gauze, Telfa pads, sterile saline, medical tape and a clean abdominal binder. Next she would take off the old binder, pull off the tape holding the sterile pads over the wounds, remove the pads and then begin pulling out the gauze that packed the wounds. Even though the gauze was soaked in saline before it was placed in my wounds, it was usually fairly dry by the time they removed it. (The exception to this was when my bile leak was severe. Then it was soaked in bile, which meant it came out easily; however, it also irritated the surrounding tissue, causing an acute stinging, burning sensation and slowing down the healing process.) As she pulled the gauze out, it was covered in blood, bile and bits of skin and dead tissue. It would stick to the wound, causing bleeding when they tugged on it. I watched her take out piece after piece, laying it on the side of the bed, creating a pile that filled a small trash can. Each time they removed old gauze from my exit wound in the front, it was as if it came out of nowhere. I mean, I knew it was coming from my body and I could feel it, but it was unbelievable to know that I had such huge holes in me. After the old gauze was removed, they would debrid any remaining dead tissue with a scalpel and tweezers, then irrigate the wound with the sterile saline. Of course, there was no way to numb the area; I felt it all. "Rubbing salt into the wound" might be an appropriate way to describe it.

Then the nurse would change her gloves and start the process of repacking the wounds. She would soak the gauze in saline and then take one piece at a time and place it in my wound. Of course it was important to pack the wound completely, filling every nook and cranny. Some nurses would use tweezers, while others just used their fingers. They would do this over and over, piece by piece, inch by inch until the wound was full. I could feel each piece of gauze as the nurse placed it in the hole, pushing into every available space. Each little push was excruciating. After the wound was packed, they would place the Telfa pad over the area and tape it down.

This process was done with each wound. I had to be rolled over on my side to care for my entrance wound. Of course, I couldn't do this on my own, so someone rolled me and then tried to hold me still while the nurse changed the dressing. Then they would roll me on my back to take care of the wounds on my abdomen. When they were finally finished, they would put the abdominal binder on and cinch it tight to hold everything in place. This process took 45 minutes to an hour for the nurses to complete; however, the doctors would do it in about 10 minutes.

Over time, as complications arose, my wounds became larger and the dressing changes, more agonizing. This was by far the worst part of my day; it was a daily pattern that created fear.

I had wound care at least two, sometimes three times a day from the time of the shooting, October 12th, until the end of March, when finally my wounds no longer had to be packed. I always hoped that a nurse might forget about it, but of course they never did. Every single dressing change was harrowing, but someone stood by my side, holding my hand, and looking me straight in the eyes giving me courage and strength. Usually, it was mom or dad, but grandmas and aunts stood to help when they were available. Most of the men in my family didn't do so well when it came to the packing changes. I even had a few friends who were "Alicia sitting" when it was time for a dressing change and my parents were out of the room. The nurses always gave them the option to leave, but they knew I needed them. One friend told me it was one of the worst things she ever experienced. She had nightmares about it for weeks - watching a friend suffer, but not being able to help.

Another daily challenge was eating. I never thought eating could become a chore for me, but it was. Because I had been shot in the liver I wasn't digesting properly. The bile that generally works its way through my digestive system to aid in breaking down my food was leaking out my wounds. I clearly remember the day when my dad praised me for eating a whole strawberry and a fourth of piece of toast. Nothing sounded good, and many times I spent my mornings throwing up. I remember thinking to myself, *Oh, Alicia, you are going to think back on the day when you thought it was hard to eat.*

Everyone knows I am a big chocolate lover, so all my friends brought in piles of chocolate and other goodies for me. Sarah came in once and said, "Alicia, you're not eating your chocolate bars!"

"I just can't eat it. It doesn't even sound good to me."

So she said, "You know she is sick when she isn't eating chocolate." Of course none of the treats went to waste, because my love for chocolate came from my dad, and Sarah and I shared that same interest.

When I was allowed to eat solids, I was required to order food from the hospital's kitchen. The food, from what my dad said, was actually pretty good. Dad was there most of the time when I ordered, so he would ask what I wanted. I knew I would only be able to eat a couple of bites, so I told him to pick what he wanted so it wouldn't go to waste. He said, "Okay!" He ordered the meal, I would eat what I could, usually three to five bites, and then pass it to Dad to finish. It wasn't intended this way, but it turned out to be a good way to save some money!

ﻋﻠﻰ

I discovered that doctors and nurses are obsessive about the workings of the bowel. Everyone who entered the room discussed my bathroom habits. When you are on large doses of narcotics and aren't eating, drinking and moving, using the bathroom becomes a huge issue. My whole world seemed to circle around my bowels. Maybe it should have been funny…but it wasn't.

ﻋﻠﻰ

Part of the daily routine was changing my sheets. Sometimes I was out of bed and it was a simple process. Other times I was in bed, and they would just change them with me there using a technique that required me to move very little. They rolled me to one side, changed the sheets on the opposite side, and then rolled me to the other side onto the new sheets and remade the first side.

I spent 41 days in the hospital unable to do anything for myself. In the beginning, I had to ask my parents to scratch my nose, because it hurt too much to move my arms. I probably had close to 41 sponge baths there. Initially I was embarrassed. I didn't want everyone to see me naked. But as the drugs weakened my mind and body, and I grasped the reality of the effort required to take care of myself, my modesty went out the door. My mom had purchased some Burt's Bees lotion and the nurses used that in place of the horrible smelling hospital lotion. It was special to smell like something besides bile or a hospital for at least a little while! Even so the bathing ritual was a chore for me.

There was one wonderful CNA who became a huge blessing to

our family. She knew how to French braid hair. Mine was a disaster and was washed in a bucket every few days. Instead of letting it air dry into a frizzy mess, Jean braided it for me. Even as time went on and I moved from room to room, she always took the time to find me and braid my hair after it was washed. That was one of the small gestures that I always will remember.

This was how I spent my days in the hospital – waiting for the next dose of painkillers, watching nurses unpack and repack my wounds, submitting to sponge baths and sheet changes, and struggling to stay alive, one breath at a time. As difficult as all of this was, one of the hardest things I had to do while at University Medical Center was the simple act of getting out of bed.

ﻋﻠﻰ

I was just 24 hours away from the shooting when they told me I had to get out of bed. Those words rang bitter and almost hostile in my ears. The question, "What?" didn't just spring from my lips, it came from everyone else in the room at the time. All I had to do was get up, not walk around, but just move to a chair a few feet from me. Sounds easy, right? Of course, it is extremely important to move if you can to keep from developing other major health issues. Besides the worry of pneumonia, one of the main reasons they wanted me to get up was because they thought I had "drop foot," which is a syndrome where the forefront of the foot drops because of weakness or paralysis of the muscles. It can cause you to lose the ability to move the ankle and toes upward and can be temporary or permanent. Nurse after nurse freaked out because they thought I was developing drop foot. They didn't understand my feet looked like that because of my years of dancing! They naturally turned out more and dropped at the ankle.

It took me several minutes to just get to the edge of my bed. I couldn't simply sit up, so we had to find a strategy to turn me while sitting me up in a way that would minimize the harm to my tender body. I sat on the edge of the bed for a few minutes before I tried to stand up. First, I was lightheaded and dizzy from all the meds and no food; and second, my breathing had to change. I had to work twice as hard taking a breath sitting or standing than I did lying down. Finally, and maybe the worst reason, was every time I sat up I felt like my insides didn't come with me. I thought things had to settle back into place before I could again try to move, much less stand up. When I was as ready as I could be, I had someone on each side and someone else pushing my IVs and holding all the tubes. It took five more minutes to get to the chair only a few feet away from me. I had to stop and take breaks just to breathe.

I will never forget the very first time I stood up. My feet were so heavy. They felt like fifty-pound weights were attached to each of them. I thought my abdomen and everything in it was going to simply fall out on the floor. My abdomen was so swollen, and I felt like I had no control over it. That was a new feeling for me. All my life I had been taught to suck it in, keep it tight. As a dancer, I was taught that my core was my powerhouse. Everything and every movement stemmed from the abdomen, and mine had been sliced and diced and pierced. Now, I had no control over it. It was a horrifying feeling.

When I finally got to the chair it took another several minutes to make me comfortable. I couldn't sit back, because it pulled on my abdomen too much. So, they stuffed pillows behind my back, under my arms and under my butt to try to make me as comfortable as possible. I always had between five and ten pillows in my room – my mom started to call me "The Princess and the Pea!" I would say I was uncomfortable, and someone would help me move an inch or two, and I would give a huge sigh of relief.

As I sat in the chair that first time and got as comfortable as I could, I thought to myself, *Is this ever going to end? Is this ever going to get any better? I cannot believe that this is happening to me.* Of course, the more I felt sorry for myself and the more I thought about my pain, the worse it became. Being surrounded by friends and family was one of the only things that helped me feel even a little bit better.

ﻋﻠﻢ

Of course, it was under the worst of circumstances, but I was able to meet many of my college friends' parents. That usually doesn't happen. Moms and dads flew to Tucson to give their own children support, and to encourage my family. Sarah and Moira's parents showed up within a few days, as soon as they could. During that first week all of the parents met up with the UofA Dean of Students, Keith Humphrey, to try to understand what was happening. They wanted to help in any way they could and find a path to move everyone's lives forward.

Dean Humphrey also came to visit me in the hospital that first week. He met my parents and asked how he could help. I told him I was planning on going back to school, so he helped me set my schedule for the following semester. He even allowed me to register for classes before anyone else! Although the shooting didn't happen on campus, the university still was incredibly supportive. I had just been shot the week before, yet there was no doubt in my mind I would be back.

The night of the shooting, my brothers told my parents that they were going to start looking for flights to Tucson. Several other people had said the same thing. Dad and mom decided to tell people to wait to come and visit until they had a better understanding of the situation. That first week, my parents stayed at a hotel near both the hospital and campus. The hotel gave them a great discount, but of course it was going to add up quickly if they needed to stay for longer than a week. My dance professor Susan had a friend, whom my parents had never met, who was going out of town until December. He graciously offered his home, so my parents, along with other family members and friends, were blessed to stay at his house for free. With his help, my parents told the rest of the family to come on down. Everyone arranged their schedules to be there that first weekend.

My brother Chris flew out a day before my oldest brother, Sean, Cousin Austin, Aunt Beth, and Grandma Ely all drove down from Cañon City. My three-year-old sister, Emma, stayed home with other family members, and my other sister, Kendra, seemed to be a world away, in the Philippines on a mission trip. When Chris arrived at the hospital, he texted Sean to ask him and the rest of the family to stay calm in front of me. Chris said it was really hard to see me – their little sister – like that, but if I saw them cry it would upset me. Chris knew I would cry. It physically hurt me, and they were all trying to help me stay as comfortable as possible.

Brothers . . . what a blessing! I always got along well with my brother Sean, who is four years older. I looked up to him and wanted to hang out with him and his friends. I spent much of my time as a young child, following Sean and his friends around the house, magically ending up in the same room they were in. Sean did not seem to mind much; he always was a caring and loving older brother. My brother, Chris, is just a year older than me. We grew up with a lot of the same friends, which meant that we spent a lot of time together. He sure knew how to push my buttons. A favorite pastime for the boys would be to stuff us girls into large, empty boxes and then flip the open end over so we could not get out. I would say that we were your typical American family. There was nothing unusual about the older brothers picking on their little sisters. By the time we were in high school Chris acted as my protector, always looking out for his little sister. I love the fact that some of my best memories in middle school and high school were with Chris. I love both of my big brothers dearly, and I know that they will always want to protect me, and most importantly, will always be by my side when I need them.

I was completely unaware of their "don't cry in front of her" strategy. When I cried in front of others and they held it together with no tears, it made me mad. I never said anything, but I always thought, *What is wrong with you? Doesn't this situation sadden you? How can you not care about this?* I was completely unaware that people were told not to cry in front of me and to be strong, because if I would have seen them fall apart it would have broken me.

Despite their lack of tears, my family surrounding me was the best thing for me. I quickly realized how the men and women reacted differently to things. The women stood and watched most of my dressing changes; the men, not so much.

Then the question "Who shot Alicia?" came up, and reality started to set in. They all understood it was not an accident, but that someone deliberately shot at someone else, and I happened to be in the way. Of course the men were very worked up about it. Rightfully so. The women just didn't react the same way. A woman's response is to nurture, and a man's response, in this case, is revenge. So, the men in my family wanted inflict as much pain on the shooter as he had caused me – their daughter, their cousin, their little sister. Chris had to leave to get back to work, but Sean and Austin started asking my mom questions about where it happened.

"We want to go down and see where it happened," they said. What they meant was they wanted to find the person responsible; he had nearly killed a close member of their family.

"No, you will not," my mom said. "You will not do anything, because that is not going to help the situation at all. How is hurting someone else going to help Alicia?"

My brothers weren't the only ones who had that thought. Many of the men who had watched me grow up back in Cañon City called my parents to say, "If you want me to come down there, I'll bring my shotgun and hunt that kid down."

Anger had taken over, but my family still said, "Look at what he did to Alicia. You don't want to be the one who would do that to someone else, no matter who that person is."

While my family was in Tucson, there were very few times they were not with me at the hospital. I was panic-stricken at the thought of being left alone in my room. I think the entire 41 days I spent in the hospital, there was maybe ten minutes when I was completely by myself. That even includes night time and naps. My family and friends took turns "Alicia sitting." I didn't care that we were calling it that. I always wanted someone with me. Even when I finally went back home and my parents returned to work, my mom called someone every day to come over and sit with me.

Thread

It had been a week since I had been shot. My family had surrounded me since the shooting, never leaving my side, so they finally decided to go out to lunch to get a change of scenery. They were concerned about leaving, but knew I was in good hands. They needed some fresh air, so Susan came that day to "Alicia sit." Moira and Sarah came to visit too.

I had complained over and over all day that something just didn't feel right. I kept telling doctors and nurses. Besides the new and unusual abdominal pain I had a gut feeling that something was wrong. I said I knew my body, and I knew it well. I knew when something wasn't right. And for me, when something didn't feel right, it wasn't. It had been a week since my first surgery, and I still hadn't been for a walk because I was in so much pain. My nurse was very diligent and persistent in calling the doctors to try to get me help. Finally they sent up a resident who shall remain nameless. She looked at my midline incision, where I had an intense and new sensation, and told me I was fine. She basically said I needed to suck it up and get moving. I had an oxygen line at the time and she removed it, telling me I didn't need it.

I was infuriated. I continued to tell my nurse something was wrong, so she finally called the doctors again. Right after my family left for lunch, Doctor Rhee came in. He pulled the curtain shut and asked Sarah and Moira to step behind it. He pulled back the bandages on my midline and popped off a couple staples so he could get a better look.

Within a second of looking, he said, "You have a massive abdominal infection. We are taking you into emergency surgery."

Moira stepped out from behind the curtain with tears welling in her eyes. Susan got on the phone and called my family, who had just sat down for lunch. They got back to the hospital very quickly. Before they took me back to the OR, Doctor Julie Wynne came into the room along with the resident from earlier to talk to my parents and me about the surgery.

Doctor Wynne said, "I'm sorry, but there is no way we could have prevented this. These things happen."

I looked over at them and said, "I have been telling you something was wrong. My nurse has been calling you all day. I said so over and over and over again, and nothing was done. You had someone come down and look at me and then dismiss it like it was nothing."

Doctor Wynne said, "I am sorry. There was nothing we could have done." I told her, "This is not directed toward you." The resident standing next to Doctor Wynne slowly lowered her head.

I was in the OR within an hour. When they had me on the actual operating table the resident came over to me, took my hand, put her other hand on my head, and said, "We're going to take good care of you. I promise." From then on any time she came in she was all smiles. She always listened intently. And any time she saw my parents in the cafeteria or outside of my room she always gave them a hug. It was truly amazing to see the changes in her, and I was grateful for that.

Before the surgery, my doctors thought I had stool floating around in my abdomen, which meant I would probably come out of the surgery with a colostomy bag. My parents knew I could handle a lot, but that would shatter me. Turned out, what they thought was stool actually was necrosis of the liver – thank God, they didn't have to give me a colostomy bag. More of my liver was continuing to die. During surgery the doctors reopened my midline incision; they cleaned out the dead tissue and removed additional pieces of fractured ribs. After operating, surgeons sewed up the muscle and fascia, but did not close the skin. They didn't want to pull, stitch or staple it back together and risk another infection. They did leave big sutures on each side hoping to eventually pull them together. It's actually a smaller risk to leave it open and packed and healing from the inside out, rather than sewing it back together. Left open, the midline was now a little over three inches wide and about ten inches long.

After surgery more tissue continued to die, and they were unable to close the midline. The doctors talked about taking me to the OR every day for debridement. The debriding process was necessary, but unfortunately I had to be lightly sedated every time. Instead of taking me to the OR for five days in a row, they brought an anesthesiologist with them. They wouldn't put me under to the point of being completely knocked out, but just where I wouldn't remember the pain. Then Dr. Rhee would take his scalpel and cut out the black pieces of dead tissue.

A couple of days later, even though I still was in poor condition, we celebrated Sean's birthday with a cake at the hospital. We have pictures of everyone surrounding my bed with his birthday cake. I felt terrible. It wasn't much of a celebration in my mind, but Sean told me it was the best gift he could have had.

Within a few days of that surgery, all my family except my parents had to get back to their jobs and their lives. My brothers, Aunt Beth, Cousin Austin and Grandma Ely left. My daily life was the same with them gone. I still had my visitors – my parents, old friends, new friends, and strangers. The infection setback really hurt my recovery. I still was unable to eat and kept losing weight, which caused continued loss of what little strength I had left. It was even harder to get out of bed, which slowed my progress. The first time they made me walk was after I hadn't walked in about two weeks. I thought getting out of bed was the hardest thing I would ever have to do... until I had to walk. Getting out of bed was even worse now that my wounds were bigger. I had a trench dug down the middle of my abdomen. My challenge that first day was to walk five to ten steps outside of my room. The feeling of being gutless was even worse than before. I felt like I was learning to walk for the first time. *Just put one foot in front of the other, Alicia,* I told myself. *Take it one step at a time.* But I was helpless. There was no way I could do it on my own. It wasn't that I didn't have the motor skills or the coordination to walk. It was that I truly felt lifeless.

❧

One thing that sprang to life, though, was the rumor mill. I was most grateful for everyone's support, but some people got their information from someone who heard it from someone who heard it from someone else. And that, of course, is not always accurate! Things started to get twisted, which was bad for my sister Kendra, who was in the Philippines. As time went by, people started posting wrong information online. She would see it and think I was doing really well when, in fact, I was not. Or worse, find out that I had another emergency surgery from someone who had posted it online before my family was able to get in touch with her.

Kendra is two years younger than me. Of course I love my big brothers, but the fact that we are both girls kept us close to one another growing up. Kendra are I are very different in many ways, but that sisterly bond has always kept us tight. When Kendra was only 12 years old she almost lost her life after being bucked off of a horse. Her spleen ruptured, and she nearly bled to death. Kendra was much younger than I was when she went through a life-changing experience. I watched, as her older sister, her grow as a woman of God, and looked up to her. She, at a very young age, could have chosen to let it spoil and darken the rest of her life, but she did not. These experiences have unified us in a way that no one will ever understand. Kendra almost died at such a young age, but she has come out of it with such poise and grace. She has been such an incredible example to me! There are not many people who have had near-death experiences, and the fact that she is my sister speaks of the Lord's plan in my life.

The fact I was shot in gang-related crime created other communication problems. The detectives could not release any information, which left people guessing. The day after the shooting, Jory Hancock, the head of the dance department at UofA, sent a mass e-mail to all of the dancers at the school to let them know what happened. He also scheduled a meeting to keep everyone up to date, but wasn't allowed to say much. Of course, not everyone came in to visit every day, because people still had their lives to live (life goes on). As much as I'd like to think that the world stopped just like mine did, it didn't. So, people acquired information any way they could, not knowing if it was accurate. Some of my closest friends didn't know how to react when they were told they weren't allowed access to information. Things became very warped for some of the people closest to me. No one was sure what they were allowed to ask. Even if they were given information, they weren't sure what they could safely pass along.

People in Colorado seemed to know more precisely what was going on than the people in Tucson. That was because my mom spent hours every day making phone calls with updates – this was before she started texting. Mom called Aunt Beth, who called the people on her list, and so on. Mom also called Sarah Ary, or Sarah called my mom, every day. Sarah was reliable to give the right information to all of the friends that I had grown up with. I had friends in Tucson who didn't know as much as Sarah did, but Sarah talked to my mom on a daily basis. There was mass confusion at the university. It often lit a little fire under both my parents and me, because mistaken information was going out. My mom found out someone had posted online that I was "doing good" on a particular day. I wasn't doing good at all! I hadn't had a "good" day in quite a long time.

One of the positive things about the mass communication, was the prayers that were taking place all over the world. But we wanted these prayers to be accurate. "Lord, please keep Alicia as well and healthy as she is," is a completely different prayer than, "Lord, please show her your presence as she is fighting for her life."

My doctors and nurses continued to help me in that fight. As time went on, I got to know them even better, and I started looking forward to seeing them every day. They were a source of comfort for me. They had saved my life twice; they were my security blanket. They didn't all have great bedside manners, but it was okay – they were not there to paint my nails and chitchat. They started to grow on me, and I think I started to grow on some of them, too. They began to realize I wasn't a complainer and listened intently to me.

Five days after the surgery to clean out my infection, I had a surprise visit. My parents had rushed from their home in the middle of the night, leaving my three-year-old baby sister behind. They hadn't seen her since, and it had been close to three weeks. Grandma Brady and Emma flew out to see me! My sweet little sister walked into my hospital room. It was the first time I was sharing a room, so it was tight space and fairly unpleasant. To get to the bathroom, I had to pass my roommate. But little Emma walked in, and the first thing she said was, "Did they take out your ribs?" Someone had tried to explain things to her. Her three-year-old mind thought I had received a bad injection (shot), but she did know what ribs were. She found it pretty interesting that some of mine were taken out. I smiled the best I could, as Emma walked to my bed and wanted to give me a hug. I was nervous about her touching me and possibly inflicting more pain. Mom helped Emma, and she did her best to give me a hug around the neck.

I had received hundreds of cards and letters that mom and dad read to me. When Grandma came, she brought all the e-mails she received from family and friends. She read some of the more encouraging ones to me. She also "Alicia sat," so mom and dad could have quality time with Emma. My baby sister also brought me homemade cards from her preschool class. One made me want to laugh, but I tried my best to hold it in because laughing hurt. "I am sorry you got shot by a bad guy," it said. The little heart-shaped card was so honest and to the point! I don't think I received a single other card that was quite so succinct and perfect.

Before Grandma and Emma arrived, I had once again told my doctors and nurses that sensations in my abdomen were concerning me. Getting out of bed seemed to be more difficult, and I had more trouble breathing. Like anyone who has undergone surgery, I had a spirometer for breathing exercises. I loathed that thing! But was told I had to use it a few times every hour to keep from getting pneumonia. I tried, but I couldn't physically take a deep enough breath to do the exercise with the little machine properly. My body just would not let me. This time they listened when I said something was wrong. Doctor Wynne ordered a CAT scan. Nothing showed up on it, so I said okay, something still felt wrong, but I didn't know how to argue with that.

A day after Grandma and Emma arrived, they, along with my parents were around my bed. The head nurse happened to stop by to introduce herself. As she stood at my bedside I had a sudden sharp pain in the middle of my abdomen, which burned with every breath I took.

"Ouch, something hurts," I said.

"Oh, you're probably fine."

"Would you mind just checking?"

So, she reached for the bed sheets and found blood on them. Picking up speed she unwrapped my abdominal binder and took off my bandages. She looked, saw the bleeding, and started applying pressure.

I didn't know it at the time, but my diaphragm had ruptured and my breathing became more challenging. The diaphragm is a sheet of internal skeletal muscle that extends across the bottom of the rib cage. It separates the thoracic cavity from the abdominal cavity and performs an important function in respiration. Immediately the nurse called for a "Code Red," the most severe situation possible in the hospital. The code called for a rapid response team, which required certain positions in the hospital to drop whatever they were doing and get where they were needed. The rapid response team arrived first and stayed until the trauma team arrived. Right after the nurse pulled the cord to call the code, Grandma took Emma out of the room before she could see anything. The trauma team worked to prepare me for surgery once again. It didn't hurt as bad as getting shot, but the burning I felt can only be described as having one spot of my body on fire. The sting in the center of my chest became more centralized as the flame intensified.

When I was in surgery, Doctor Wynne went to my mom in tears and said, "I am so sorry. I don't know how we missed this. We checked it. I just don't know how we missed it."

Once again after surgery I awoke feeling disoriented, out of control and drugged. I needed pain medication but could not focus enough to find the words to ask for help from the nurse. Yet, I remember everything. Time after time, nurse after nurse, doctor after doctor, friend after friend, and family member after family member told me that one day this would all be a bad, distant dream. I would not remember it. Here I am, easily recounting little details; I guess I am supposed to remember it. All of it. Every moment is crystal clear. They moved me from recovery into the Intensive Care Unit, which was my sixth hospital room. Grandma Brady, who was seventy at the time, sat next to me in a chair the entire night. I woke up during the night and thought I was somewhere else, but I remember Grandma being there. I can feel the emotion and the confusion and the pain of that night.

Sadly, because of the latest setback and its fallout, Grandma and Emma cut their trip short. Emma wasn't allowed in the ICU, which made it difficult to keep track of her while watching me. My parents were unhappy, because they didn't get to see much of Emma or my grandma, but they understood the need to return home. Like I have said, my nurses were incredible. But there was one who seemed a bit rougher than the rest of them. I happened to have this nurse the day Emma and Grandma were leaving. They stopped by the hospital again to say goodbye and talk with my parents. Since Emma was so young she wasn't allowed in the ICU, but they certainly couldn't leave her in the waiting room by herself! So Grandma brought her into my room anyway.

My nurse jumped on my parents and grandmother, saying, "What is she doing back here? She is not allowed back here."

So my dad said, right to her face, "Gee, Attila the Hun, huh?"

She didn't like that much and of course my mom said, "Randy!"

When the nurse walked out of the room everyone smiled and laughed a bit. Funny!

We were all thankful to have the chance to see Emma and Grandma. It was rough not only for Emma to be away from her Daddy and Mommy for so long, but for our parents to be away from her. I know it gave mom and dad peace of mind that we had family and friends back home they could rely on to take good care of her and give her lots of love.

I was agitated that all privacy flew out the door once I entered the hospital. It was dehumanizing to need help to bathe, use the restroom, brush my teeth, and even comb my hair. And then there was the hospital gown. Not only are they ugly, they leave your backside completely exposed and I wore one 24 hours a day. Others had to do everything for me, there was nothing I could do about it, so I just let it happen. A sense of innocence was taken from me, but I appreciated that I had people to take care of me. When I look back at pictures, I can't believe I lived like that. I don't understand how anyone could.

Several people had called to ask if they should fly to Tucson to help out. In the beginning we had so much help there were almost too many people. My family did need the support and especially the prayers, but when others came from out of town, the hospital was the only place they could all be together. More visitors didn't necessarily mean more help. Back in Cañon City, my friend Sarah Ary had been faithfully calling my mom every day to get an update. When she heard about my diaphragm rupture, she realized that I might not live through this. She wanted to visit me.

Mom told Sarah if she came she would be sitting by my bed every day, watching dressing changes, helping me use the restroom, and helping me sit up and lay back down. She told Sarah to prepare herself, because I was not the same Alicia that she knew.

Sarah understood all of that and still decided to come to Tucson for a four-day trip. The day before she arrived, the doctors determined they had to give me a feeding tube. I had lost more than fifteen pounds despite the threat of a feeding tube, so I told them to go ahead and put it in. My dad sat up with me through that night, while they were having trouble getting the tube in. Inch by inch it went through my nose, down my throat and into my stomach. Now, I sometimes forget all the machines, monitors and tubes hooked up to my body. Back then, just seeing all those gadgets, smelling the scents, and hearing the beeping weighed me down and made me tired.

When Sarah came to the hospital, the first thing she witnessed was my chest tube being removed. The chest tube was placed in my right lung after my diaphragm ruptured to drain the fluid that had built up. There was about four inches of actual tubing inside me.

One of the doctors came in and said, "Are you ready to take your chest tube out?" He came over and took out my stitches. He told me to take a deep breath, and then he started pulling. It was like pulling your fingers out of a Chinese finger trap. Sarah was always given the choice to leave the room, with a doctor asking her, "Are you sure you want to watch this?" And thankfully, she always stayed with me.

No one wants to see another human being in a broken, inhuman-like condition, especially your best friend. But Sarah always stood by my side. I had heard from several people that it was just too hard to see me in the state I was in. But then, having Sarah come for four days and spend every single day with me, watching everything that took place, made me realize what a wonderful friend she really is. I do think a lot of it was her personality. She never shed a tear in front of me. She stayed so courageous for me. That might not have been the case once she left my room, but I know both my parents and I drew so much strength from her during her visit. Sarah was able to spend some time with my roommates, Sarah and Moira, whom she already knew from the year before when we vacationed together. During this trip, she also met Jake, Danielle, my doctors and other friends. It was exciting to have my two worlds intertwining together. I knew that it was exciting for her, too.

To this day, Sarah and I still always joke about that feeding tube. I was still losing weight, and it was an ongoing battle between the doctors and me. They knew I was a dancer and were almost suggesting I wasn't eating on purpose. The stuff they fed me through that tube was a brown bag of mush. When Doctor Wynne told me they were giving me the feeding tube, she also said I had free reign to eat whatever I wanted! Then she mentioned fast-food. I am not a big fan. For some reason, I was confused and thought they were going to mush up fast-food and put it in my feeding tube.

I kept looking at Sarah, "Please don't let them do that. I don't like it. I don't want it."

She just said, "Okay."

We laugh now, because I was really concerned about that! I did not want that food put into my body!

Normally, Sarah and I spoke with each other on a regular basis, and it had been over a month since we had last talked. I wanted to make the most of our time together so I attempted to have meaningful conversations. Later down the road, Sarah told me, "No one understood how close you were to dying, Alicia. People just didn't want to believe it." She had conversations with friends who said, "Oh, when Alicia gets out of the hospital," and things like that. Sarah told them, "I used to think the same thing, but things will never be the same for her again. Her life will never be the same. She won't just get out of the hospital and then bounce right back." But that is what most people thought. Because Sarah saw my condition, she was able to comprehend the dire truth of it.

Sarah did have a hard time seeing my wounds, but it bothered her more that I just wasn't her old friend; Ashley Parnau told me the exact same thing. I was stuck in bed, weak, completely dependent everything surrounding me, working to keep me alive. I wasn't laughing or going my usual 100 miles per hour. Sarah said it was those four days when she truly realized that if I survived, my life and all of our lives would never be the same again. Before that realization hit, she denied such a thing ever being possible.

After Sarah left, I was finally healthy enough to move out of the ICU. The wound care floor of the hospital had extremely small semiprivate rooms so they put me on the oncology unit where there were large, private rooms. This was my seventh room. Not just my seventh hospital room, but my parents' seventh hospital room. They had hauled all of my stuff – cards, pictures, and knick knacks that made my room a bit more comfortable – all around the hospital for me. They also moved around a green chair, the only place I had finally able to find some comfort while sitting up. It was also the chair my mom slept in for about 41 straight nights! Doctor Wynne told the nurses to give me the largest room available; it was huge! It was nice to finally have some space to give us room to breathe as I continued my stay in the hospital.

ﺷﻞ

One day, my mom took all of my cards and the clippings from our hometown newspaper and taped them up on the wall. We were settling in, thinking we were finally going to get to stay in the same room longer than a few days. It was a good change for us. But I soon discovered the room was so big it echoed, and the way it carried sound was too overpowering for me. It gave me horrible anxiety. Even when people came in or left the room, I would jump when the door closed. This was the beginning of my experiences with Post Traumatic Stress Disorder. Every loud sound made my heart skip a beat, and that room carried the noise and made it seem louder than it really was. I asked my mom and dad to tell others to shut the door more quietly. While it was a nice, spacious room, it was a big open space that was simply too big for me.

Lots of visitors still came to see me. I remember Sarah, Moira and another good friend, Jess, being in this particular room a lot. It's strange that I might not remember what time of day it was, or what day of the week, but I definitely remember things by what room I was in. I was always in the same spot in each room, so I had a lot of time to take in the life around me. I recognized everything around me was changing, and I wasn't. My friends would often come in and just sit by me or do their homework. I had one friend who told me she would come in and just sit and watch me breathe. When they walked in the room I always asked how they were doing. I truly wanted to know. Just because we weren't able to spend every day together didn't make our friendship any less. I hadn't been outside in weeks, and wanted to know what was going on in the real world. In general, people seemed afraid to tell me how they were doing. It was hard for them to talk without crying, and if they were having a good day, they felt guilty expressing that to me. How do you say, "It's a good day," to someone in my situation? Most of the time, though, I dosed off and on while trying to hold conversations. Once one of the girls said to me, "It's okay, Alicia. Just sleep."

I appreciated every visit, but I was beginning to wonder if I would ever leave the hospital. It seemed that I wasn't getting any better physically. Mentally, I started to get worse. I didn't want to hear any talk about "that night." I didn't want to hear whispering voices, whether it was about me or not. I always thought it was. My anxious heart and mind just couldn't take any more.

Susan, who had been loyally visiting almost every day, played the bad guy. In the beginning she was the bouncer at my door, saying, "Okay, you only get a few minutes in there with her." Or when someone came to the room with tears in their eyes she told them they couldn't come in crying. So when my mom suggested fewer visitors might be a good thing, Susan passed the information to all the dancers. It's not that I didn't want to see anyone at all. I just thought if I had more quiet time and time to rest, my anxiety might start to subside.

Unfortunately, the request was misconstrued. Our desires were misunderstood in the communications channels, and when certain people just stopped showing up, my feelings were hurt. I believed people stopped caring. With fewer people visiting and getting less information directly from my parents, the information was even more warped than it was in the beginning.

We hoped I was going to start climbing uphill, but my weight still was dropping. I was always sick to my stomach and I spent a lot of time throwing up. Most of the time I still couldn't get up to use the restroom, and after my catheter was taken out, I had to use a bedpan or a bedside toilet. I was also having my dressings changed twice a day. Doctors and nurses also "stripped" the drain tubes in my abdomen, which was excruciating. The tubes were not actually attached to anything inside me, they were sutured to my skin. The tubes drained out all the unnecessary fluids inside my body. They could get clogged, so doctors and nurses started at the top and squeezed the tube all the way down, pulling on it to make certain it kept draining like it needed to.

My entrance wound was still the same size, but my exit wound was enlarged by the seven inch incision they had made during the surgery to repair my diaphragm. When my diaphragm ruptured, the doctors went in through the exit wound to fix things. Again, they closed the muscle and fascia around the bullet hole, but not the skin. My midline incision was not healing as fast as they would have liked, so they used a wound vacuum, which is exactly what it sounds like. It was placed in my midline wound, where it used a controlled pressure to promote healing. It sucked my body back together, like a vacuum, while also removing excess bacteria and promoting good blood flow. Since my eating habits hadn't returned, a nutritionist came to see me. She provided special drinks to make sure I was getting as much nutrition as I possibly could. They also gave me a special purple mixture in my feeding tube every day that was very high in vitamins but made me sick when I first took it. My daily activity was getting up and getting into my special chair.

On the morning of November 4 – Election Day – I was sitting in my chair resting. Doctor Rhee came in and started looking at my wounds.

He said, "You have got to get up, and you have got to try." And that was that. He also told me I was going to be very addicted to painkillers, and wanted me to go off them "cold turkey." I am not a person who just gives up and I was trying. Unfortunately, I was so debilitated, movement was next to impossible.

A constant fear hung over me. I felt scared and uneasy; something was amiss. I know now it was God keeping me on my toes, keeping me alert and prepared for what was to come.

Right after Doctor Rhee left the room, a pain management specialist walked in to see me for the first time. She spent almost an hour going over my chart, the meds I was on, and how often I was receiving them.

After studying my records she said, "Well, the problem is that you are still in too much pain! We need to increase your meds." I was right on board with that.

My mom asked about becoming addicted to the pain killers. The doctor said that yes, I would be addicted, but we would deal with that when the time came. The most important thing now was to manage the pain enough to promote healing.

My parents were still my backbone, and they now needed all the support they could get. One of my mom's best friends, Jane Mattox, flew out a few days before on a Friday to visit and lend her support. She came at the perfect time.

The worst was yet to come.

Chapter Six

I have set before you life and death, now choose life.
– Deuteronomy 30:19

PAIN ENGULFED ME IN THE HOSPITAL, I could not escape it. Interaction with my family, friends, nurses and doctors diverted my attention occasionally but I lived in my own world of incoherence and sorrow.

I don't remember thinking about specific things during most of my stay there. Despite the meds I still was present in conversations, even though they lasted just a few seconds or mere minutes. When I wasn't sleeping I drifted on a horizon of thoughtlessness. I did not think about how my family and friends were dealing with this. I did not think about God and ask why this was happening to me. Indeed, I was well aware of all the things that were happening around me, but I could not participate more fully. I was now always the observer, even to my medical care, and was never capable to be a participant. It was not my choice – my mind, body and spirit always were consumed with the anticipation of what was to come.

Things look different to me now. Today I see the Lord was clearly communicating and working through others the entire time. He was always there and never left my side, even though I didn't feel His presence until my final medical emergency. He was not only working through the prayers that were being answered every day but through the hands of my magnificent doctors, who helped save me over and over again. During that time I received cards from all over the world. I had visitors I had never met but whom had just heard about the shooting. They came in to offer a prayer, a "hello," to lend support in any way they could. They gave us what we needed most, hope. Just one in a lengthy string of visitors was the pastor of a nearby church who came in one day when just Dad and I were in the room. He told me the story of his daughter, who had multiple abdominal surgeries and was told she would be unable to have children. But now, in her late 20s, she was several months pregnant with her first child. I know what I felt on the inside didn't always come across on the outside. I was incredibly grateful for the encouragement and stories of all those who came to share.

It wasn't until Tuesday, November 4th, 2008 that I realized the Lord had power over the situation the entire time. I had no idea what day it was, let alone Election Day, until a nurse mentioned it to me. Day after day and night after night my life had been the same. I felt I went nowhere, while everything outside the hospital continued to move with the fast pace of the world.

That was the day the doctors told me to get up, get out of bed, and get going. It was the day they were particularly hard on me, telling me I had to tough it up and move. To me, they were saying I wasn't trying. That same day a pain specialist came in and upped my meds. Yay! This was a packed day! Everyone had come and gone, leaving my dad and me alone. I always joke that my dad was "reading," because he was most likely napping along with me. As I lay resting in my hospital bed, I heard an audible voice coming from my left side.

"One more time," the voice said. I did not recognize the voice. I knew it wasn't my dad, and there was no one else in the room. I didn't even bother to open my eyes. I knew who it was. God was telling me that something else was going to happen, preparing me for the worst. But for the very first time, a restful peace came over me. I was okay knowing that something else was coming.

I continued to rest calmly and didn't say anything to anyone about the voice. Soon my parents went out to dinner, while Sarah,

Moira, and Jess came to "Alicia sit." We watched the movie SWEET HOME ALABAMA together. It was so nice to watch a movie and share a bit of the normalcy we used to have. Truth be told, I didn't watch much of the movie, but they all came in and sat next to me in the uncomfortable chairs as I lay on my bed. I know my friends wanted to stay longer, but I was really tired from all the activity. When my parents returned my friends left, promising they would be back in a couple of days to visit again. My dad and our friend Jane left to return to the home where everyone was staying, leaving my mom and me at the hospital. I was getting ready for bed, which meant that instead of sleeping two hours at a time I hopefully would get at least four or five hours of uninterrupted sleep. It was hard for me to "go to bed," given that I already was in bed most of the day. I ventured outside that bed only to my chair, which was about ten feet away. Like always, I was on edge, because I could not shake the thought that one more big hurdle was coming my way. My nurses always told me to relax and try to get some sleep, but I could not forget that every bad "crash" my body suffered was at night. Well, night was looming once again, and this thought in the back of my mind said I wasn't through suffering.

I was being tucked into my bed with ten pillows and what I called "my little treat," another dose of meds. I was so anxious at night I had panic attacks, making it hard to doze off. That difficulty was compounded with one of the side effects of Dilaudid, which is itching. My skin didn't just itch, it crawled! I felt like I had hundreds of little worms crawling all over my body, and I found it impossible not to pick and scratch at them. So the nurses gave me Benadryl, an allergy medicine, when I went to bed each night. The Benadryl, given straight into my IV, took away the itching and helped me relax. I was tucked in and drugged up, ready for the night. The nurse that gave me the Benadryl was headed toward the door when I said, "I think I'm leaking."

There was no quick response, because I had mentioned this several times over the last few days. It was usually nerves trying to wake back up, which felt like something wet was sliding down the side of my abdomen. I also had trouble with the Kerlix for my dressing changes, which sometimes were soaked with more saline than usual. But then I said, "I am leaking a lot." There was no pain, but it felt like someone had dumped a bucket of water on the side of my bed.

My mom got to my side first, because she was closer. When she pulled the covers back to look, she found a pool of blood at my side. This was maybe only ten seconds since I first said I was leaking. The nurse saw the blood, rushed over to pull the emergency cord, pulled her gloves back on and started to feel around my wound. She immediately applied pressure to see if she could stop the bleeding. Blood continued to spill out onto the bed, and I could feel my life draining away. It wasn't slowly trickling down my side; it was as if someone had turned on a faucet and let it run. I felt the light in my face start to leave. I felt the nurse find the spot to somewhat plug the bleeding.

"Right there." I said.

"This probably really hurts," she said.

It did. She was pushing as hard as she could on an open wound.

"That's okay. You can push harder," I told her.

Since the nurse absolutely could not even move her hands, she wasn't able to do anything else to begin to stabilize me. If she moved her hand at all I would start to bleed again, and this time I would probably bleed out within a matter of seconds.

My mom ran into the hallway, yelling, "We need help!"

Familiar faces rushed into the room, including the nurses and CNAs that I had for most of my stay there.

My mom came back into the room and took my right hand. I looked at my nurse and said, "Please don't let go. Please don't let go."

She said, "I won't. I won't."

I knew the pressure she was applying was the only thing keeping me alive.

The rapid response team got there quickly. They piled into the room along with many others from the floor. There were so many familiar faces, but they looked different now. This time, they looked at me with defeat in their eyes. Many of them were hanging their heads. They didn't have to say what they were thinking. I knew. *This poor girl is going to die.*

Just about seven minutes later, the trauma team arrived. Dr. Rhee walked in, and I had never been so happy to see somebody in my life. I never thought I would say that about him, but it was true. Before this, he had given me a lot of tough love. I knew if anybody could save me, he was the one. When he walked in the door, a trace of relief seeped into my brain.

Dr. Rhee came to my side as the nurse kept the pressure on. I know her little arms were extremely tired, because she was putting all she had into pushing on me. When Dr. Rhee told her to let go so he could look, his face changed, and his eyes flew wide open. "That's arterial," he said. Then he grabbed a wad of Kerlix and shoved his fist into the wound at my side, opening it to several times its original size. He repeated this process seven or eight times until my abdominal cavity was packed. Then he used his fingers to search for the spot that was gushing, discovered it, plugged it with his index finger and stopped the bleeding. For some reason I decided I wanted to look. I started to lift my head up, but he quickly stopped me and said, "Don't look."

My mom stood by my side, calmly holding my hand in the few minutes this all took place. She asked one of the nurses to get her cell phone so she could call Jane, who would tell Dad. And then the phone tree would be started along with the all-important prayer chain.

My dad walked into the room a few minutes later. He stepped in to see his little girl covered in blood and surrounded by people who were trying to save her. He went ghost white and started to hyperventilate, reaching for something to catch himself. His legs were giving out. My mom saw this and yelled at a nurse.

"Get him out of here now!"

I thought he looked like he was having a heart attack. Mom knew he couldn't take seeing me like that, so some nurses helped him out of the room. Jane went to sit with him.

There were probably twenty or more people working to stabilize me. As all the doctors and other nurses worked around me and talked, I started to realize what had happened. I had an aneurism, basically an enlarged artery, in my liver. It had just ruptured, spraying life-giving blood with every heartbeat.

I had only one IV site at that time. I was still gaunt. I hadn't eaten. I needed blood and other fluids right away. They started giving me blood in the single IV I did have and tried to get another

IV going. At the same time, one of the residents pointed to the monitors and told Dr. Rhee, "Look." My stats were falling fast. Normal blood pressure is 120/80; mine tends to run low at about 90/60. At that moment it read 50/30. Everyone glanced at Dr. Rhee but kept working.

My mom was holding fast to my hand. She had so much adrenalin pumping through her body that her hand was shaking, which caused mine to shake. She continued to look in my eyes, telling me that I could do this, and that she loved me. Then she said, "You're the strongest person I know. You're the bravest person I know."

Dr. Rhee turned to my mom and said, "So are you."

I had to go back to the ICU before surgery. Dr. Rhee and my nurse switched spots again. He took her hand, placing her finger on the appropriate spot. Because she was so small she was able to climb onto the bed with me when they wheeled me out. As we started to move, my world went black. I lost all vision.

I lifted my head off my pillow, wide-eyed, and said, "I can't see. I can't see."

I was still holding my mom's hand. I was talking, awake, and alert, but my vision was completely black. My mom just held tighter and tighter and said, "Yes, you can. Yes, you can."

In that moment I felt two hands slide under my head to support me. This was the instant God gave me the free will to choose: Live or die. I felt His presence, saying to me, "Alicia, if you want to let go, then let go, and I will take you back into my hands. But if you want to fight, then fight, and I will lift you up. This battle is not yours alone."

I chose to fight. In that split second I fought harder than I have ever fought for anything in my life. I fought and held on one more second, lifted my head up an inch higher, and then my vision came back. I slumped back against my pillow and knew I would survive.

My dad was outside the door when they wheeled me out of the room. He came to my side as we flew by, but I told him, "I'm going to be fine. I love you." He probably was not convinced.

They took me into ICU, because they still had preparations to make before they could get me into surgery. Dr. Rhee had called in a favor to one of the vascular surgeons who lived about 45 minutes away. Dr. Smyth wasn't even on call that night, but he came to help with the surgery anyway. They would go through the femoral artery in the groin up into the liver, where they would use platinum coils to plug the artery. Dr. Rhee said Dr. Smyth was the best man for the job. The aneurism had happened in a branch of the hepatic artery, which supplies 20 percent of the blood needed by the liver.

While we waited for Dr. Smyth, they continued to work on me in the ICU. All I wanted to do was close my eyes and rest, but every time I shut my eyes, someone said, "Alicia, you have to stay awake." I was completely surrounded by people packed into that little room. The nurse continued to use her hands to plug my wound; Dr. Amini and Dr. Rhee were at the foot of the bed making phone calls to get the surgery set up. One resident was on one side placing an IV in one thigh artery, while another resident worked to place another IV in the other thigh. One would be used to get fluids in, while the other would be used for the surgery. My parents weren't allowed in the room while they were putting the IVs in, because the area had to be completely sterile. I had no idea what they were doing until I heard and felt a loud "snap!" as they pushed a large needle into each thigh. After one of the residents placed the needle, he stopped for a second to look at me and took a deep breath. He lightly rubbed my arm, as if to say to me, "It's okay." I appreciated that he took that moment to stop to comfort me. They covered me with blankets to keep me warm. I did not think I was going to die, but still began to wonder if I should ask to see my parents. *Should I tell them how much I love them? Should I be saying my goodbyes?* I wasn't sure what to think. In the end, I didn't say anything. I didn't want anyone to think I was giving up, because I certainly wasn't.

Eventually I faded off, but they did allow my mom to come sit with me before I went back into surgery. There were only a few people in the room now. While I still was conscious the whole time, I don't remember the last twenty minutes before surgery. It was just my mom, the nurse and Dr. Rhee who were left in the room with me. Dr. Rhee sat on a stool with his hand plugging my artery until it was time to operate.

That night was the first time in my life that I fully surrendered to the Lord. I had asked Jesus to come into my heart when I was a little girl, but this night I fully understood what it meant to let go and trust His Kingship. He was in control. My mom and dad later told me their prayers changed that night.

As I headed into surgery, they no longer said, "Lord, please save our child." They now prayed, "Lord, we surrender. Thy will be done. She can't take this anymore. Please take away her suffering."

My mom passed this on to others as she asked for prayers. She told people, "We can't be selfish anymore. If it is God's will to take her, then we have to let her go. She can't live like this any longer."

My parents were amazed to find that after this prayer, the Lord gave me back to them.

I awoke the next day to find I was intubated, too weak to breathe on my own. The next few days are pretty blurry for me – really the only time in the hospital when things aren't clear – but I do remember that tube. My hands were tied down, because the natural reaction is to pull at something that is lodged in your throat. When I opened my eyes in confusion, my parents and a nurse explained why I couldn't move my hands. I should have been so heavily sedated I would not be able to come around and should never have known what was going on. But I did know. I was awake and thinking, *Am I even breathing? Or is this machine doing it for me?* My mouth was 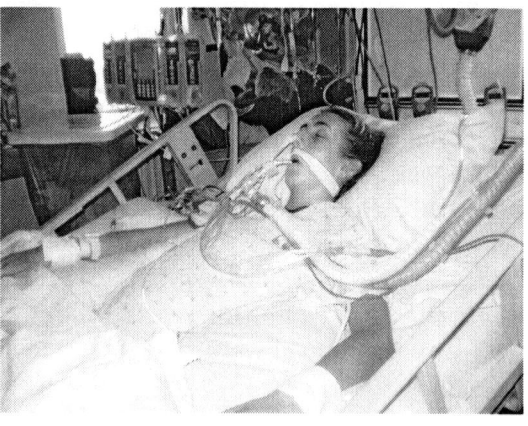 wide open but filled with a giant tube. My hands were held down, and I could not move. The emotional trauma finally hit me, and I was nearly swept away in a tide of anguish and sorrow. Tears ran down my face and my mom wiped them away, whispering to me that I should just relax. That moment was the most powerless I have ever felt.

A bit later I tried to tell mom and Jane that I needed ChapStick, which was difficult since I couldn't talk or use my hands. I tried to move my lips as best I could. After playing the guessing game for awhile, Jane figured out what I needed.

The nurse came in and said, "What's going on? She isn't supposed to be awake!"

Later Jane told me, "You're the only person I know that can be intubated, with her hands tied down, and still boss people around."

Emergency surgery the night before was only to fix the rupture. I was too critical to try to perform additional work, so they took me back into surgery the day after on Wednesday to open me up and clean everything out. After that surgery they waited to be sure I was strong and stable before they extubated me. A nurse came in and said they were going to take the tube out.

"It's going to feel like you are choking, but just keep breathing out."

It was like a suction cup as they pulled it from my body. Even today, it makes me gag to think about. Of course, having something like that down your throat is painful. I continued to hurt even after it was removed. That made it even worse to try to talk.

I was still in ICU when Dr. Smyth came to see me a day or so after I was extubated. He talked to us, mainly my parents, about what he had done during the surgery. I remember watching him draw a picture, but the only thing I really remember him saying was they had put platinum coils into my liver to stop the bleed. He had to try several different shapes before he finally found one that worked. It was shaped like a tornado, thicker at the top and smaller as it spiraled down.

Thankfully, I wasn't so heavily sedated after the extubation. Things became clearer again, but I started running a fever of 104 degrees. My body was fighting against white blood cells I had received from all the transfusions, about eight units of blood and another four units of plasma. My body didn't like the donated blood. They set the temperature of my room at about 65 degrees and brought in two or three fans to continually blow on my body. I had only a single sheet to cover myself. Anyone who came to visit brought a coat or asked the nurse for a blanket. This became known that when you came into Alicia's room you were going to need a jacket of some kind!

My entrance wound was healing. The midline incision had been reopened so there was no progress with it. Sadly, now my exit wound was unbelievably huge. I still would not look at it. Everyone described it to me "as big as a grown man's fist," which makes sense, because my doctor's hand had been inside. My liver was exposed, and I heard people talk about the color of it. They told me the tissue surrounding it looked better. I tried to not imagine what it looked like, because I couldn't possibly create such an image in my mind. It was months down the road when I finally looked at a picture of how awful it had been. When I looked at that photo I thought, *I have no idea how I survived that.*

The first few days after surgery Dr. Rhee was the only one who changed my dressings. He didn't want anyone else touching them, and neither did I. Toward the end of the week, my nurse Aubreena said she was going to do the dressing change that night. It scared us all to hear that, and my mom excused herself for a moment. She went into the hallway to cry. Of course, Aubreena did an amazing job. She was a nurse I had had many times, and I was glad she was the first one to do this. But it was a huge step for me. Once again, Dr. Rhee had been my safe place, but it was time to start moving forward.

Speaking of moving forward, they had me out of bed by Friday evening. I must admit I hated everyone that day, but I knew I had to do it. I didn't want to get pneumonia on top of everything else. I know it was evening, because Aubreena is in the picture of me walking for the first time after the aneurism, and she always worked the night shift. Mom and Aubreena helped me out of bed, and a CNA came along for the short walk just to hold the machine that read my vitals. His only job was to keep an eye on my statistics. I was so thankful Aubreena was the one to help me start to walk. She was young, so I was very comfortable with her. She always was kind and understanding to whatever my needs were. Just like most of the nurses who cared for me, Aubreena was excellent at what she did.

While I was once again fighting for my life after the aneurism, news of the catastrophe spread faster in Colorado than it did in Tucson. The phone trees were working at home again. In fact, my mom called our family, our pastor and my friend Sarah Ary the night of the rupture and told them to get everyone out of bed and ask them to pray. Susan also knew, but for some reason, Sarah and

Moira didn't know. Classmates were asking them if it was true I had suffered an aneurism, and they had no idea. Some channels of communication were wide open and flowing, while others weren't working at all. I know some people were upset by the way they found out or how long it took, but it was totally out of my control.

Many of the people who did find out came to see me. I had an exciting visitor in the next day or so, the President of the University of Arizona, Dr. Robert Shelton. He came to meet me and my parents and to see how I was doing. The support the university continued to give me was more than we could have expected. Dr. Shelton brought me the cutest little stuffed duck that quacked when I squeezed it. He said he had looked for a Wildcat – the UofA mascot – but couldn't find one that made any noise, so he brought me the duck instead. The quacking noise was annoying, but I put it to excellent use. You see, I had my call button to call a nurse, but sometimes it took them awhile to get there. Truth be told, by the time I left the hospital, my mom knew my entire routine down and could do almost everything a nurse could do, except give me pain meds. And she spent almost every night I was in the hospital sleeping next to me in a chair. If I needed something and my mom was sleeping, my voice wasn't strong enough to wake her up. A low whisper was about all I could manage. Instead, I would take the big remote that holds the call button and bang that on the side of the bed to wake her up when I needed something. Real nice, I know, but it was effective. When I received the duck, I started using it as a "call button" for my mom! I'm sure she didn't like it much, but she let it slide.

Right around the same time Dr. Shelton visited me, Moira's parents came to town. I was still in ICU. My parents wanted to step out for a bit and get a bite to eat. Moira's mom, Debbie, used to be a nurse. Her dad, Richard, is a pain specialist. So I was very comfortable having them stay with me for awhile. The timing was bad for them! They ended up helping me move to a new room. You see, so many people are in and out of the hospital, when a patient is capable of leaving the ICU, they boot you out to make room for someone else. Since my parents were gone, Richard and Debbie graciously packed up all of my stuff, grabbed my chair and helped move me to my new room.

I was back on the oncology floor. This time I was really frightened to change rooms, because every time I moved from ICU to a regular room, something had gone wrong. I felt secure in the ICU. There, I was hooked up to a lot more machines that check everything going on with my body. Most of the time in the ICU, I had one-on-one care from the nurses. The patient-nurse ratio is a lot different on the other floors. When I had the aneurism they had to work hard to get another IV line started, but when you are a patient in ICU you already have two or three. While I was scared, I finally felt the worst was over. For the first time, I didn't think that every time I moved or took a step, something might explode or rupture inside me.

Because I was settling in to my new room, we asked Susan to let the dancers know I was once again ready for visitors. Once I was in my final room, I began to make very slow, but steady, progress. I was able to have a conversation with someone on a level higher than a whisper. I started to hold conversations for more than a few seconds or a minute without falling asleep in the middle of it! Life was indeed starting to look up. Still, I had not yet seen my wounds and didn't fully understand how much my body had changed.

My high school choir teacher, Todd Albrecht, sent me a giant poster he had made for fundraising back in Cañon City. It had pictures of me dancing and in choir shows, as well as other fun photos. My mom hung it up on the wall of my room. I remember several people making comments on the poster, but one doctor's comment distressed me. Dr. Amini had seen me almost every day since I had come into the hospital. He came into my room, looked at the poster, and asked, "Is that you?"

I thought, *Wow! I must look so different. People can't even recognize that it's me in those pictures.* Sadly, Dr. Amini was not the only one who asked if I was

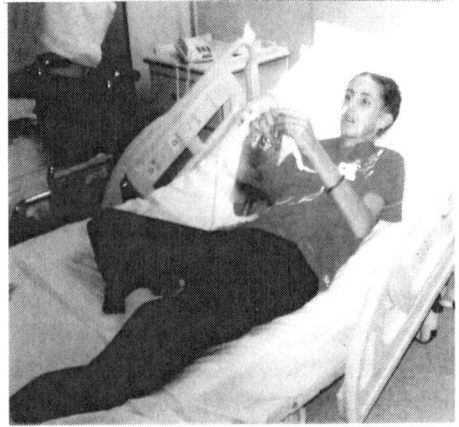

the girl in the photos.

I still had trouble with my weight. Eating continued to be a chore because I seemed to always be nauseated. My doctors were hoping my wounds would close on their own, because they didn't want to do another surgery or procedure if they didn't absolutely have to. So we waited a few days to see if my body could begin to heal itself, but it kept leaking bile. The flow seemed to speed up, with bile soaking through my Kerlix packed in my wound, the bandages over that, the abdominal binder, and through my hospital gown. A few days after I was transferred back into a regular room, Dr. Rhee decided to do an MRI to figure out the problem.

Well. I can't even tell you how many tests I already had done while I was hospitalized. It always terrified me to submit myself into someone else's hands. I know the techs who run the tests are skilled in their specialties, but because my wounds were covered, they did not understand how fragile I was. Usually, I was wheeled down in one bed and then transferred to another for the test. "Get in," they would tell me. "I can't by myself," I said. So they tried to move me, not knowing my injuries, and always ended up hurting me. Needless to say, it was scary for me to hear another test was ordered.

This time, I was taken down the same day Dr. Rhee ordered the test. I always have been claustrophobic, but I now had been confined to a room for months at a time with people hovering over me twenty-four hours a day, seven days a week. That made it even worse. So when we got to the MRI, I asked if they had to put my head in the machine. They told me no. I was put on the machine and they started it, but as I was going into the MRI, they put me in feet first, then continued to my torso, my chest, and then started to put my head in. I started screaming as best I could and put my hands up, trying to stop me from going in further.

I said, "Get me out."

I started crying and told them I understood I didn't need my head all the way in when they were looking at my liver. They took me out and back up to my room and waited until the next day to run the test. That day, they had to knock me out, but I had the test done.

Sadly, the test showed I still had damage to my liver. My bile ducts were very enlarged, which led to the bile leaking. Dr. John Cunningham, my gastroenterologist, decided to do a procedure called an ERCP, or Endoscopic Retrograde Cholangiopancreatography. Normally done with the patient on their stomach, my wounds made that impossible. It had to be done with me lying on my back. The technique uses endoscopy, instruments to examine the interior of a hollow organ or cavity of the body, and fluoroscopy, an imaging technique used to obtain real-time moving images of the internal structures of patients through the use of a fluoroscope. The surgeons determined I needed a tube to help drain my bile duct, so they once again placed another tube into my body. This time, the tube started a centimeter from my bile duct, went up through my duodenum (a short portion of the small intestine), through my stomach, up through my esophagus and out my nose. This lovely little tube drained my bile out of my body into a little bag, which someone had to empty a couple of times each day. I had to carry that nasogastric tube with me for three weeks! To this day, I still have a small point in my nose from that tube, which was really hard and had been taped to my nose. The gastro doctors even made signs and posted them around my bed, saying: "Don't Touch My Tube!" If the tube had been moved even a little bit, it could ruin the process of what it was trying to fix. Once again, I was incredibly uncomfortable. I could feel it at the back of my throat every time I swallowed. The only good thing… the tube was pink!

I was becoming more alert by the day. I'm sure I was more fun to visit. My friends and family came back in to visit me, and this time I felt like I could interact with them. I remember Sarah, Moira, Danielle, Jake and Jess visiting several times. They came in to sit by my side and hold my hand. I was awake enough to enjoy their company. This is when smiling started to become a normal part of my day. Every once in a while I tried to laugh. These are everyday things we all take for granted, because every time I smiled or laughed it created horrible pain for me. It was almost as if I had to learn to smile all over again.

I also was encouraged, because I was learning to do my own daily activities. I couldn't do them all every day, but adding in one thing at a time was a huge step forward. I finally was beginning to brush my teeth or wash my face. I helped with my sponge baths. Unfortunately I still was losing weight. For the first time I was able to stand up and get onto a scale. I weighed somewhere around 95 pounds. I remember looking at those numbers and not believing them.

My head continued to emerge from the fog that had cloaked me. I no longer slept the entire day away. Daily life started to change for me. Indeed it seemed to be looking up. I now looked forward to seeing my doctors and nurses. I was not just a patient that had been wheeled in and wheeled out within a few days. They had become an integral part of my life and I had become important to them. I was not only the patient whose case they would use for years to come as they taught new residents, I was the one they never gave up on, they fought tirelessly for, against incredible odds. I didn't dread their visits or shrink in fear for what new pain I was about to endure when they walked in my room. I was grateful to see them, even when I knew the visit might mean a little discomfort for me. Dr. Rhee even called me his "little prima donna." I wasn't their only patient; I wasn't their only gravely wounded patient. We tend to only remember them for what they have done during our time with them. We forget what the rest of their day may have looked like. They may have just lost a patient. During my stay in the hospital, I know my family and I developed a new admiration for not only those doctors, but for all in the medical profession. I know my parents enjoyed their company, even though it was just a few minutes each day. The medical team's visits had become routine, and mom and dad liked to see them even if it wasn't to discuss my medical issues.

A few days after my aneurism, my Grandma and Grandpa Ely and Aunt Beth came to Tucson. A day or so after that, my Grandma and Grandpa Brady, my Uncle Rex Brady and family friend Matt Conditt came down from Colorado. It was pretty packed in my room, and visitors had to take turns coming in and out during the day. It was refreshing for my parents to have so many familiar faces, and support close by. If they had shown up a week or two earlier I wouldn't have been able to handle it, but it was nice to have so many members of my family there again.

After that last big crash, my anxiety started to ease and the walls of protection started to come down which allowed me to share my experiences the night I was shot, and even about some of the events that had just taken place in the hospital. I no longer kept it all bottled inside. I woke up many mornings to find everyone in my room just sitting over in the corner trying to stay quiet. My mom told me later they often cried as they listened to me whimper in my sleep as the nightmares assaulted me day after day. Sometimes, one of them came over to my bed to try to wake me. By now I wasn't fighting so hard simply to stay alive, and PTSD was starting to take hold, especially during my dreams. It seemed no matter if I was awake or asleep I could not escape it. They were incredibly vivid. I was dreaming of being shot over and over and over again, and the dreams were so painful they woke me up. Even after I opened my eyes, the sting of the bullet remained. My body and mind would not let me forget what it felt like. To this day, I still have those dreams. I don't think the feeling of being shot is something your mind and body can replicate in a dream, unless it took place in reality. So when someone says, "I had a dream last night, and I was shot. It felt so real," it almost makes me laugh. They have NO idea!

By the time I moved into this room, I had been hospitalized for about 30 days. That's a long time to be in bed. I still had my PCA button, which was my best friend for a long time. I always think of Jake when I think of that button, because he would visit me and try to hold my hand. I always made him take my button, too! It was right there with us. He would always crack some joke, "Don't worry Alicia, I won't take it away."

I had been on my back for a long time. I was lucky I hadn't developed other problems, like pneumonia, drop foot, or blood clots. I had a reality check one day, though, when a nurse came in to check me for bed sores. I thought, *I'm being checked for bed sores? Me?* I know bed sores are caused by not moving enough. *That's not me!* I thought. But still, I couldn't roll myself over. I still needed help getting in and out of bed. The nurse lifted each leg, arm, my neck, and then she started to roll me onto each side. I just couldn't do anything to help, and that was one of the worst feelings. It only happened the one time, but I will never forget that feeling.

Fortunately I had no bed sores, but my exit wound was as large and painful as it had ever been. My wound dressing changes were even worse, but other things were looking up. The nasogastric tube continued to drain all the excess bile from my body, so I wasn't quite as nauseous as I had been. Every once in a while I actually thought of something that sounded halfway decent to eat. My family and friends were so great with running out to get me anything that I wanted. They were willing to go anywhere to get me something to eat, even if I ate just a couple of bites, because at least I was willing to try to eat. Unfortunately, the hunger came and went – as soon as the food arrived in my room, I no longer wanted it. Once, my grandpa mentioned McDonald's hash browns. That sounded good to me, so he went out and brought me some. Another time my friend Corey Campbell was there, and we were all talking about Olive Garden. I said that sounded good, so everyone jumped at the opportunity to feed me.

Corey said, "Do you want that? I'll go get you some."

So he ran out and got me pasta. By the time he returned I was no longer hungry, so I saved it for the next day and took a couple of bites. It truly was the thought that counted – even today, I still appreciate their eagerness to make me happy.

The time I specifically remember is waking up one morning and craving a donut. I hadn't had a donut in years. If I was going to eat that junk, now was the time. My dad spent over an hour searching for a place to get me some. He finally found them and brought them back. Surprisingly, I ate the whole thing. I think that was the first time since I'd been hospitalized that I ate an entire anything. That was the most I had eaten in a very long time. True, there was no nutrition to it, but at least I ate something! Although the nasogastric tube helped with my nausea, I still had very little appetite. Eating was still a chore. After a week or so I stepped back onto the scale to see if my weight had changed. I was still losing weight. I couldn't believe it.

I told my mom, "I'm eating some now, so I don't understand why I am still losing weight."

My mom just reminded me that my body was working so hard at trying to heal itself; every calorie was going toward that. Then the next thought that popped into my head was, *Oh, man, Dr. Rhee is going to be so mad at me!* My body continued to waste away.

I have so many memories from that room. For example, the dog. Therapy dogs are often used in hospitals. I know the pets are a healing remedy for some people. It just didn't work for me at that time. My friend Jess was in the room sitting right next to my bed one day when a woman came in with her old, slobbery dog. She brought that dog right over to my bed and put it in my face! I didn't want to be rude and shoo her away, but it was not therapeutic for me. I did not want a slobbery dog in my face. The lady kept talking about how sweet and cute her dog was, while Jess sat there trying not to laugh. She knew I did not like it at all. She could tell I was thinking, *Please, please get this dog out of my face!* We still have a good laugh when we talk about that day.

There was another woman who helped me relax on a regular basis. This tiny old lady came to my room once a week to massage my feet. Every time I changed rooms she would seek me out. That meant so much to me! It was so calming, and I never felt calm in the hospital. She was wonderful.

One of my favorite memories was with my mom and one of my night nurses. This night, she brought in another nurse who was training and asked if she could stay to watch my dressing changes. I told her that would be fine. My regular nurse started to change the dressings on my midline wound. It still wasn't anything that someone working outside a hospital wants to see, but the size had shrunk and it wasn't nearly as big as it had been. It was nothing compared to my exit wound! By that time, my mom had learned so much she probably could have filled in as a nurse. Mom was talking to the new nurse about how bad my midline was originally and how much it had healed, not thinking it would bother the nurse because of the line of work she was in. The nurse just stood there nodding. She never even saw my exit wound. Suddenly she said, "Will you excuse me a second?" and she was out the door.

My night nurse kept working on the dressing change and said, "I hope she is okay."

My Aunt Connie Foster returned to the room – she had been out getting something to eat – and asked, "What's going on out there? There is a nurse passed out on the floor."

We all started cracking up! That was the first time I laughed like that in a long, long time. The rest of the time I was hospitalized

I repeated the story to every visitor and doctor. We all had some good laughs about that.

While it still hurt to laugh, I was working hard to get my smile to come back. Smiling is a part of everyday activity, but you don't realize how big a part until you just can't smile any longer. You forget how many muscles and how much energy it takes just to put a smile on your face. As my time in that room went on, my smile started to become easier. Even the simple things were hard, like a yawn. Sneezing or coughing hurt terribly. Anything that came from my abdomen hurt, and I was so glad to be regaining some of those simple human characteristics.

Once I had a big group of dance girls come to visit. They were asking questions and, as usual, my mom was giving them every single detail they wanted. Maybe more, because hospitals are not for everyone – the smell, sound, feel and even color can make some people very ill at ease. So my mom was talking about what my wounds looked like and giving details of my recent trials, because I hadn't had many visitors for some time. Mind you, the dancers weren't looking at my wounds, just hearing about them. Suddenly one of my friends started to rock on her heels and said she needed to leave the room. As she headed toward the door she started to walk faster, and she stumbled. As she reached for the door she fainted. Her head smacked the doorknob on the way down. Luckily we were already in a hospital, so my mom looked at me and said, "Well, Alicia, you better call for the nurse." Several nurses came running and they got smelling salts to awaken my friend. All the nurses and girls were surrounding the door, and my mom said, "We should move away from the door, because if Randy comes in right now he's going to have a heart attack. He's going to think something else happened." So we cleared everyone out, and my mom went to the emergency room with my friend. She ended up with staples in her head.

Shortly after that, my doctors decided it was time to wean me off my pain pump. There is no joking around when it comes to this method of medication. Running out wasn't funny. The box that holds the liquid medicine is locked, and not everyone has a key. The nurse who comes in to change the meds always had to bring a witness to make sure they handled the narcotics appropriately.

Liquid meds were shot straight into my veins through my IVs, so the change to taking medication orally was a huge one for me. Instead of finding instant relief, I had to wait 20 minutes or more for the medicine to take effect. That was rough. I still wasn't eating much, so a lot of the time I just threw it all back up.

I was continuing to do more of my daily grooming routines. Instead of lying in bed all day, I tried to sit up in my chair for longer periods of time. I was starting to interact with the world a bit more enthusiastically.

Our family friend Matt was still visiting, and one day he brought in his laptop . My sister Kendra was still in the Philippines. Every time my body had crashed she asked if she should come home but was told it was probably the last emergency and that I would to be okay. Then disaster would strike again. Honestly, there wasn't anything she could do for me besides pray, and I already knew she was doing that. So Matt got Skype up and running for me. I got settled into my chair, and Kendra and I were able to see and talk to each other through Skype. This was the first time we had seen each other since we had both left Colorado the previous summer. I just saw her, and we both started to cry. We only said "Hi" and "I love you," but I was so happy to see her! That day meant so much to me.

My doctors began talking that I would soon be ready to leave the hospital. Of course, I was very excited! A few days before my discharge my mom and Grandma Ely bought me a nightgown. It was a little, light green nightgown, but it meant so much more to me. I was thrilled, because it meant I was separating myself from the "patient." This was something that belonged to me. It didn't open all the way up the back and leave me exposed. I had been wearing identical hospital gowns for close to 40 days, and I finally had something of my own. Life was looking up!

Sometime during my final week in the hospital, Grandpa Ely took me outside for the first time. I had no idea where the medical center was in relation to everything else in Tucson. When he took me out I realized how close to the university we were. I could see UofA! One of the first connections I made was, "I am so close to the dance building, and people have been telling me they don't have time to come and visit?" That was a sad realization for me, but one I would later understand.

I was supposed to have the nasogastric tube removed a day or two before I left the hospital. I went to the gastro doctors full of hope, but they told me it wasn't closed enough for them to be able to take it out. I was crushed. Not only was it terribly uncomfortable, but I sure didn't want to leave the hospital with that tube hanging out my nose with a bag of bile attached to it! Sadly, I didn't have a choice.

The day before I was set to leave several friends visited me. Hailey and Sarah were there. I was showing them how I could finally bend my legs on my own. I was so proud of myself, because I hadn't been able to do that since I had been shot. I had finally seen how skinny my arms were; no wonder they took my blood pressure with a child-sized cuff(3 ½ to 5 ½ inches). I knew how thin I was, but I still hadn't seen my legs. I finally looked at them that day and realized how skinny my thighs were. I started to cry. I never thought I would be looking at my thigh and crying that it was too thin! But the sight of my own body shocked me. I really hadn't seen myself in the mirror. I rarely got to use the actual bathroom, so I never saw a true reflection of how much I had changed.

A couple of physical therapists came in while my friends were there. They needed to ensure I could walk far enough before they could discharge me the next day. While I was very nice to everyone in the hospital, or at least I think I was, they were the one exception. I completely understood that I needed to be at a certain physical point before I left, but I also knew it was the PTs job to help me get there. They had only come in one other time to help me, and that was before the aneurism. I was told they would be in every day or several times a week, but they weren't. And now they told me I had to get out of bed on my own, stand on my own, and walk around on my own?

I said, "I can't do any of that."

They asked, "Then who is going to help you?"

I told them my mom, dad, and a million other people would be there to help me. They again told me to try my best but that I really should get up and do it on my own. I tried to sit up before asking my mom for help.

One PT said, "You have to do this on your own."

I finally told him, "You don't have a gaping hole in your body and an entire side of crushed ribs. So don't tell me what to do."

Then my mom helped me sit up the rest of the way.

I stood up on my own, but it took me awhile to get halfway standing straight. My straight was now the Hunchback of Notre Dame. This was no exaggeration. My sightline, according to how straight I was standing, was down at the floor. When I started to walk my friends came to walk with me. I was extremely hunched over but wasn't doing it on purpose. I truly was working as hard as I could to please them, but the PT started tapping my back and telling me to straighten up. This just went on and on and he was really starting to annoy me and starting to frustrate me. I finally turned and swiped at him and said, "Don't touch me."

Hailey and Sarah were trying their best not to laugh by then. I did walk as far as he wanted me to, then we went back to my room. By then the girls were laughing, because they know me and knew I was trying my best. They knew he must have really gotten on my nerves for me to take a swipe at him! I sat back down on the bed.

"We are just trying to help you," the PT said. I did know that. I hadn't really had a problem with anyone until that point.

But, I told them, "You are telling me that you aren't going to discharge me if I don't walk a certain length. But, none of you have come in to help me but one time? And now this is what you're saying?"

After I said that, they realized it was true. They probably could be in trouble for that, so they finally signed off on my discharge orders.

The next morning the doctors who came in to discharge me weren't my normal team. The doctors always are on rotation, and it had changed. I got approval to leave, but when it became real, I was so scared. One of the doctors asked if I was ready to leave. I thought, *I don't know! Maybe I'm not ready. This has become my home.* Not that I loved it there in the medical center, but leaving was a big change for me. I honestly didn't know if I could do it. It shocked me to realize they were going to let me leave with a huge open wound. All the paperwork was ready by late that afternoon. Mom and dad packed up everything and took it down to the car. Mom brought a T-shirt and a pair of sweats for me and helped me change. I got in my wheelchair and they took me out to the car, putting a pillow over my stomach to protect my abdomen. After 41 days in the hospital I was getting to leave! We took Grandma and Grandpa Ely's car, which was a lot bigger and safer than mine. I remember being scared to even get into that car. The drive was very slow, because every little bump was painful. We were off to the Ronald McDonald House, where we would be staying for the next two weeks.

The Ronald McDonald House was about a five-minute drive from the hospital. Someone had mentioned it to my parents and suggested it might be a good place to stay. The house is a wonderful organization for families of hospitalized patients as well as those of us still under treatment or not quite well enough to live at home. It's a big house, more along the lines of a hotel and full of separate bedrooms and common areas. It was brand new and had only been open a few months. Normally the cutoff age for the patient is 18, but in October 2008 it was changed to 21. So my family and I were able to stay there. It was only $15 per night, but that minimal fee was waived if someone couldn't afford to pay it.

My parents and I stayed in one room, while my Grandma and Grandpa Ely stayed in another across the hall. They had made arrangements to stay as long as we needed. Each room had two queen-sized beds, a television, small refrigerator and full bathroom. Our room was equipped with handicap access. This house had about 30 private rooms upstairs with a free laundry area and computer area. Downstairs was a giant playroom, a computer room for kids, and a giant kitchen. The kitchen had two community refrigerators full of food, but there also were several other refrigerators and cabinets that were assigned to particular rooms where we could keep our own food. We had access to a stove, oven, and microwave, so we could cook anything we wanted. Also, every day a different volunteer group came in at dinner time to make a big meal for everyone. They were community groups, church groups, individuals, and businesses. Once a week a group of ladies came in to bake, so goodies were always available. There was so much food in that house. There were always leftovers. While I didn't see much of the kitchen at that time, I know my family was so thankful. I don't know what we would have done without the Ronald McDonald House.

Some asked why we didn't just stay at my apartment. There were several reasons. First, it was too far from the hospital; second, there was no room for my parents; and finally, it was on the second floor. I was still wheelchair bound, and that would have been impossible.

The house had rules like no eating in bedrooms and no visitors upstairs, but once they saw me, and how weak I was, they made a few exceptions. I still had my nasogastric tube in, and the first week there I didn't leave my room much. They allowed my parents to bring food up to the room. The oral meds still made me sick to my stomach, so if I was hungry at all I needed to eat right there. Taking me downstairs would take too long.

This amazing place finally gave my parents a little space to breathe. They had chairs right outside the rooms, so they could still be close without us being on top of each other. They could go downstairs, get on a computer, or read. It was a comfortable place. They didn't have to sit in hard chairs all day or even sleep in a chair! They finally got to spend some time with me in a place that felt a little bit more like home. We were all incredibly grateful.

Being at the Ronald McDonald house was a huge change from being at the hospital. I wasn't quite sure I was going to be able to do it. As soon as we arrived, my parents encouraged me to walk more. They stopped my wheelchair a few feet from the door and asked if I could walk the rest of the way. The hospital doesn't have many open spaces to walk, but when you are released you have to do things on your own. Not only were most of the people no longer at my service, but there were certain tools that were gone, too. There was no extra portable toilet by my bed. There was no bed pan. I had to walk all the way to the bathroom. Maybe that doesn't seem like a long way, but it was! The bed no longer moved up and down, and I was scared to death to have to lay flat. Not only was it painful, but I couldn't get up by myself for any reason. I just wasn't capable. It was a terrifying feeling to realize how different things were. But it was all for the best, because it made me get up and move. I think if I had never left the hospital it would have been months until I was able to get out of bed on my own.

A nurse came once a day to change the dressing on my wound and make sure things looked as they should, but the rest of the time my mom did my dressing changes. She had learned from not only watching it done in the hospital, but she also had started to help out while we were still there. By the time we left, she had the process down perfectly!

The first week at the house all I wanted to do was sleep. But it was very important to try to get on a normal schedule now that I was out of the hospital. Of course I still needed sleep to heal, but I also needed to get out of bed and try to get out of my room. In the beginning I slept through breakfast and then did not want to do anything for the rest of the day. It's so hard to get up and get going when you don't have anywhere to be! Mom and dad encouraged me to get downstairs for at least one meal a day. Everyone there was so kind to me, but I felt very out of place. I was the oldest patient there. Most of the others were little kids, but I still looked younger than many of them. I was helpless and so others approached me as if I was a young child. I didn't have much energy to smile. I just wasn't myself, and having children come up and talk to me like they were the adults was very strange. I felt so out of place.

While we were at the Ronald McDonald House, my parents were invited to a UofA football game. They sat with Keith Humphrey, the Dean of Students, and at halftime were invited into the President's Box! I know it meant a lot to them, and it was nice for them to get out. In turn, that gesture was very special for me. I also remember my parents brought some special UofA cookies back to me that no one else could get! I wasn't able to eat the cookies, but we took some pictures of them, and I am pretty sure that dad polished them off.

There was one Tucson woman who had heard about the shooting from a family member in Cañon City. She had visited me in the hospital a few times and had brought us several meals. She worked at Kohl's and offered us her discount to go shopping. I needed new clothes badly. Nothing I had was going to fit; in fact, everything was going to swallow me up because I now weighed just 90 pounds. Just like any other girl, I loved shopping. I didn't try anything on that day, because it would have taken me an hour to try on one shirt and a pair of pants. But it was still a nice treat for me. It made me feel like a girl again. It was a bit different from a normal shopping trip. My mom pushed me in a wheelchair. I shopped in the juniors' and little girls' departments, but I was so happy to be there! I remember buying size 0 jeans that still were baggy on me. The kindness of strangers continued to positively impact my life.

My parents had talked to my dance professors several times. While we were at the house, my professors called and asked if I could come to the school as a surprise for everyone, just to say "Hi." So my parents and I went to campus for the first time during a meeting in the dance theatre auditorium, which allowed me to meet up with all the other dancers and professors at the same time. It was nice to see my friends, but hard to enter in a wheelchair. I still had the tube up my nose, so of course people on campus stared. It was a big change from walking the campus as a confident person to becoming a shriveled-up version of myself. I didn't want to look anyone in the eye, but it was great to see all of the dancers again, especially in that familiar environment. I remember everyone coming up to me to say hi, being so scared to touch or hug me. I felt welcome, but that world seemed almost alien to me now. I was there, but I wasn't a part of it anymore. I didn't know when I might belong once again.

We got the biggest surprise when we got back to the house. Around the corner came Jim and Kris Thulson, who are the pastor and his wife at the Evangelical Free Church in Cañon City. My parents have attended that church for 28 years or more, and all of us kids grew up there together. It was so uplifting to see them! The Thulsons just said they felt drawn to come to Tucson to see us and that everyone in Cañon City sent their love. Jim asked if there was a message he could take to the congregation.

"Tell them thank you for their prayers," I said, "and that I can't wait to be back home."

It was such a Godsend to have them there and so enriching for my parents. They provided an extra shot of vigor. Jim and Kris Thulson are people of such great faith and strength. They were only there a day or two, but it was a wonderful time.

Friends came to visit me at the Ronald McDonald house, but it always was awkward. They weren't allowed upstairs, so I had to make my way downstairs and sit either in my wheelchair or on a couch. I was always really uncomfortable. Once in a while a friend would come upstairs to "Alicia sit." I was so excited when my friend

James Jeffery came to visit me there. He just couldn't handle the hospital setting. He is the type of person who gets queasy when he hears the word "blood!" So his visit meant a lot to me.

After about a week of living at the house I went back for a checkup and to see if the nasogastric tube finally was ready to come out. It already had been in a week longer than it was supposed to be. I was absolutely miserable with it, so I was very excited to have it removed. My bile duct finally had healed enough. They were able to take it out. The hated tube was gone! Then I had to wait in the recovery room until they gave me permission to go. I had another appointment to get to after that.

While I waited in the recovery room, my friend Jamie Reed surprised me by walking through the curtain and to my bedside! She had flown to see me for just a day. My mom had mentioned that Jamie was going to visit, but I had forgotten. I still was not always with it. Later on, Jamie reminded me one of the first things I told her was about the teddy bear I had with me.

"I named him Gunner," I said, "in honor of everything that has happened." That gave her a good laugh!

When Jamie first went off to college she wanted to be a pediatrician, so she was really excited and interested in the medical side of things. So when I went into my next appointment with my trauma doctors she was able to come into the room with us. I was still in my wheelchair, but when they called me, I got out of that chair and walked to the room. I was so proud of that. Dr. Amini came in to check on me that day. He said things looked good and made an appointment for another checkup the following week. Jamie saw my wounds and said it was shocking to see any human, much less a friend, injured like that. She couldn't believe that the first thing she saw when they removed the bandages from my exit wound was an unrecognizable black and gray chunk. It was my liver. There it was, still inside my body but on display for everyone to see. Jamie was able to handle it. I was so excited for her to meet at least one of my doctors. Now my life had been separated into two different worlds, the Alicia before the accident and the Alicia now, the wounded Alicia. I was always excited when friends got to meet doctors, or friends met friends, family met family, friends met family.

When I first left the hospital I was told we would have to stay in Tucson about two more weeks to see how I was doing. Then we could talk about me flying back home to Colorado. I knew I would have to find a surgeon in Cañon City who would take me on. The chances of any doctor taking on a case like mine were very slim, especially in a small town, but we did find Dr. Timothy Brown. He was not only a great physician in my hometown, but he also was a family friend. He decided to take me on as a patient. It's a good thing, or returning home would have been a lot more challenging.

We had an exciting night planned after we left the hospital the day of my checkup. The mother of one of the dancers from the UofA had connections to get us a free night at The Westin La Paloma, which is a nice resort and spa in Tucson. It was nice Jamie was still there; she had come on a good night. We were so fortunate to end up with a suite! We didn't arrive until late because we got lost. The women in my family have no sense of direction, and of course my dad wasn't going to stop to ask for directions! Once there we made our way into the lobby area for dinner. We had to go down a set of stairs, which I couldn't do, so they had to take me down on the wheelchair lift. I couldn't believe I had to do that. I am sad to admit this, but I was embarrassed as I was taken down in my wheelchair. But, we had a great meal! That was the first time I really had a meal since I had my tube out. I didn't clean my plate, but I finally was eating and enjoying it instead of eating because I had to. I was excited that I was eating without getting sick!

Our waiter was curious as to why we were there. He could tell I had been, and still was, sick. I was very thin and still moved slowly. It was a random day of the week to be staying for just one night, so he finally asked why we were there. My parents told him a bit of the story. He was so sweet. After we had dinner and got back to our suite he sent up a bag of treats along with tickets for a complimentary breakfast.

Back in our room Mom and dad gave Jamie and me the big king-sized bed, and they took the living area that had a bed that folded down from the wall. We rented a movie. I clearly remember that night. It was the first time I was able to eat chocolate for the first time in months! After the movie, though, I had trouble sleeping even with a friend right there and my parents in the next room. Jamie later told me that's when she realized how different my life was going to be, because even small noises terrified me. She kept asking what I was afraid of.

"Someone's going to break in," I said, just like I was a little five-year-old girl again.

Jamie said, "We are in a nice resort and we are safe. It's gated. You're going to be fine."

I wished I could believe her.

That new way of thinking had become reality to me. Most people probably thought it was unrealistic, but it was my life. Many times people said to me, "Do you know how low the chances of someone coming and breaking into your house or something like that are?"

And I usually responded with, "Do you know what the chances of me being shot in a drive-by shooting are?"

My way of thinking had completely changed overnight. While some people probably thought it was something I could control or wish away, it just wasn't.

Jamie had to call my mom in several times that night because of my dreadful dreams. My poor parents never got any sleep. My dreams were so clear and gruesome. Now I woke up not knowing the difference between my dreams and my reality. They were a battle for me then and continued to be months and months down the road.

In general, that night was a lot of fun. I was so thankful to get a little mini-vacation, but the night itself was a normal night for me. That's how I spent most nights. Not sleeping well. The next day was back to reality. Jamie had to leave. I was sad to see her go so soon, but glad I got to see her for a bit.

The night we spent at The Westin La Paloma was just a few days before Thanksgiving. My parents had discussed what they were going to do for the holiday and decided Dad was going to fly back home to be with the family and Emma. Plus, Grandma and Grandpa Ely were going to stay with mom and me. It looked like I would be coming home in a week or so. I was very upset that my dad was leaving. I didn't want him to, but I knew he needed to be with my baby sister and the rest of our family. So he flew home.

The Ronald McDonald House celebrated Thanksgiving with a special dinner, but one of the CNAs invited us to come to her house instead. Jean was the CNA who had braided my hair for me once or twice a week while I was in the hospital.

So my mom, grandparents and I went to Jean's house for Thanksgiving. We met her whole family; they surrounded us with love and welcomed us in. It was wonderful! I remember my grandpa standing up to give a toast and saying, "This is so amazing. Our family has been through such a rough time. Thank you for welcoming us into your home." Truth is, we were perfect strangers. But they didn't care, and they knew we needed their help. We will never forget what they did for us. That was the first Thanksgiving in my life that I didn't eat until I got sick. I was stricken for other reasons and did end up back in the ER for the rest of the night. My abdomen was so swollen we were fearful that another complication had arisen. After hours and hours in the ER, one doctor who did not know me asked if I was pregnant! No! That is not why my stomach is so swollen! I have been in the hospital for the past 41 days! Several tests later, it was determined that I had gas. That was all that was wrong!

Right after I had been shot my cell phone exploded with texts and phone calls. I tried to have my parents call and text people back, but it was just too much. I asked them to turn my phone off. It was turned back on Thanksgiving Day. Trying to connect back to the world. I remember looking at my phone and reading all of the thoughtful text messages along with hearing the many voicemails I received from friends with their families in the background. Truly, I had so much to be thankful for.

My grandparents left the Saturday after Thanksgiving. They had driven to Tucson, so of course they had to drive back to Cañon City. Several other people offered to come out and stay for the week, but my mom thought we would be fine for just a week. It looked like I would be going home the next Saturday.

Before the trip home we wanted to get together with everyone who was in the car that night. We had no idea when we would all be back together again, so my mom, Susan, Sarah, Moira, Jake, Danielle, and I all planned to meet up one night for dinner. So far I had avoided taking a real shower, because I knew it was going to be very hard and tiring. But I really needed one, and I needed to actually wash my hair. I took my first shower. First, my mom wrapped my abdomen in Saran Wrap. Then I sat in the handicapped-accessible shower trying to wash my hair while trying to keep my abdomen dry. I was scared to death to get my wounds wet, fearing that water would sink into my holes and cause me more pain. When I got out of the shower I saw myself in the mirror for the first time. I started to cry. I had seen my sunken face and had finally gotten used to that, but I had not seen my full body. I was emaciated. I could see every rib in my chest. When I got out of the bathroom I told my mom I looked like a Holocaust victim.

I was so excited to go out with everyone and to hang out and chat somewhere other than the hospital or Ronald McDonald House. It was the first time I put on makeup and wore something other than sweats. I got to wear my new size zero jeans, which I knew would never happen again in my life. It was nice to feel like a human being. It was a wonderful night to just be with these people for a while. My mom; two best friends; professor, mentor and friend Susan; and now two new friends who I still didn't know well but was now attached to. I truly owed them my life.

When we finished eating, they all walked me out to the car to say our goodbyes. They helped Mom put me in the back seat since she would not let me sit in the front. I put a pillow over my stomach so the seatbelt would not rub it. The pillow also doubled as a cushion for me, and I took it with me everywhere. I was so bony that it hurt to sit on a hard chair for long, so I always took my own pillow and sat on it!

A couple of days before we left Tucson I went back to the hospital for my final checkup. We already had booked seats on a commercial flight, but a friend and client of my dad from Cañon City offered to fly us home in his private, six-seat airplane. We thought it was a great idea. We wouldn't have to go through security checkpoints, which would have been really hard for me. Instead of flying into Denver International, which is two and a half hours away from home, we could fly directly into Fremont County Airport, which is just ten minutes from home. We wanted to make sure it was safe for me, because the private airplane was not pressurized like the commercial planes. The doctors said it would be fine to fly. As I was being examined for the last time, Dr. Wynne looked at me started to cry. She said, "You're one of the best patients I've ever had. You never complained." Then she gave me a big hug. Tears welled up in my eyes and, of course, my mom cried too. I simply said, "Thank you." That was the best thing I heard in that hospital, and I will never forget it.

Finally, my mom wheeled me around the hospital for a bit. We went from floor to floor and said goodbye to whoever we could find. Then we left.

My last night in Tucson was spent at my apartment with Sarah and Moira. It was exciting yet a little odd going back. I hadn't been there in more than 50 days. I was only going to be there one night and then be gone for who knew how long. We packed up most of my clothes and whatever else I thought I might need. Of course I loved spending some time with the girls! We spent our night together doing our favorite thing – watching a movie. We ordered in pizza and enjoyed cheesecake that our neighbors had brought over.

The next morning was December 6, 2008. Finally, I was going home, two long months after the shooting. Sharon came to pick us up for the drive to the airport. Sharon and Jerry Moyer were friends of Grandma and Grandpa Ely. They were from Cañon City but wintered in Tucson. My grandparents had called them the morning after the shooting, and they were at the hospital even before my parents arrived. They had told a little white lie and said they were my aunt and uncle so they could get in to see me, trying to get information to give to my family members. Sharon and Jerry had picked up every single person who flew in from out of state and took them to and from the airport. So at last, Sharon came to pick us up and drove us to the little airport where Mark Greksa would pick us up in his little six-seater. We drove right up next to the plane.

We wanted to bring home my child-sized wheelchair, but it didn't fit with the rest of our luggage, so we left it behind. Mom and Sharon helped me get out of the car, wheeled me even closer, and Mark picked me up and carried me safely into the plane. We said goodbye to Sharon, as mom and Mark got me as comfortable as I could be in the small space. There were two seats in the front and four in the back. I was sitting in the back where the seats faced each other. Mark took our suitcases and put them in the back and next to me, making sure the weight was distributed evenly.

Mom hopped in the front. Small planes are not pressurized, so it is also extremely loud. We put on headphones so we could hear one another during the flight. The small plane represented one more adventure that we would not have been able to have without the kindness of another. Mark proved to be a most willing participant. He had flown in to Tucson the night before and stayed at a hotel, paying for everything himself. Mark took us down the runway, up into the sky and we headed home for the next phase of my recovery.

Chapter Seven

And now these three remain: faith, hope, and love. But the greatest of these is love. – 1 Corinthians 13:13

MARK THOUGHT THE FLIGHT MIGHT TAKE TWO or two-and-a-half hours, but turbulence extended it to more than three hours. Smaller airplanes don't reach as high in altitude as commercial airliners, and the turbulence can be quite severe at lower altitudes. Mark knew the bumps and bouncing around would take a toll on my body. He tried his best to avoid the unstable air and veered off course to make the flight as comfortable for me as possible. Zigzagging around the turbulence added a little extra time to our flight.

I napped for about an hour soon after we took off from Tucson. When I awoke we were starting to make our way through the magnificent Colorado Rockies, and I was in awe of God's creation. The amazement took hold and wouldn't let me go. We weren't flying above the mountains, we were flying through them! I was back home! I couldn't stop staring out the windows and truly realized why Coloradans believe we live in "God's Country."

I had enjoyed very few chances to be outside since the shooting. This trip reminded me of God's majesty. My eyes saw with a new appreciation, and I realized it was like seeing everything for the very first time. *I almost missed the chance to ever see this again,*

I thought. I grew up in these mountains and had taken them for granted, but I never will take this breathtaking sight for granted again.

We neared the airport, and Mark said, "It looks like you have a crowd waiting for you." I tried to look out the window, but was not in a position where I could see anything. As we were landing my side of the plane tilted toward the crowd. I saw people waving, smiling, jumping up and down, holding signs and banners, welcoming us home. I was not expecting this! I thought only my dad and grandparents would be waiting for us at the airport. Our local news radio, KRLN, had aired the following:

It will be a royal homecoming on Saturday for Alicia Brady, a junior at the University of Arizona in Tucson, who has been battling for her life after being shot October 12th in a drive-by shooting. Mark Greske, owner of the Royal Gorge Railroad, is flying Alicia and her mother Dena from Tucson in his private plane, with arrival scheduled at the Fremont County airport at 2 pm Saturday. The community is invited to meet the plane, welcoming Alicia home for the holidays. A graduate of Cañon City High School, Alicia is enrolled at the UofA on a prestigious dance scholarship. Her father Randy Brady credits the class I Trauma team at the University Medical Center with saving Alicia's life after 6 surgeries and 41 days spent in the hospital. Brady and his wife, Dena, were at their daughter's side throughout the hospital ordeal. Brady said, "It was touch and go for a long time. We nearly lost her a couple of times while she was in intensive care." Tucson police suspect the shooting to be gang-related, but as yet have no one in custody.

My mom looked back at me and smiled, and then a huge smile came over my face as we touched down. As the airplane slowed to a stop my family, who had been patiently waiting for over an hour, took off sprinting toward us. My uncle Rex had the video camera to record everything that was happening, knowing this would be a moment to remember forever.

Dad rushed to the airplane door and hugged me, and I immediately began to shed tears of joy. Then he took me in his arms, carried me out and sat me in my new, oversized wheelchair. Finally I began to receive huge hugs and kisses from my brothers and proud grandparents. Aunt Beth had rushed to my mom's side and placed little Emma in her arms. "Mommy! Mommy!" Emma shouted. I don't think Emma let go of our mom the rest of the night, holding onto our precious mother as tightly as she could. The family stood together by the airplane, knowing this was one moment in time we never would forget. We were all sharing in the joy of my return, which had been a long time coming. Finally my grandparents started to push me toward the crowd.

People began to applaud as we came closer. The local newspaper was there to write another story. Some of the people who were there I knew well and had known them since I was a little girl. But there  were others whom I had never even met before. Uncle Rex continued to run all over the place with the camera trying to tape everything. He didn't want to miss anything! As I wheeled right up to the crowd of people everyone just stared at me. No one was certain of what to do now that I finally was home, so it was an awkward moment. I finally reached out my arms, and people started falling into a line to embrace me with hugs and kisses.

I was so happy to be home! I had been so homesick in those last couple of months, even more so than when I had first gone away to college. I was back in my hometown with my community family. They had watched me grow up and stood by my family throughout my ordeal. The love and hope that they brought all of us was more than we ever could have asked for, not only that day but in the months before and throughout the days that would follow. My dad said it well in one newspaper interview. "We are all created in God's image," he said, "but some of us are better bearers of that image than others." People like this show us all that the good in the world can and does outweigh the bad.

I had to say a quick "hello" and "goodbye" to everyone who had given me such a warm welcome. It had been a long trip, and my body was worn out. I needed to get settled in at home. We headed toward the car, and everyone wanted to help. There were close to eight people helping me to get into the car, buckle me up, and shut the door. I knew I was going to have all the help I needed in my new phase of recovery. We started toward home and, at last, we arrived. My childhood home never had looked so good. Although I don't remember everyone who came over that night, I do know a lot of people followed us back to the house.

I was able to walk into the house and was surprised to see it decorated with **Welcome Home** signs. I settled in the best I could. I couldn't do much, so I just sat on the couch while everyone else seemed to be in a tizzy around me. Uncle Rex gave me the videotape and said more people had been at the airport before we landed but had to leave because we were so late arriving. Once I settled in I watched this video of everyone saying "Hi" to the camera. They told me they loved me and were sorry they had to leave. For the first time, the tears I shed were tears of happiness, overwhelmed with gratitude.

Once everyone had left the house except my family, my Aunt Sandy, who is a nurse, checked my wounds. Through my family and the church we knew several nurses and others who would continue to check my injuries and come over when we asked. Mom would be doing all of my dressing changes. I was so relieved to be home, but I don't remember much of that first night other than getting settled in and watching the video. I know my whole family was happy to be reunited, and it took everyone awhile to get settled.

We spent the next week getting more comfortable at home and trying to figure out where to go from there. How could I progress? How could I live while still needing help with every single thing? Family members needed to get back to their own lives. I was now in a house that had not been built with handicapped accessibility, and things were going to be harder. I couldn't fix a meal for myself, get in or out of bed, stand or sit, get dressed, shower, drive, or open doors. I still was wheelchair bound, although there wasn't much room for that contraption in our house. I had to have someone with me at all times.

That first week we tried to figure out doctor appointments and physical therapy sessions. We also worked to establish a new routine for me. We had to determine a baseline, figuring out just how much I could take care of myself and how hard I should push my limits. I still couldn't do muc h of anything. If I could have had things my way, I would have stayed in bed all day and had someone wait on me hand and foot.

The next morning I realized for the first time just how much my family's world had revolved around me. The phone rang and, for some reason, no one got to it in time. Our answering machine picked up. I heard my Aunt Beth's voice on that recording. She said, "This is the Brady's house. If you are calling about Alicia, please call this number or this number, if it is about something else please call…" It was a family answering machine, yet it was all geared toward me. My family home had become an office of information for those seeking news about me. Most phone calls were about the shooting. Not only did my mom spend hours every day making phone calls in Tucson, but so did my family and friends here in Cañon City. I realized it wasn't just my house or my friends and family, but this entire town was turning around the Brady's. Everyone came together to support us. True, I liked to be in the spotlight while on the dance stage, but I didn't like this, everything revolving around me for this reason. Now it finally was time for a change. Life needed to resume.

Dad slowly was getting back into his line of work. He's a real estate agent, so he works on commission. That was a blessing because he was able to leave work when he needed to, but financially he needed to get back in the game. He hadn't sold anything in months, which meant no paychecks were coming in. He did his best to get back into work and that change of pace. It was a big change for him and for us all.

Mom, an elementary school music teacher, didn't have to go back to work until the second week of January. She ended up missing 12 whole weeks of work. When she left for Tucson she didn't have a lot of sick days available. She used up the two weeks she had accrued and then used the maximum twenty days allowed from the school district's sick leave bank. After that, gracious teachers from all across the district gave her some of their sick days so she could stay with me and continue to receive a paycheck. I learned something moving: The day an e-mail was sent to all the district's teachers requesting sick days for my mom, her own school's e-mail system was down. By the time the teachers in her own building received the request, so many others already had given days that she didn't need any more time from the teachers she actually worked with. From the time of the shooting, throughout my return home, three full months, she did not lose a single day of pay. That was remarkable.

When my mom came to stay with me after I was shot, the school district had to find a long-term substitute teacher. Because she was gone for so long, the sub had to meet a "highly qualified" standard that usually doesn't apply to substitutes. Married couple Con and Norma Miller, who both held lifetime teaching certificates but had retired many years before, came out of retirement to do her job. Con taught band, and Norma taught general music. Mom had been good friends with their daughter, Alicia, who tragically was killed in a car accident. I had been named after her. This was another thread in the tapestry of our lives.

My parents, Emma and I were the only ones living at home at this time, but family came to visit daily. My oldest brother, Sean, was there every chance he had when he wasn't working. My brother, Chris, who lives in Denver, came home as often as he could. Grandparents, aunts, uncles, cousins, and family friends streamed through the doors to help out as much as possible. It was wonderful for everyone to spend time not just with me, but with one another.

I had "talked" with Kendra via Skype the one time in Tucson, but that was all. She had lived the same nightmare that we all had, but Kendra had endured it on the other side of the world with no close family nearby. It had been so rough for her. She was finally coming home! Kendra got home just a few days after I arrived. My grandparents picked her up from the airport, and we got to see each other for the first time in months. It seemed as though we were seeing each other through new eyes. We both had gone through life-changing experiences we never would forget, and we knew just how fortunate and blessed we were to be able to embrace one another.

The night she came home we curled up next to each other as best we could to watch a movie. She had a weird rash on her legs and decided to see a doctor the next day. They discovered she had a staph infection. We had to be separated, because my open wounds were susceptible to her infection. It could be fatal to me. It seemed so unfair. After she had been gone for months on end, Kendra once again had to leave the house. She went to stay with Grandma and Grandpa Brady. Friends from church came over that day to disinfect the house, working for hours to clean everything. Kendra had to be gone for a week, before she finally was able to come back home. Being separated from her once again was disheartening to the entire family.

After arriving at home, I was again surrounded by people; we had an abundance of help. It seemed though as huge crowds gathered at dinner time each night. The church had planned out full-course meals for us four or five days a week for about a month, and three or four people helped prepare the meals each night. Family members came to help set up for each meal and then cleaned it all up. Staff members from Skyline School, where my mom taught, also helped provide meals for our family. Tireless volunteers helped relieve the stress on my parents and my entire family. We were able to enjoy some time together. Besides all the prayers, it was one of the few ways people could help. When everyone saw how thin I had become they all were very eager to feed me anything and everything they could. They brought over hearty meals and calorie-laden goodies. We had massive amounts of food. The entire first month I was home our dinner table was packed with people and an entire tableful of wonderful food! It was incredible to know so many people cared.

Just like in the hospital, visitors had become part of my daily routine. Many people volunteered to come and stay with me during the day or help with anything, but there really wasn't much else to be done. More than anything we needed fervent prayer. The power of prayer already was so apparent! I was told that the night my aneurism happened my mom had called Pastor Jim Thulson right away. She told him, "We need prayers right now, as many as we can get." He passed the news on as quickly as he could. Several visitors from our church told me, "When we got the news, we all got out of bed in the middle of the night to pray for you." And here I was, still alive, proof positive that prayer works.

Just before Christmas the church gave us a huge care basket with all kinds of food for the holidays as well as staples for everyday use. It contained probably between $250 and $300 in groceries. Soon after that was the first time I was able to go to services in my home church. My family and I sat to one side. Pastor Jim stood in front of the congregation and welcomed me back, and my church family stood and applauded, many with tears streaming down their faces.

My medical issues continued to rule my world throughout my first few weeks at home. My first appointment to see Dr. Brown occurred only a few days after I returned. He examined my wounds and was very encouraging. He said he would be able to take good care of me and always was available to see me. More than once I felt I needed his attention, and although they didn't have an appointment available, they fit me into his schedule. Dr. Brown took as much time as we needed at every appointment. He never was in a hurry and always sat down to talk and answer questions. After that first appointment we made another to come back in two weeks. His main encouragement to me was to eat. He said my body still was healing and not only needed to gain the weight back, but needed the nutrition to heal properly. I knew, and I tried.

I also saw Dr. Ellen McCormick several times. Her office also always worked me in, and several times they wouldn't even take the co-pay fee for insurance. They just saw me for free.

Perhaps the most difficult part of that first week home was going into physical therapy. I had been in PT for a lot of other health issues before, but never for anything as basic as learning to balance on two feet or walk standing up straight. Now, PT became my hardest activity, and it was something I had to do three times a week. I dreaded it.

I came to realize the entire community had followed my story through the local newspaper. The first article appeared when I was shot, and every time my body had another crashed they wrote another story to tell people what had happened. They followed us the entire time we were in Tucson. The reporter even called my mom several times while I was in the hospital, so she could get as accurate of information as she possibly could. Because of all those stories, many people outside the church knew of the shooting and watched my recovery from afar.

As the weeks went by, I was able to get out a little more. We never went anywhere without someone approaching us to talk about what had happened. Many times when we went out to eat someone else picked up the tab and paid for the entire meal. Sometimes we knew who it was and other times we had no idea. One day we went to Waffle Wagon, this amazing little restaurant in Cañon City famous for its breakfasts, to find it already had closed. They opened back up just to feed my family! Other times we would go places where no one knew us, and I felt people staring at me. People, and I can't exclude myself from this, are so judgmental. They would openly stare at me as I walked hunched over, this tiny little thing unable to take care of herself. Their disgust was written all over their faces. "Wow, that girl needs to eat!" I wanted to respond to those who gave me the nasty looks, but I sure didn't have the energy to do that.

This was the first time in my life I realized how easy it is to be judgmental. I realized if I didn't know me or my situation, I probably would have been thinking exactly the same thing. Maybe I shouldn't be so quick to judge others.

During my hospitalization and the long months after, I received hundreds of cards from people all over the world. Those cards and letters were such a blessing to me! They really picked up my spirits. I spent hours and hours reading and rereading them. There were cards and letters full of love, hope, encouragement, and shared stories of hardship. I still have every single one of those cards, and I love to get them out and look at them from time to time.

Soon after I returned home, a pharmacist at Walgreens named Helen started to help by paying for some of my meds out of her own pocket. The first time my mom talked her, Helen related she had lost her own parents when she was young. She said the entire community had come together to help and support her and her siblings. She said she was "paying it forward" by providing my meds at no cost to me. Helen still pays for prescriptions for me to this day.

Everywhere we went we heard, "We are thinking of you," and "We are praying for you." One day my dad was in the grocery store and one of the doctors I had when I was a little girl came up to him, gave him a big hug, and then walked away. In addition to the love and emotional support my family had received, others knew we needed financial support, too. An account was established in my name at Wells Fargo Bank just a few days after the shooting. Jim Thulson, my pastor, and Todd "Mr. A" Albrecht, a family friend and my high school choir teacher, were instrumental in setting up the account. People gave money to Mr. A or dropped it off at the church, or sometimes just took it to the bank. We never knew who gave because they decided not to keep a list. The financial help was a blessing from the entire community.

Mr. A mentioned my name at every concert they did at the high school. He also held fundraiser raffles in my name during those shows. Never one to turn down a challenge, Mr. A decided to organize a concert just to raise income for the Alicia Brady Fund. Of course it was a big show, because that's what Mr. A does. He started planning one show but quickly it grew to two. Favorite performers, Cañon City High School graduates Jim DiMarino and Richard Barth, cleared their schedules so they could be part of the concert, and the show quickly sold out. Mr. A added an afternoon concert. Even at $15 a ticket, it also sold out!

Amazingly, 120 performers participated in the concerts including other CCHS alumni, the Fremont Civic Choir, both high school choirs, and close personal and family friends. Even my own mom performed! They participated in a rehearsal in the morning, a three-and-a-half hour show in the afternoon, and another three-and-a-half hour show in the evening. People, many of them elderly, had to stand for long periods during each concert. There was not a single complaint. It was an incredible benefit concert and a joyful day of praise. Between the concerts and other donations, the people of Cañon City – including many people we did not even know – had donated thirty-thousand dollars to us. Almost every dime went to my medical bills. Those bills would not have been paid without everyone's help.

I welcomed the audience to both concerts. It was somewhat difficult for me, because for the first time in my life I was attending a show as an audience member and not as a performer. I thanked everyone for being there and told them all how proud I was to be part of such a great community. I sat in the audience with tears streaming down my face the entire time, but they were tears of joy. The most memorable moment for me was when one of my good friends, Ashley Adkisson, got up on stage and started to sing, "I'll Stand By You." She looked me right in the eye as she started to sing, "Why you look so sad? Tears are in your eyes? Come on and talk to me now." I never will forget the look in her eyes as she sang those words to me.

I was overwhelmed by the faith, hope, and love that filled that auditorium. The kindness of my community and my friends, who had stood by my side, simply overwhelmed me. It was a concert to celebrate the power of prayer and God's love. It was a day I never will forget. I truly was touched, and there never will be a way for me to thank them all for what they did. For that one day I was able to rest in hope, knowing that maybe things aren't going to go just as I planned, but I had the understanding that I always would have the love and support of my family, friends, and community.

Yet even as I sat and watched, I dreamed about the day I would return to the stage. Many people knew the severity of my injuries and thought, "That poor girl. She will never dance again." But I was determined to fight for my dream. So I watched and dreamed, not knowing that my uphill battle had only just begun. My physical wounds were grave, but I had no idea how deeply my psyche had been damaged.

This was the beginning of what would be some of the most mentally torturous moments of my life.

Chapter Eight

It's not the load that weighs you down, it's the way you carry it. – Lena Horne

FINALLY SETTLING IN AT HOME, I WAS trying to get some normalcy back into my life. Everyone was telling me to "get on with my life," but I didn't know how. I was twenty-one years old, but I wasn't an average twenty-one year old. I wasn't active. I wasn't going out with friends. I wasn't independent. I had no sense of self. Instead, I was lost and teetering on the brink of serious depression. Post traumatic stress disorder had taken up permanent residence. Find normalcy? I didn't know what that meant. I didn't know what "getting past it" might entail, so I sure didn't know how to begin doing it. I wanted so badly to look at my future and see a bright and clear path, but I just couldn't. It was unimaginable, so I took it day by day and everyone else took it day by day with me.

Returning home meant trying to find a daily routine. I tried to put myself on a daily schedule. I went to doctors' appointments and physical therapy a couple of days each week. Once a week they also checked my wounds along with the PT. I went from strenuous dancing twenty-five hours or more each week to dreading PT as my hardest and most vigorous activity. I had been at the top of my game, a dancer at a prestigious school, and now had to work on the simplest of things, gaining strength and mobility. I was like a child who needed help just to walk straight. All eyes were intently on me as I worked on putting one foot in front of the other. I couldn't balance on both feet on my own. When I was six years old I could do more on one leg than most could do on two. I had spent years working on balance, strength, muscle tone and mobility. Now, therapists helped me work on stepping over small cones or stepping up onto a four-inch platform. I needed help going from one end of the room to the other, sitting and resting in between. It was not only hard for me physically, but it was embarrassing for me to stand next to people three-times my age that could do more than me. It was now my harsh reality, and it was hard to bear. Every PT session was a battle. I had once been a graceful dancer, and I now moved like a toddler, discovering my body again/how it worked, what I could do. I didn't know if I ever would find that elegance on the dance floor again. Or in life.

Life went on. I still needed help taking care of myself. Each morning I needed someone to help get me out of bed, because I still couldn't sit up on my own. Eventually I figured out a rocking method to get myself out of bed. It was close to a year later before I could sit up without assistance. I didn't have the energy to stand long enough to fix myself something to eat. Even pouring the milk was a challenge for me, because a gallon of milk was too heavy. I couldn't shower on my own and managed to shower only once a week; it was so exhausting for me. Every time I showered we had to cover my wounds with gauze pads and then wrap me in Saran Wrap. I sat on a shower stool, but even then it was hard for me to lift my hands above my head to wash my hair. Not only did it wear my arms out, but raising my hands pulled too tightly on my wounds. Once out of the shower I needed help getting dressed and putting on my shoes. I still relied heavily on others to do almost everything, which meant I always needed someone with me to "Alicia sit."

Most mornings I woke up sick to my stomach, which made it that much harder to eat. This often became a vicious cycle for me. When I didn't eat I didn't get my meds, or if I did I would throw them up. When I didn't have my pain pills I did not want to budge an inch. Poor nutrition and the massive amounts of anesthesia I had endured had been cruel to my body, and it was starting to take its toll. Dark circles stained under my eyes, and my hair started to fall out in clumps. Once I was in the shower and my mom came in when she heard me scream. Hysterical, I handed her a big chunk of hair. She said, "It's not that bad, Alicia." Then she left the room and cried. I had been so grateful to all the nurses and CNAs that had taken such great care of my hair. I did all that I could to keep it healthy, and now this. I was shedding all over the place. I woke up most mornings to see my pillow covered in hair. We ended up cutting it in a very short, textured style so that it was not so noticeably thin. It seemed as though I was losing myself one small piece at a time.

Maybe they were petty, but the little things sometimes angered me more than the bigger or more significant problems. I remember once looking in the mirror and finding a gray hair. I could not believe it! I thought, "OH! You ... Look at me! I am twenty-one and you gave me gray hair!" It was only one strand, but I was not okay with that. My mom joked with me that I had given her a few gray hairs during that time too. She is older than me, so in my opinion, that's allowed.

Mom also continued to provide wound care twice a day, morning and night, which meant I couldn't go anywhere. Not that I really wanted to go very far from my home – I still was too scared – but I couldn't have even if I had wanted to. I had to be with someone who could do a dressing change for me. It still was a big ordeal even after all this time. I would lie down, then my mom would put a towel under me, take off my abdominal binder, pull out old dressings, rinse the wounds, open the sterile gauze, pack it back in the wounds, cover it up with new pads, tape it down and then wrap the abdominal binder around me again. The medical tape we had to use sticks like glue. Having that peeled off my body twice a day was no fun.

Emma started to come in and watch my dressing changes. At

first Mom wasn't sure if she should see such a sight, but she didn't seem fazed by it. Emma liked to pretend she was the doctor and helped my mom. Then, after my dressings were finished, she would lie down next to me and have my mom pretend to change dressings for her, too. It was her way to be a part of what was happening in our house. Eventually, Emma said she when she grew up she wanted to be a doctor, so she could help people like me – people who had been shot.

I rarely had my abdominal binder off, but the doctor suggested I try to start wearing it less. I felt it was the only thing holding me together, inside and out! When I got out of the shower or after a dressing change I would try to walk around for a bit without it. I remember thinking, "I will never again have muscle tone back in my abdomen. I will never again be able to have control over it." My body was tiny from all the malnutrition, but my stomach was extremely swollen and protruded, compared to the rest of my body. Most of the time I walked and moved like I was pregnant, with one hand on my lower back and one on my abdomen. My swollen belly always seemed to be in the way!

I already had come off a lot of different medications but continued to take large doses of narcotics. I took one hundred milligrams of OxyContin twice a day and two milligrams of Dilaudid every two hours. I was on different meds for nausea, acid reflux, and tons of stuff to get my bowels moving.

Time went by, but things remained difficult. Just like at the Ronald McDonald House, I had to get up and move. I had no choice. I didn't want to, but I had to. Not only did I need help getting in and out of bed, but I required assistance sitting down, standing up, and opening doors in houses, restaurants, and cars. I still needed a wheel chair for weeks after I arrived home. I was unable to drive, so even though I was out of the hospital, I still felt I had no freedom. To be honest, I didn't care about that, because I wanted someone by my side twenty-four hours a day, seven days a week. The thought of being left alone made what little hair I had left stand up.

Visitors continued to flood in every day. Most were family and friends, but others were mere acquaintances, people I had only seen once in my life, or maybe never met before. They listened to me tell my story. Even at that far down the road no one had let a tear fall down their check while in front of me. I kept thinking, *Wow. I don't understand why you're not crying. I guess it doesn't bother you that much.* I didn't know the agony they endured holding their tears in. My mom had continued taking pictures of me and my wounds while at the hospital and at the Ronald McDonald House. I still hadn't looked at my wounds or the pictures, either, for that matter. Visitors often looked at those pictures and said, "Wow! I can't believe this." I just said, "Yeah. I don't know what it looks like, but I can tell you it didn't feel good."

Sometimes my cell phone or the house phone would ring and I didn't answer. It was unkind for me not to answer, especially after all that everyone had done for me, but I just didn't want to see or talk to anyone. I knew people were there to offer encouragement, love, compassion, and prayers, but when someone would come in and say to me, "You look so good!" I knew I didn't look good. I would have preferred to hear, "You know, Alicia, you look fragile, but you are alive. You will become stronger as the days go by." Such encouragement might have been better than trying to create a false image for me.

Sometimes I was honest and said, "I really don't feel good. I am struggling." But other times I put on a happy face, because these were the people who cared deeply for me and had gone above and beyond for me and my family. I wanted so desperately to be cheerful for them, but it was a grueling challenge. Those were the days I didn't care to see anyone.

There were a few words that I heard from almost every visitor, family member, and friend. Words that were meant for comfort, but cut deep. "I wish I could take this pain from you. I wish it could be me instead of you." I would never wish this upon anyone.

Fortunately, I did have days when I found moments of joy. They didn't come often, but I found a spark of delight when someone I hadn't seen or talked to in years walked through the door. That elation usually lasted only a few seconds. My emotions were up and down all over the place. I had no control over how I felt.

I realized there was a major difference in the way different generations treated and approached me. The older crowd looked at me sincerely and said, "You are a miracle." I knew they meant it. While those around my age leaned more towards the, "You're going to be fine" mind set. I think the older generation understood better, just because they have lived more life and seen more struggles. My life altering event had been one of the first to shake my friends' worlds. Most believed, like always, it would pass, and all would be restored. We all thought the same way. We are young, we can't die. It seemed to me that people my age really had no idea just how close I had come to dying. They didn't know how sick I was. Not to say they did not love or care for me any less, but they didn't understand how hard I was going to have to work to get back to some semblance of normal life.

As people came and went from my house every day and told stories of their lives, I slowly realized the world was turning without me. I was no longer on board a world full of life, energy, and cheer. My world had stopped dead in its tracks. I was stuck with no way out and no place to go. I had lost a life that I never would get back.

Up until then I had been so stubborn and headstrong that nothing would change MY choices in life. I knew where I was going and how I was going to get there. I would not allow anything to get in the way of my dreams. In the hospital I thought this entire experience was just a "time out" for my life. I thought I quickly would piece everything back together and get back on the same road that I had traveled my entire life. Now, at home, I knew things never would be the same.

I began to mourn the life I had lost. I felt sorry for myself. A part of me was gone and I knew I never would get it back. I didn't know how to deal with this knowledge except to grieve and mourn, like losing anything else of great importance. My heart was broken. I dealt with it the only way I knew how. I dug myself a deep hole of self pity.

Dad had returned to work a few weeks after these realizations set in. That was hard enough to get used to, but then mom went back to work and I really struggled. She had become my shelter. I was attached to her in a new and previously unforeseen way. We all know our moms have their own special powers, but my mom is Super Mom! I can't count the number of times people had come up to me and said, "Your mom is one strong lady. You are lucky to have her." She even had to stay with me when my sister Kendra was heading off to her first semester in college. Normally, our mom and dad would have gone with her together to get her settled, but Kendra knew I needed one of them here with me. So my dad and uncle, Preston Troutman, took Kendra to college in Missouri, while my mom stayed home with me. I know mom really missed not being able to take her to college, but Kendra understood. I was grateful that she did. Now, Dad had returned to work and now mom had to return to work. It was a change that had to happen, but a change that hit me hard.

About mid January, I had someone coming to the house each morning to help me dress and take me to physical therapy, then take me back home. Medically speaking, I could be alone for a few hours a day. Once I was dropped off I grabbed whatever I wanted to eat or drink, really anything I needed, and put it all on the table by the couch. I settled in, not needing to get up but maybe once to use the bathroom. I still hated standing up. I was hunched over like a worn-out old lady. Every time I stood it still felt like my organs had to settle into place and my breathing had to adjust, but my wounds felt as if they were going to rip apart. So I avoided standing as much as possible. Not because I was too physically weak anymore, but because of the pain it caused. Most of the time, in fact almost every day someone offer to stay with me the rest of the day, but normally I declined. I just wanted to be left alone with my thoughts, which only dragged me deeper into the depths of my despair.

I lay around all day, depressed, despondent and even fearful. Most of my day was spent replaying the entire ordeal in my head over and over again. I relived the shooting, my hospitalization, my complications, and my surgeries. Many times the memories came as flashbacks, and I couldn't change my focus. I was obsessed by wondering what went wrong. *What could I have done to avoid this?* I cried. *What could I have changed*? I cried all day long. All day. I remember thinking about how many tears my body had. *Will my tears ever run dry? How can one person cry so much?* Then the biggest question hit me.

Why? Why me? And how? How could this possibly happen? How could such a powerful, all-knowing God allow something like this to happen to me? I had been a little girl born in a small town who loved God. I had not lived a perfect life, but I had accepted Christ into my life when I was just six years old. I didn't understand it. I sobbed, *What is the point?* I did not see how this experience could possibly supplement, or deepen the meaning for my life or what I could do to be proactive in my healing. I simply sat and thought about all the hurt and damage I had been through, the bottomless sorrow my family had been through, and all the harm that I knew still was coming our way.

I was without hope and defeated. PTSD had now set in with a certain fierceness, and it settled in to stay. In addition, I was coming off my meds, a journey that took me to a vastly dark state. I suffered ruthless withdrawals and my body hated me, but I knew I needed to get off the drugs. I didn't sleep well anyway, but coming off the meds made my nighttime a living hell. I couldn't sleep. When the doctors told me to start cutting back they gave me specific instructions to be taking a certain amount by an exact date. My mom then took whatever was left and dumped it all down the toilet. They were gone. I was weaned off the Dilaudid first and then OxyContin. Of course, the longer the drugs were in my system the harder it was to come off. The withdrawals included panic attacks and heat flashes – to this day, my temperature changes drastically from the vast trauma my body endured. I don't do well with temperature fluctuations, whether cold or hot. My body now associates those changes with panic attacks and sometimes, even death. I was very fortunate that I was able detox on my own, with the help of my family.

I began to look at my day-to-day progress and was very discouraged. I needed reminders of how far I had come from a week ago, a month ago. I knew that was the only way to truly measure my improvement, but it was difficult when I had to take everything else day by day. It was a lot to wrap my head around and soak in. Yet, I had to manage my life. And now I was supposed to be progressing forward? That's what everyone was telling me to do. Nothing really registered with me. I couldn't put one mental foot in front of the other. People constantly told me, "It's in the past. It happened. You'll get over it and move on." NO! I still lived with the physical wounds, and I didn't think I was just going to get over it. It still wasn't real to me, so I didn't know how to begin to move forward mentally, especially when I wasn't yet healed physically.

I had a difficult time dealing with family and friends, but I did the best I could. My wounds, my physical world, my PTSD and my depression were all I knew at that point. I felt that I was an unpleasant daughter and friend many times, but nevertheless my situation was the only thing I could talk about. It was my entire life. So when people came in and wanted to visit with me I had to talk about it time and time again. It besieged me. Just like in the hospital, people weren't sure how to act toward me. No one wanted to talk much about their lives for fear it would upset me; night after night the topic of conversation always centered on my grave situation.

As if I didn't have enough problems, I still was having trouble eating. I couldn't gain weight. This was a new thing for me! I had been a dancer all my life and was so careful about what I put in my mouth. I had always been very health conscious and then, suddenly, I was told, "You're too skinny! You're too skinny! Eat anything and everything that you want!" That was a big mental change and a challenge for me.

The confident Alicia Brady that everyone knew, that I knew, was gone. The new Alicia Brady had lost all independence. Occasionally we went out in public to a restaurant, and I found myself unable to even look people in the eye. I walked past others with my head down, gazing at the floor. That's not who I was. I had become ashamed of how I looked and afraid of people. Afraid of what they thought of me. I had been cut off from life. Now my world was a forged reality that I had created from the shooting. When we were in the car and someone pulled up next to us, I thought they were going to pull out a gun and shoot us. That's not a common or natural way of thinking, but it had become my new way of thinking. It got to the point I would not even leave the house unless it was with my family. Eventually, I didn't want to ever leave the house. *What if something happens again, and I can't get to the hospital fast enough?* I was terrified of being around others. I was living in a fantasy world. What had happened was surreal; I had created a dream-like world to go with it. I made everything fit the crazy scenarios that I played out in my head. Everything and everyone seemed to bring unsteady and unwanted nerves to me, so I withdrew into myself. I stayed as far away from reality as I could and felt sorry for myself.

I also began to suffer, once again, from claustrophobia. The claustrophobia began when I was a little girl and my siblings and I played in giant boxes. We put pillows in them and rolled each other around. The boys thought it was humorous to put the open end on the ground so I was trapped inside and could not get out. I didn't think that was funny at all. That's where it really started, but it got worse the night I was shot. When I was in the car and was shot, my entire world immediately closed in. I had a fear of not being able to get out. Then I was in a hospital room for months, confined to a bed with people always hovering around me. I never got to go outside. And now I was confined to a house and always had people around. The first time I went to a movie theater after the shooting I had to sit on the end of the row, because I was too claustrophobic. Those rooms are huge caverns with high ceilings, and it terrified me.

One night at dinner we had a packed table, and everything started closing in on me. Heat overtook my body. A panic attack was taking hold. I got up from the table as quickly as I could and headed into the other room. My mom saw my face and asked if I was okay. I didn't answer and just kept going. By the time I made it to the other room I couldn't breathe. I began crying uncontrollably and tried to scream. It was the first time that happened, and I just let go. All the women in my family came to my side and comforted me as I sobbed into their arms. I had been holding it back for a very long time. During that panic attack I felt all the doors had been shut in my life. Nothing was going to open back up for me. It was all over. I didn't think I would be able to pick myself back up.

I had no idea how to deal with this. I knew I needed help. I know that no one expected me to deal with it on my own, so when my mom and dad suggested counseling I was right on board. Amanda Koleman was from our church and had willingly offered her services at no cost. I was able to share my thought process and feelings with her. I told her I didn't understand why I was so angry and that others didn't understand what I was going through. The Bible tells us to seek wise counsel, and that's what I was doing. Seeking wise counsel and being proactive in my healing. That's how I see it now, but then, I saw it as, "I am crazy! I need some help." While a lot of people have a hard time admitting they have seen a psychologist, it wasn't difficult for me at all. That was because my circumstances were so unusual, and there were very few people I could talk with about it. It's not every day that you meet someone who has been in a drive-by shooting. I needed someone who could give me advice that would help me move forward. Right from the beginning I told Amanda I had no idea how to deal with it, and I needed guidance.

Amanda was the best thing for me at that time. She helped me work through as much as I could in the limited time we had together. There was only so much that my mind and body would let me process. I quickly learned I did not have to set aside anything that had happened to me. In one ear I was hearing, "Let it go!" But from my counselor I was hearing, "You don't have to let it go right now. And you shouldn't be expected to let it go right now. This is something that did happen to you. Let it shape you. You have to work with it and work through it. You can't just push it aside like it didn't happen." I finally understood that I couldn't just let it go like it was something that was going to float away from me. I also learned I could not rush my healing. I had no control over how fast I was healing, either physically or mentally. Amanda told me the things I needed to hear.

As we spent more time together I soon realized that much of the healing process was showing through in my dreams. My dreams were very much in line with my place in the healing process. Those dreams started out evil and horrifying, just like the day I was shot and the days I spent in the hospital. In my dreams I was shot at, stomped on, stabbed, and even attacked from doctors with giant needles. I always woke up aching, as if it were real.

In one dream I was in the back of Jake's car, just as I had been the night I was shot. It all happened exactly the same way. I went through the same motions of seeing my friends, getting into the car, and then being shot. But instead of being driven off to the hospital my shooter opened the car door and dragged me out. The car took off without me. Then, he put the gun back to my already bleeding body to finish the job. I finally awoke, drenched in sweat and stifling a scream.

Dreams like this were common for me. They happened almost

every night. I had been keeping a journal, and one entry started to change how I perceived that dreadful night. Amanda tried to help me understand that I had not been the target. I drove myself crazy, starting to believe that maybe I was the one they were shooting at. Why else would I have been shot? Maybe he actually was aiming at me. I told Amanda I had dreamed that I was at a gathering with a crowd of guys that I didn't know. I was the only girl there. There was a set of six guys who all looked the same. I was sitting there with them just having a casual conversation. As the discussion ended I was about to leave, but a fight broke out. Somehow I was shoved to the floor, and then everyone was fighting on top of me. The people who had been outside came in and joined the fight. I was trapped underneath everyone at the bottom of the pile. I couldn't get out.

"Listen to what you just said," Amanda told me. "You were caught. You were trapped underneath all those people that were fighting. They weren't trying to fight you, Alicia. You were just in the way."

We talked about how that dream was a way for God to show me that I had been caught between two rival gangs. I finally began to understand I was not the target. My dreams started to become a way for me to understand where I was in the healing process.

One day in late December I was sitting around – like usual – and I heard air escape from my exit wound. It started happening daily, and then it started happening several times a day. It got to the point air whistled out of the wound every time I moved. I didn't know what it was, so we went back to Dr. Brown to check it out. He told us it was a fistula, an abnormal connection or passageway between two lined organs or vessels that normally do not connect. A fistula had been created from my colon to my exit wound. The sound I was hearing on a regular basis was gas leaking from my exit wound. Dr. Brown said fistulas usually heal on their own and that I shouldn't be too concerned about it unless stool started to seep out of it.

One night while I was on my computer I once again heard the sound of air escaping. This time it felt like something wet had come out. I looked down at my shirt and abdominal binder to see a light brown color right where my exit wound was. I yelled for my mom. She came running and looked at it, told me to sit down on the couch, and got on the phone with the doctor. I sat there with my heart pounding and my throat tightening, thinking, *Not again. Not again.* I thought I was going to be rushed back into emergency surgery. My dad came over to me and took my hands trying to calm me down as my mom spoke on the phone.

Luckily, I didn't have to go in that night. But the next day they were going to prep me for surgery, and the following day I was going in for a colonoscopy. Dr. Brown was going to try to plug the fistula at the same time.

The doctors in Tucson had said, on two separate occasions, that I might need to have a colostomy bag. I thought I was past that scare. But here we were again. I thought to myself, *I can't deal with that. How can I live?* That was the one thing that would completely break my spirit.

The next day I had to do the "lovely" bowel prep. It made me twice as sick as it makes the average person. I remember getting ready for bed when something trickled down my side, a most unwelcome, familiar feeling. I looked down to see stool dripping out the side of my body, falling all the way to my pajama bottoms. It was gut wrenching, as I watched stool spill from the side of my body.

We had arranged for Pastor Jim and the elders of our church to come over and pray with us that evening. *How small Cañon City is* I thought, because the elders included my middle school principal, teachers from elementary and high school, counselors, and even our county sheriff. They were all praying with my family, along with other family and friends. *I am so lucky and blessed to be surrounded with so much love and prayer.* We prayed and prayed that the procedure was going to work.

The next day I went in for the surgery. Normally the procedure doesn't knock the average person down for very long, but it hit me hard and made me incredibly sick. Dr. Brown performed the surgery and then I was moved into the recovery room. I stayed there a long time, because it took them awhile to get my pain under control. Soon after I was moved into a regular room, I heard air leaking from my wound. Discouragement flooded me because I knew that it had not worked. It happened to be New Year's Eve.

Friends and family were putting their own celebrations on hold while they waited to hear from us. I was sent home from the hospital around eight-thirty that night. Of course I couldn't go out or do anything for New Year's Eve, so a few friends hoped they could come to visit me. Mom and Dad took me home and got me comfortable on the couch.

My sister Kendra invited a few friends over for the evening. Most young adults were going out for the evening, definitely not staying at home with their parents. Yet, there I was. I settled in on the couch for the night, and in walked Sarah Ary! Mom had communicated with her that day, because the minor surgery had taken its toll on me. Sarah came and sat with me as we all watched the TV. I know I wasn't good company, because I got really sick and started throwing up. Most people would have left the room, but Sarah stayed right next to me and held my hair while I threw up. Shortly after that, in walked my friend Ashley Parnau. She came and joined us as we sat on the couch and enjoyed our show.

There were some M&M candies on the table in front of the couch – we had so much food in the house because it was a holiday. I reached for the candy because I was feeling better, just having thrown everything up, and it was chocolate, and I hadn't had anything to eat in more than twenty-four hours. My mom asked, "Are you sure you want to eat those? You just threw up."

I said, "Yeah. That's the point. I threw up, so I feel better now, and I can eat all the chocolate I want."

With a smile on my face I enjoyed those M&Ms! Sarah and Ashley continued to sit there with me on New Year's Eve – that's all we did. We sat on the couch the entire night, because that was all I could do. I don't even remember if we made it to midnight, but they stayed with me until I went to bed. I will never forget that. It was one simple example of my friends coming to my side and being there for me. I certainly didn't know how to react to things, but neither did they. No matter what, they were always there for me, even if it was in silence.

I had planned to go back to school in Tucson starting in January. But the surgery was unsuccessful, so we were praying the fistula would heal on its own. The next option was going to be a colostomy bag. My wound was still leaking stool, so that slowed the healing process. I still had a hole in my side. I realized there was not going to be a quick fix, that my physical troubles were not going away any time soon, and that I wasn't going to get to go back to school. I was devastated again.

Another journal entry:
I wasn't sure if I was ready to go back to school, and now I know I am not. I have a fistula that still isn't closed, and is stopping my exit wound from healing. I am not going back to school this semester. This means I won't graduate on time. For the first time I am very angry at the person who did this to me. I realize how much has been taken from me. I can't go back to school. I can't take care of myself, and I also feel like I am going to lose everything I have ever worked for. I wonder if I am ever going to have my life back? I feel like there is nothing I can do to help myself heal physically. I am stuck. There is nothing for me to do.

The realization slowly set in that I might never dance again. I sure was willing to try, but who knew? I might not graduate from college. I might never again get to actively partake in my dreams. Anger had taken over. Everything I had worked so hard for seemed to vanish. I looked at myself and said, "Now what? If I can't go back to school what do I do? What am I working toward? What am I going to do with my life?" Of course the first and obvious part of that was to heal, but there was no motivation behind it. Why did I even want to be healthy if I couldn't dance?

I don't want this to make me a bitter person. I have no joy in my life right now. All I know is this pain and suffering. Some days I am numb to everything. Other days I can't stop crying. I wonder if there will ever be a day that I go without crying; a day when I don't have a flashback or think about all of this. This is going to make me a better person or tear me down. Right now I am so depressed. It's hard to live through these moments of pain and be able to push myself to the best of my abilities, while I sit and watch others live their lives.

By now I was managing to gain some weight, but I knew I still didn't look all that great. I talked to Sarah and Moira, who were back in Arizona, as much as I could. What actually was a brave face they were putting on for me during that time, I had mistaken for them pushing everything aside and trying to move on with their lives. Meanwhile, I had to face the trauma every day. I so desperately wanted to be back with them and have my "normal" life back, but I couldn't. I was torn apart by the thought of everyone in Tucson living as though nothing had happened. It made me think that no one else wrestled with this, because no one shared with me. I later found out it was because no one knew how to share things with me.

I know that the world keeps on turning without me. It's hard when my roommates, who were there that night with me, act like it never happened. I don't know how they are dealing with it, or how they really feel. I, on the other hand, have to face it. I have to deal with this. I will have to carry it around with me for the rest of my life. I know that everyone has to get along with their lives and so do I, but I didn't know it would be so fast for some. I am not sure if it is my place to say something or not. People my age have a hard time grasping the reality that I was on my death bed several times. It's really frustrating to me because they don't understand. They all tell me that it is going to be okay, and it's not. I am probably never going to be okay. I can't get them to understand what I have to deal with and what I am feeling.

There were some positive notes. One day around this time my friends Ashley Adkisson and Sarah Ary wanted to take me out. I finally got to wear clothes that were not sweats, and Ashley came over to curl my hair and put on my makeup. When we left the house, of course they put me in the back seat of the car – just like my mom had instructed them to! We took lots of pictures, and then they took me out to lunch. It was one of the first times I went out without a family member. We spent the rest of the day together watching movies and talking. The thing I remember the most from that day was feeling like a young woman of 21. I didn't need to have a parent with me. That day was simple, but meant so much.

When mid January rolled around, my mind continued in its dark state, but my body was getting stronger. My exit wound still had not closed, because it continued to leak. I went into Dr. Brown's office a couple of times so he could use silver nitrate sticks to burn off hypergranulation tissue, which was basically the overgrowth of granulation tissue around my wound. He took sticks that looked like giant matches and stuck them right inside my wound, burning off the bright red, blistery looking tissue. I could smell it smoldering. Ultimately, when he burned the tissue off, the wound became even bigger. That wound had been beaten over and over again and was having a very difficult time healing.

A friend who came to visit me around this time asked me, "How is your relationship with God?" I didn't know how to answer that. At that point, I didn't even know how I felt. I spent time praying and wondering. But I didn't spend time in God's word every day, growing in His knowledge and wisdom. To be quite honest, I didn't want to. I was fine without doing that. I couldn't and didn't even want to try to understand why these things were happening to me. The simpler the answer was, the better. I still believed in God. I knew He existed and that He continued to love me. But I didn't want to comprehend the hurt that I had been through, because instead of drawing me closer to him I thought it would drive me further away. How could I understand His love for me and yet continue with the torture I was in? I didn't see how they could possibly go hand in hand.

By February, my exit wound still had not closed. But all of the others finally had! Now, I just needed help getting in and out of the shower. I had a hard time stepping over the tub, and we sure didn't need me falling. Another reason was that I still couldn't stand the thought of accidentally seeing my own body in the mirror, so mom came in and helped me as much as she could.

My dad isn't the most expressive person I've ever known. I still hadn't seen him cry throughout this ordeal, just hyperventilate! Finally, when I wasn't so fragile, Dad gave me a daily hug that seemed to last five minutes. I was able to be hugged, a tender, light hug. He hugged me like it was the last time he ever was going to see me again. Although he hardly ever said it out loud, I knew in those moments how much he had been hurt by all of this, and just how much he loved me. His hugs said it all.

Anytime my mom and I would be riding in the car somewhere she would take my hand and say, "It's not right, and I am so sorry that this happened to you. But I know God will bring good out of this." Once I looked at her and started crying. Clearly, I cried a lot!

This time was different. I said, "I don't understand why everyone tries to hold it in around me. I don't want people to not show their feelings. I would rather people cried with me."

And for the first time, my mom started crying with me. She wasn't feeling sorry for me. Her empathy was far greater than anyone else's could have been.

I continued on in this pitiful state of mind, thinking I wasn't going anywhere with my life. I didn't know if I would dance again, and I didn't know what I was going to do. My parents asked the daily question of how I was doing. I didn't have much to say, so I usually shrugged my shoulders, wallowing in my deep and disturbed pit.

One day around this time I decided it was time to look at my exit wound. Others had seen all my wounds over and over again, and seeing their reactions made me wonder if I could handle it. I had seen my other wounds after they had closed, but this one still was open. I had put it off for a very long time. Finally, one day during dressing change, I decided to take a look. I was lying on the bed in my parents' room. They have a mirror right next to the dresser, so when my mom stepped out of the room for a second, I glanced over to see my reflection.

My exit wound had shrunk to only the size of a quarter, but I still was shocked. I had heard family, friends, and doctors talk about it for months now. I couldn't help but stare. Was that really my body? The hole was bright red and almost perfectly round. It looked exactly like someone had taken a cantaloupe scooper and dug a chunk out of my side. I was glad I finally had seen it but still avoided looking at it as much as possible. I had seen it, and that was that. I didn't need to look at it – or any of my other scars – for any kind of reminder. I knew they were there. I couldn't forget.

The daily question of "How are you?" came up again, and this time my mom shared her concern for my state of mind and well-being. Mom said, "Alicia, I don't know what you are going through. I can't understand it. But I do know that if you continue in this state that you are in and continue to let the joy be taken from your life, this will make you a bitter person. That's exactly what the devil wants. He wins." Her words lit a fire in me. Not provoking me in rage, but igniting me to not let this fallen world get the better part of me.

I finally realized I wasn't just feeling sorry for myself, I was becoming resentful. I was so far in a hole of self pity that I was reaching a place from where I might never return. The further I dug myself in, the harder it was to get out. The devil had his death grip on me, and the evil things in this world were taking over my life. I was indulging in self pity, which was spilling over into resentment. I soon would resent anything and everything that crossed my path. I came to recognize that I did have a choice. I could choose to let this make me bitter or better. The impact of the gun shot had shaken me to the core and had torn me apart, not only physically but mentally, emotionally, and spiritually. It had destroyed my way of thinking. It had drawn my focus from what was good and from the Lord. I knew I had to change.

What I needed to do, all I could do, was take one step forward instead of one step back. I needed to move forward instead of staying in place. The only way I knew to do that was to make a change, a big change, because the daily life that I lived was not going to move me forward. So, I decided to go back to Tucson.

This decision of mine spread through town like wildfire. People came to me and said, "I don't think you should go. I don't think you are ready." They constantly asked my parents, "Are you really going to let her go back there?" My parents just said they couldn't make me stay, and explained that I was a grown woman. I needed to make my own choices, and I couldn't stay here forever. Of course they weren't thrilled about me going back, but they knew I needed to make this change in order to move forward.

I made that decision at the end of February. Soon, another great family friend, Grant Adkisson, asked if he could put on another benefit concert for the family. We were a bit hesitant at first, because the people of Cañon City already had done so much for us. Asking for more financial assistance was hard to do, but to be honest, we needed it. All the money already given to us was gone, spent on medical bills, flights to and from Arizona, and doctors' appointments. It sure wasn't spent on family vacations.

I had grown up with the Adkissons and was very humbled that Grant had asked permission to do this. Putting something like a benefit concert together is a lot of work, and I knew he already was a busy man. Yet he managed to pull it off in grand style! The concert took place the day before I would return to Tucson. It was another great turnout and raised a lot of much-needed money for my family. We all loved the country-style concert, because I grew up listening to country music. Grant even invited R.W. Hampton, one of my Grandpa Brady's favorite singers, to be a part of it. His participation made the event extra special for us all.

Mom and Dad decided to throw a going-away party for me. It was similar to a graduation party. I was graduating from home and being sent off again. We believed that everyone should be invited to the send off, because it wasn't just the immediate family that had been a part of my healing. It had been the entire town! We wanted to thank everyone and let them know how grateful we really were. Mom made special cards and mailed them out to everyone, inviting them to share in my send-off. I wasn't necessarily going back to school just yet, but I was going back to Tucson.

It was a big stride forward, one I was ready to take.

Chapter 9

Failure is not when one falls, but rather when he fails to get up. – Omer Kayani

I WAS GOING TO RETURN TO THE place where so much had been taken from me. I was determined and unwavering in my resolve to get it all back. No one else could do this for me, so I had to. Not many understood why I would want to go back there, but no one was going to change my mind. I knew I had the love and support of all those who came to my "going away" party, including the reporter who came to write another story for the newspaper. Our home was packed with people celebrating the next step in my recovery. It was a wonderful day for all of us! I wasn't sure what to expect once I returned to Tucson, but it was time to pick up the pieces I had left behind and begin mending my life back together.

Mom and Emma were going with me for a full week to help me get settled in. Dad and Sean took us to the airport the morning of March 7, 2009. While it seemed like another lifetime I had only been back in Colorado for three months. I had seen almost every emotion from my dad over the past few months. I had seen him hyperventilate and turn both ghost white and beet red, but he rarely got misty eyed. I hugged him to say "goodbye" and looked up at him to see tears welling in his eyes. This was more difficult than when he had dropped me off at college, but he knew at that time, Colorado no longer held what I needed in my recovery. My dad had faced brutal reality and knew I could be ripped from his life in the blink of an eye. As hard as it was, he once again let his little girl go.

Once we were in the air, mom asked me how I was feeling about my return to Tucson. I thought I might panic when we landed, but I didn't. I was oddly surprised at the calmness I felt. Feelings of excitement seemed to take hold as I was eager to be back and anticipated seeing all my friends. I happily thought about living, once again, as most twenty-one year olds do. It wasn't fearful like I thought it might be. I realized my fear was not directed at Tucson itself; it resided deep within me. I was afraid of people, of not having control over myself or my situation, of holding no power over the actions and reactions of others. But I felt this way anywhere, not just in Tucson.

After we landed, the drive from the airport was what got my veins boiling. We had to drive by the area where I was shot. When we came to that stop light and I saw the intersection of 36th and Campbell, a rush of terror came over me and panic set in. That was only the first of many times – from then on, every time Sarah, Moira and I were together and we drove through that intersection, the car was dead quiet. We never said anything to each other. The silence was haunting. To this day, none of us have ever returned to the actual location of the shooting.

Overall, I did amazingly well going back. I knew it was not Tucson or the University of Arizona that had pulled the trigger. It was a single person who had made a split-second, reckless decision that destroyed my life. I had always thought I was in control, but I finally realized I cannot control the choices others make. I can only control how I react. I guess, in a way, this realization was my reaction. It might have been slow, but it was there.

I was returning to the same apartment with Sarah and Moira. Both had talked to their parents about the decision of whether they would return to the UofA for the Spring semester. Once I told them I was going back, they both decided they wanted to stay, too. Moira told me more than once, "Alicia, if you would not have survived or if you hadn't come back, I would not have returned to school here, either." I needed them as much as they needed me. We had a long road of healing ahead of us, but we were all going to be in Tucson once again. It was, to say the least, a miracle.

The night we returned, we went to meet with Moira, Sarah, and Moira's family for dinner to celebrate Moira's twenty-first birthday. We planned to just have dinner and then head back to my apartment to go to bed. When we walked in, everyone had already made it to the restaurant. I walked over to give the girls a hug, and Sarah, Moira and I immediately started to tear up. When I hugged them the tears rolled down my cheeks. I never had been one to cry much,

let alone in front of other people. I was not like my mom and Kendra, who cry over everything, including commercials. But I had become very emotional, even in the little things.

I was there. Back. But it was different. I couldn't embrace my best friends with a giant hug. I had to give the slightest hug by leaning in, leaving the lower half of my body far away for fear of having my abdomen touched. The girls were all dolled up and ready for the night, and I was in my sweats. I had on no makeup; I was tired and worn out. I looked that way. I was sad to recognize that a few months ago I would have looked just like them. We had a quiet dinner, catching up. In many social situations, I now saw how people were afraid to speak up and talk about what they were feeling. That night was no different. No one wanted to mention the exciting night they had ahead. I knew the girls were eager to have fun, but no one said anything. I knew it was to keep me from feeling left behind.

Soon after dinner my mom asked if I was ready to leave. I wanted nothing more than to be there for Moira's big night, but I knew I couldn't handle it. We said goodbye and headed back to our apartment. Along the way I knew that this all wasn't just going to fall back into place like I had thought it would. Things were different, life was different. I had a lot of work ahead of me, taxing work. All of my friends were out celebrating my best friend's birthday. I was close enough to attend, but still too mentally and physically wounded to partake in it.

I didn't yet know how to make this transition. I didn't want to hold others back in their daily lives, but I sure didn't like being left behind. That was the thing I had feared the most while I was still at home – I was afraid I would be forgotten and passed over.

Mom and Emma helped me unpack, settle in and establish some sort of daily routine during that first week back. Since our mom had been gone from Emma for so long after the accident she didn't want to leave her behind in Cañon City. Emma was struggling every time mom left the house. Her young mind didn't quite understand that now when mom left the house she would return in a few minutes or a few hours, not in a few months. Bringing her along was fine with me. It was always enjoyable to have Emma around. She tends to keep the mood light!

We worked to figure out a schedule that gave me something to look forward to and keep me going every day, but not so much that it would wear me out. My body was still in the process of healing. In that week we planned to visit all of our "helpers" and newfound friends from the past few months. We met up with Susan, Dean Humphrey, Jake, Danielle, and several dance professors. We visited the trauma doctors and a new psychologist. I also started working with an on-campus physical therapist who I had worked with before when I had hip problems. We even asked Michael Williams, one of my Jazz dance professors, if we could go in to watch one of his classes. When I first walked in I was rushed by people running over to say "hi." It stimulated me to be back in a dance environment, but more than anything I was in high spirits to be around so many loving and familiar faces.

Sarah, Moira, and I had all kept in touch while I was in Colorado, but face-to-face conversation proved to be much different than by telephone. At first things were awkward between us. I know I talk about these girls almost as if I am married to them, but like in any relationship, we had to work at it. We had been separated, not by choice, for a very long time. Tragedy always leaves its mark, and we were not spared. We were different people. This new unease was so foreign to all three of us. We had spent every waking moment together, and now we didn't know how to act around each other. They didn't know what to say about the shooting. What was appropriate and what was not. What do you say to comfort but not coddle? How do you encourage and support without downplaying events of the past few months?

One night Sarah and Moira were making a run to the grocery store, an event that used to include all three of us. They figured I probably would not want to go along. After all, it took some effort for me to make a run to the store, and they knew that. My mom had noticed the difference between us and knew she would be leaving soon. It was going to be hard on her to leave, but she knew it would be just as difficult for me. She was trying to help me make the transition to once again living without her. So she said, "Alicia, do you want to go?" I knew right away the girls felt horrible for not asking me to go along. It seems like such a tiny detail in my recovery, but now I believe if I had said "yes," it would have been a huge leap forward for me. But I said "no" and then felt like I was a guest in my own apartment. I didn't feel that I lived there any longer. Problematic things like that happened many times.

Our relationship continued like that for the first week. With my mom and Emma there, we didn't get to spend much time together, anyway. One night, when Jess was over, I was in the middle of my dressing change and the girls asked to see my wounds. Of course that brought up the chain of events and all that happened that night. It was the first time all of us talked about the shooting. It was the first time in all the months I had spoken about the shooting that I could recall the same exact feelings that I had the night that it happened. The moment I started to talk about it I was flooded with them, and I knew why. These were the girls sitting next to me when it happened. I had told my story many times but never talked about it with them. The stark facts of what had happened hit me harder than ever before. This was real. As I continued to talk about the detail of that night with certain ease, they all realized I was okay with that conversation. It sprang deeper as Sarah and Moira recalled other details of that night. That broke the ice for us, but there were only a few more days before they headed home for Spring Break.

A week after I returned was the UofA's Spring Break, so both girls already had made plans to return to their home states. Sarah had grown up in a town close to Chicago, Illinois, and Moira lived in Huntington Beach, California. Some of my Colorado friends planned to drive my new car down, stay the week with me, and then drive my old car back. While I was back in Colorado I bought a "new, to me" Jeep because my little Saturn was not a safe car for me to drive anymore. If I were to get in an accident with my sturdy Jeep I would have a lot more protection.

Mom and Emma also left around the same time the girls did. Just like with my dad, it was harder for my mom to leave me this time. This was one of the most difficult things she ever did. She asked me to text her whenever I went anywhere and to call her when I got in for the night. I was more than happy to do so. Although I'm sure she would have been more at ease if you could have had a tracking device on me, I didn't want her to worry all the time. I knew the importance of being well aware of my surroundings. I knew the chances of being mugged, robbed, or a victim of another violent crime were small. Mom knew staying in Tucson was the best thing for me, so I dropped her and Emma off at the airport for their flight back to Colorado.

The day after my mom left, three friends from Cañon City, who I had grown up with, Sarah Ary, Ashley Parnau, and Ashley Adkisson, arrived for the week of their Spring Break. During that week there were a couple of times my mom tried to call me, but either I didn't have my phone with me or just didn't hear it ring. My mom tried to stay calm but panicked and ended up calling the other girls several times just to make sure I was alive. This new separation was extremely hard on Mom. Having these girls with me was a nice transition, and I was so excited we were able to make the timing work out! I had become more comfortable with my injuries, and now I was surrounded by people who knew me well. They knew, like few people in Tucson did, what I could and couldn't talk about and what my physical limitations were. It was a great shift for me to see my two worlds converge yet again.

The girls drove my new Jeep down. It was a fairly relaxed week, because there wasn't a lot that I could do. We spent our days lying by the pool. It was a lot warmer in Tucson than it was in Colorado. I wasn't allowed to get into the pool. For the first time in my life I was wearing a one-piece swimsuit. My wounds were not completely healed, so I didn't want to expose them to the sun. I also didn't want to scare other people away! We watched movies, enjoyed dinner out, and went to the Colorado Rockies' spring training there in Tucson. We simply enjoyed each other's company. These were the friends who had stayed by my side. Through thick and through thin. They were with me in this completely new phase of my life. They were the ones back in Colorado who had given me the encouragement needed to go back to Tucson. Here they were with me, in Tucson, helping me find some peace in the midst of the chaos.

I had finally seen the wounds on my body, for the first time, just a couple of weeks prior to returning to Tucson. My exit wound was just a bit bigger than the size of a quarter. They didn't have to be packed any more, but they still needed to be cleaned out and covered. So Sarah, Ashley, and Ashley helped me. Someone turned on music as I lay on the bed. Sarah usually was the one to don the gloves. All three girls crowded around me, dancing while they collectively changed my dressings. Now, there's an image for you!

My mom had sent with them a basket full of individually-wrapped gifts, enough for me to open one a day for a full month. Mom told me it was something to look forward to every day. And I did! There were little things like chocolate, weights (only three pounds), movies, and gift cards to some of my favorite Tucson restaurants. I was excited to open something new each day.

After the girls left, it was time to do everything on my own. I was allowed to drive, and had a time or two, but didn't really want to. I wasn't always comfortable, because I couldn't twist well enough to see behind me or side to side. I still didn't have much motion in my torso. Once I was off my meds they allowed me to drive again, but I don't think I was the safest person on the road! I always allowed others to drive instead.

I settled in to my new way of life. Not one that I had ever planned for, but I was living it as best as I knew how. I had missed an entire semester and had to withdraw from all my classes. Now, I was missing the spring semester – I was going to miss an entire year of school. But I wanted to get back and catch up, start completing the classes I had withdrawn from the semester before. Although I wasn't actually enrolled as a full-time student, I worked at my own pace and spent a few hours each day on my academics. I was enrolled in independent study. Dean Humphrey offered that path for three reasons: I could continue to work in the Dance Office, see a physical therapist on campus, and get my own individual parking spot. It was the best possible way to stay connected to UofA and continue my studies.

I returned to working in the dance office a few weeks after settling in. I worked only five or so hours a week, but it put some spending money in my pocket. Most importantly it was a way for me to be around the dancers again and soak up the dance environment. I spent time answering both phones and questions about the dance program. I continued to see all the work that happened behind the scenes and everything the staff does to make this prestigious program run successfully.

Although I now was involved with dancing it was complicated for me to be there. I was in a unique position. It wasn't anything like it had been before – I wasn't involved twenty-four hours a day, seven days a week now. I wasn't even dancing. I wanted to immerse myself in it once again, and I couldn't. It was challenging and difficult to watch dancers pass me by every day, whether they were in the office or walking past me on campus. I missed wearing my leotard and tights. I never thought I would say that! I missed going to class. This world was part of my past, and I wasn't sure if it would continue to be my future. I didn't know if I would ever dance again. I didn't let those thoughts devour me, because if I couldn't return to dance I had no idea how I was going to confront and work through that new reality. I still planned to work toward a degree in dance. I was a little over halfway there.

Springtime at the UofA is extremely busy for the dance department with show after show. That year I didn't go to all of the shows, but I could have. I felt unsupportive to my fellow dancers, but it hurt to watch. My head already was full of doubt and confusion. Dancing and watching others dance always had inspired me – now, as I watched, I was reminded of my loss and my damaged body. I did go watch a single show that my roommate Sarah was in. It also was full of friends from what would be my graduating class. As I watched them dance I was miserable that I wasn't on stage with them yet still grateful I had the chance to watch them. I remember thinking to myself, *Lord, I hope I will get the opportunity to do that again, even if it is just one more time.*

Because of my injuries I was able to get a very special parking spot. Not that I would want to be shot again, but I did receive a few nice perks! The University of Arizona has about 37,000 students and more than 51,000 people including staff. There are only about 19,000 parking spaces, so it is obviously not possible for everyone to have a parking permit. Even those who have a permit aren't guaranteed a parking spot on a regular basis. Parking there is a nightmare, not to mention expensive. Technically I was a student, so Dean Humphrey pulled some strings to get me my own parking space. They took out a parking meter that was right next to the dance building and put up a sign that had a permit number on it. That was my number. It was my space around the clock. Of course I felt very special, because not even all of the dance professors had a special parking permit. Because it was my space I could have called a tow truck if anyone else had parked there.

The softball stadium was right next to the dance building. Softball is another sport at UofA that is very popular and prestigious, which meant most parking spaces in that particular area were very popular and rarely available when a game was happening. Once during a softball game someone parked in my space. I didn't want to have them towed, so I asked the announcer to broadcast the car's make and license plate number to move their car. Thankfully, they did. I don't think I ever would have actually had a car towed. I'm not that insensitive, but it was nice to know that I had my own spot!

My return to the campus allowed me to see more of my friends again. My parking space was not only close to the Dance Office but was near the library and physical therapy, too. It also was within walking distance to other places in my daily routine, which allowed me to get in a bit more exercise. In general, walking around campus allowed me to engage in more social interaction. I had spent the last few months at home, alone, not socializing. I needed help to return to the real world.

In addition to my physical therapy sessions, I also started doing Pilates, a complete physical conditioning program that incorporates coordination, strength, balance, flexibility, and endurance training – all the things I had lost. I had done some Pilates mat work in high school, but the UofA dance students use the program a lot. We did a Pilates program based on Ron Fletchers, who is a former Martha Graham dancer and studied directly under Joseph and Clara Pilates. I worked with Pilates instructors who had worked with Ron. The complex program improves overall body alignment and posture, moving in a way that is closely related to dancing motions. This was exactly what I needed! I couldn't do the mat work, because it requires you to use your own body weight and I still couldn't sit up on my own. Instead, I started working on the Pilates reformer, which is a piece of equipment designed to assist through a range of motions. It helped me get my strength back and helped with posture. Most people think of Pilates as doing a sit up or a crunch, but it is about strengthening the entire body. Even someone like me, who had holes in her body, still was able to get through the motions with assistance. I did Pilates three times a week to start building some core strength again. That was the most vital part I needed to rebuild, not only to support the rest of my body but to maybe help me dance once again.

Pilates was starting to help me with flexibility again. Even to this day, when I am teaching, my dance students assume I am naturally flexible. I always tell them that I work at it every single day. It seemed almost impossible for me after the shooting happened, because I had to start all over again at square one. When I got home from the hospital my body was tight and stiff. I couldn't even sit with one leg bent. My muscles were too inflexible to sit cross legged. I had been on my bed with little or no movement for almost fifty days. From being a dancer to not moving at all, my flexibility was gone. I worked diligently to get it back. I remember the first day I attempted to stretch. *There is no way I am ever going to be able to do what I used to do*, I thought. I couldn't even sit with my legs straight out in front of me. But I worked at it. People still tell me on a regular basis, "Oh, you're young!" Assuming that is why I had mobility to my body. Yes, I am young, but it does not come naturally. I work relentlessly for everything that I have. Pilates was the first step in opening the door to see that I could get some strength back, even if it was just a little.

I continued counseling with a new psychologist. I'm sure

switching psychologists often is not recommended, but I had moved a couple of times, so I really didn't have a choice. Each counselor that I saw gave me a fresh and new way to look at my life and my situation. The best thing my new psychologist did for me was make me understand that being honest was the best thing I possibly could do. Honesty would help me work through my problems and guide me into the future. Whether they were right or wrong, my feelings were all mine. I couldn't control them, and I had to experience them. Whether I was angry, happy, sad, or mad, I had to express my emotions. I knew I was not getting permission to use others as a punching bag, but she helped me realize that suppressing my feelings was only going to hurt me in the long run.

Mostly, we talked about my roommates, the two who were affected most by my emotions and reactions at that time. I was back in familiar surroundings, but things simply were not the same. I lived with Sarah and Moira. I loved these girls, and I wanted our relationships to grow. I knew they felt the same. The awkwardness had lessened since the night before Spring Break, and things were easier between us. Conversations came easier, but still we weren't quite able to connect with one another about the shooting and its aftermath. None of us had any idea how to start that conversation, but it was one we needed to have.

One day my psychologist told me, "Just express exactly what you are feeling, even if it is completely unfair and unreasonable. Just tell them, because if they truly care about you, they are going to listen. At least you are being honest with them."

Most of the time what I was feeling was completely irrational and unfair to others. I worked hard to express myself more openly and honestly. Communication between us became easier. I would say, "Hey, guys, I don't feel like going out. I don't really want you to go out without me. I would rather you stay here, even though I know that's not reasonable. But that's how I feel." Of course they always understood. They wanted to help me in any way they could. While all three of us had forever been changed by the shooting, we finally began to understand its effects on one another. We slowly became "us" again. I had forgotten what it was like to have that much fun! I missed laughing so hard that it hurts. I had missed them.

As we spent more and more time together, "that night," as we called it, came up more and more often. We never forced the conversation, but each time we talked about it, our discussion became deeper, longer, and more poignant. There was a night when we all sat around and cried together for the first time, realizing that we were blessed to be back together again, but that it had fatally injured all of us in some way. My friends were not over it, either. They were still hurting, just like me. None of us had known how to deal with it or express our emotions. Now we became able to lean on each other and talk freely about the good and the bad.

Both Moira and Sarah said to me, "I hate that this happened to you. But, Alicia, if it was me, I would not have survived. It was you for a reason." I still struggled to understand that reason, but I was able to move forward with my life.

Eventually we started talking about the official police report, which taught us everything that had happened that fateful night. It became evident that a miracle had occurred when no one else was injured. We had survived hell on earth, a gang-related shooting. Jake's car had been swiped by an automatic AK-47. Four bullets had hit the car, and detectives tore it apart to find the slugs in different places. We were horrified to learn one bullet had stopped in the back of Jake's headrest, mere inches from entering his brain.

Once they finished searching the car they released it back to Jake. Not only did it have bullet holes, but a door panel was off, and there was blood everywhere. He later told me that after staying up all night at the hospital he drove his car home the way the police had given it back, dismantled, and then washed away all the blood. He couldn't stand to see it and smell it. I told him I was so sorry that he had to do that. Then one of the girls told him that they would have helped. Jake said, "That is not a sight I would have wanted anyone else to ever have to see."

∼ℓ∼

The girls and I continued to remember small details of that crazy night. Once Sarah and I talked about what type of gun an AK-47 is. I knew it was a big and powerful weapon but knew no specifics. We decided to go online to look it up. We thought we knew what it looked like, but we weren't quite sure. We found it online and saw how big and menacing it is. We realized this is the same gun our military uses. We discovered it is an assault rifle, and its only intent is to kill.

I wanted to know more about the weapon that forever changed my life. A family friend, Marc Mattox, allowed me to interview him on the ballistics and specifications of the AK-47. Marc is a retired parole officer and fire arms instructor.

Marc showed me the civilian version of an AK-47, which means it does not shoot automatically like a machine gun if the trigger is squeezed and held. The AK-47 is legal. It is a semi-automatic, so the shooter must pull the trigger every time they want to shoot it. The bolt of the gun cycles back and forth, picking up another round while discharging the fired round. Shells are held in the magazine, the device that stores and feeds rounds. The magazines may be integral to the firearm or removable. Marc said most people call the magazine a "clip," and said although they are used interchangeable, this truly is a magazine. It looked like a banana clip and was just like the one on the AK-47 that shot me. That magazine holds about thirty rounds.

It is very difficult, but not impossible, to possess a fully automatic weapon in the United States. Marc said it can be done, and I believe a gang member would know how to get his hands on one. My police report said I was shot by an automatic, but anyone without much training could pull the trigger so fast you might think it was an automatic. In this way, an automatic and a semi-automatic may be almost indistinguishable. There is a delay of only a couple of tenths of a second between each shot.

No one that night could have said with any certainty how close together the shots were. When you are hit and your body goes into panic and shock, who knows what you will hear and what you won't? In fact, I only heard one shot that night. That was the first one that hit the car. It was the same round that hit me.

Modern ammunition has a shell that is usually made of brass and is typically the bigger part. The other segment is the projectile, which is also known as the bullet. The primer ignites the powder charge and is located at the center or head of the cartridge case. When the trigger is pulled it releases the firing pin, which then strikes the head of the case causing an intense fire. That flash fire causes the powder to burn rapidly. The powder burns most of the way down the barrel, and the expanding gases force the projectile down the barrel to be released. This entire process happens very rapidly, within a split second.

This particular weapon is commonly used. It was developed in 1947 by a Russian infantryman named Mikhail Kalashnikov. The letters AK stand for "Avtomat Kalashnikov," which means "Kalashnikov's Automatic Rifle." It also was known as a Russian Assault Rifle. It was cheap yet reliable and simple to clean, maintain and fire, so it quickly became famous. Its use was widespread and, soon, the rifle was in use around the world.

Bullets: A projectile, or bullet, damages and kills in many ways. One way is through exsanguination, which means literally bleeding to death. Someone could take a bullet that wasn't necessarily a death blow, yet still bleed to death before receiving medical attention. Another method of shooting death is through organ destruction. If shot in the heart, chances of survival are very low, but death may not be immediate. The body normally takes several minutes to stop all of its functions. Another way to die from a bullet is a process called hydrostatic shock. As the projectile is moving toward a target it is pushing a column of air ahead of itself and off to the sides. This natural phenomenon is commonly observed in wind tunnels. Motorcycles, airplanes, cars, and many other modern-day inventions create such turbulence. A bullet moves much faster than any airplane ever could move, and it creates an incredible amount of turbulence.

A typical cartridge for the AK-47 is 7.62mm diameter by 39mm length. It weighs only 123 grains and moves at 2,300 feet per second. It is effective within 380 yards and has an accuracy of 3 to 5 inches at 100 yards. Its penetration is 27 inches at meters. Its rate of fire is 600 rounds per minute. The projectile has a tendency to remain intact even after making contact with bone.

Most people know what a small .22 handgun is. Well, a little .25 auto pistol is closely related to that, and the .25 is the gun that James Bond used. Mark said no spy in his right mind would carry a gun that small. It has a velocity of only 760, compared to 2,300. That gives an idea of the difference between weapons. An AK-47 has almost four times more velocity of a .25. The auto pistol has 64 foot pounds of energy at the muzzle, and its diameter is 6.4mm.

It is not the speed of the projectile that does the damage, it is the energy. It is hard to distinguish them, but speed plus weight equals energy.

The further away you are from a bullet the less power it has. Many people told me I was lucky that the bullet went through the car first, because it hit sheet metal and took some of the speed away. But the fact that it went through the car, skidded along Sarah's leg and ended up in the back of a headrest after hitting me says that, most likely, I absorbed most of the impact. The shooter probably was no less than 100 yards away. He wasn't trying to hide.

Bullets have both internal ballistics and external ballistics. The internal ballistics is, quite simply, mathematics. The bullet for the AK-47 weighs 123 grains and is pushed by 20 grains of powder, so it will achieve a muzzle velocity of 2,300 feet per second. At 100 yards out of the muzzle, velocity drops to 1,800 feet per second. When you do the math that is 800 foot pounds of energy that is exerted on whatever it hits, whether it is a plastic wall, a car, or a human being.

External ballistics is a lot more complicated. This is the study of what happens when the projectile leaves the muzzle. For example, rifles have "rifling" inside the barrel. If you look down the barrel, you will see little striations that spin the bullet to give it stability. If the rifling is clockwise the bullet experiences something called "spin drift" as it leaves the muzzle. Spin drift carries the bullet where the shooter aims. Most shots under 100 yards usually hit the target. When the target is 200 or 300 yards out, the shooter must raise the muzzle and shoot to the left or right to achieve the target.

The entrance hole is 30 caliber, and the exit is aggravated because the bullet seems to be getting bigger. As the projectile goes through a human being, it moves parts of the body and blood with it. The bullet still is pushing that column of air and the turbulence that goes with the bullet along with it. That also is part of external ballistics.

The faster a bullet is moving the greater chance it has of continuing to move in the same direction. Consequently, an AK-47 most likely will go in and out because it is moving so fast. A handgun bullet moves a lot slower than a rifle bullet. There are many cases where people are shot with handguns in the hip, and then the bullet comes out their right shoulder, for example. It bounces around in the body. But if a rifle bullet were to hit you in the hip, chances are it would go out the other hip. So in the case of a handgun bullet, everything that it hits has to be accounted for, because it all changes the course of the projectile.

The effect of the speed and the diameter of the bullet create an air of turbulence around the projectile as it moves through the air. That air, along with the bullet, enters your body and disrupts blood vessels, muscles, tissues, bone, and everything else it encounters. So in and of itself, the projectile is doing considerable damage, but the harm is exacerbated by the turbulence of the air around it.

This is the weapon that is used all over the world, mainly by the military. But Marc gave me this piece of information: The semi-automatic is available at your local gun store.

That brought us to another sobering question: How does someone get their hands on that kind of weapon? Not only was it an automatic AK-47, but it was complete with a banana clip. Police had detained a suspect while I was in the hospital. He was only seventeen years old, but the member of a well-known gang. He was in custody for attempted second-degree murder. Detectives told us he was shooting at a rival gang across the street, and our car was caught in the crossfire. The detectives said all information pointed to him. They were positive he was the shooter, but they didn't have enough evidence to hold him. None of his gang members or even the rival gangs would speak up against him, so he was released a week later. The case remained open.

اللہ

My life continued to move ahead. I had more daily structure now and was in charge of making my own schedule. If I felt too overwhelmed, I backed off a bit until things once again things were under control. Some days, Sarah and I decided to spend the day together doing nothing. It was always a day that I could count on to bring some amusement, which was wonderful. Just like back in Colorado, I had time to think and to over think what had happened to me. I was up and down from one minute to the next. Here is one of my journal entries about a month after I returned to Tucson:

> I am back in Tucson. It took me awhile to feel like I belonged here again, but now things are going pretty well. I have a million thoughts running through my head all that time. What am I going to do if I can't dance? Why did this happen? What if they never catch the guy who did this? I am so up and down all the time. Sometimes I feel like I won't be able to fit back in and work in this world. Other times people are so helpful and encouraging. I remember all they have done for me and I don't want to give up. I want to give back everything that I can. But how can I do that? I have days that I feel so great that I am waiting for something to strike me down. And then I don't think that I will hold up. While I am pushing forward there is always a little voice in the back of my head telling me I can't.

Clearly, from this journal entry, my emotions were all over the place. That's how I actually remember it being most of the time. Life didn't seem so serious as I spent more time with the girls and other friends, but there was always a piece of me that believed I never could make a full recovery. So many people continued to cheer me on. Their comments would lift me up, but I soon crashed back down wondering how I possibly could do and be what I wanted. Here is another journal entry from around the same time.

> How do I do what I want when I physically can't do those things? Before the accident I felt untouchable. Now I am insecure. People say you can be whatever you want to be. I just don't know how I can do that with my wounded body and mind.

I was surrounded by hope and lifted up in prayer. But that still did not take away the thought that I might never dance professionally.

Are you kidding me, I thought. *It might not be physically possible.*

At night, my dreams continued to parallel my healing process. Once again I was submerging myself in the world of dance, so I thought about it all the time. I think I was subconsciously telling myself – and God was also saying – "No, Alicia, you are wrong. You can dance! You will recover from this. You will be able to move freely without pain once again." But, I couldn't believe it. I had no reason to. Here is another journal entry from the end of April.

Lately my dreams have been back and forth from dreams of old friends, being shot, and now dancing. They are usually related to my daily feelings. They have become a huge part of my healing. I never know what to make of them because I will be dreaming that I am taking dance class and then the next dream will be me getting shot. It's hard for me to put these feelings somewhere or to react to them because I have so many. Again, I am waiting for myself to break. Even if it is years down the road.

I had many good days, but I never felt I was completely stable. Something felt off, and I wouldn't find out what that was for years.

All I wanted was an ordinary, routine life, to be able to do what all the other twenty-one year olds were doing. I wanted to get past my initial grief. I thought I could force myself to heal more quickly, but slowly came to realize I could not. It wouldn't take mere days, weeks or months. It would take years. I wanted the shooting to stop dominating every aspect of my life. I thought I might break down eventually, but I was dealing with life right there and then as best I knew how.

Another journal entry about my dreams:

I had a horrifying dream last night. I was walking on my sidewalk and was randomly held up at gunpoint. For some reason I ended up lying down. The man with the gun kept teasing me with it. Waving it in my face, until he finally shot me in the side of the head. It didn't kill me right away, but I started to bleed out, similar to the night I had my aneurism. I knew I was dying. Dying alone on a street. Right as I was taking my last breath in my dream, I woke up.

I suffered from dreams like this all the time. Anyone who could get into my head and see the dreams I had over the years would think," Psycho girl! What is wrong with her?" My dreams of being shot, stabbed, and beaten continued, but the worst were my dreams of being attacked by gangs. There were groups of 20 or more men who chased me down, and I never got away. Occasionally I had the rare dancing dream. Those were my light at the end of the tunnel, but they toyed with me. My emotions were all over the place.

In addition to spending time with Sarah, Moira, and the other dancers, I started spending more time with Danielle and Jake. I was surprised to find myself so attached to them and was grateful for these new and blossoming relationships. We had come together in the strangest of ways, but we got along like we had all known one another for years. We went out together, celebrated birthdays, went to movies, and enjoyed dinner out. Without a doubt we always found the lighter side of life all together, living to the fullest together, but rarely did we ever talk about that night. Once again, we all knew how fortunate and blessed we were. We were just happy that we had lived to enjoy moments like that together.

While I was recovering in Colorado I had hoped for the opportunity to get to know them better. I wanted them to be more than acquaintances. I wanted to share with them just how much they meant to me. The truth is, if Jake and Danielle had not been in the car that night, I would not be here today. I will be forever thankful to them, and I know my family and friends feel the same way.

The day after the shooting I had received a giant card from all of the dancers. Most of them had signed it, sending their love. They also made similar cards for Sarah, Moira, Jake, and Danielle. On Danielle's birthday we were all together over at her house celebrating. She had saved the card they made for her. It was hanging on her wall. As I read it I came across a signature from one of my ballet professors. James Clouser wrote, "It is people like you who restore our faith in humanity." I couldn't have said it better. My own faith in humanity had been shaken after all I had been through, but my friendships with Jake and Danielle reassured me that hope and compassion still existed.

Things were going as well as they possible could, considering it had been only about six months since I was shot. Even though I lacked a tangible goal, I was determined to just keep moving forward. My only goal was not to slide back. I continued to heal both physically and mentally.

I seemed to be doing well "hanging in there." I was almost on a high from no longer being bedridden. I was being social again. I was able to walk out in the sunshine. I wasn't running marathons or walking for miles on end, but I could walk from building to building on campus. That was huge for me! I was healthy enough to go out with friends on the weekend. I offered to drive because I had my handicap permit. No matter where we went, we always were assured of a close parking spot. I admit that driving friends around on a Friday night and pulling into a handicap spot wasn't the best use for that card, but as I was able to walk farther and my stamina got better, we started parking in regular spots. I'm sure many people questioned why loads of girls stepped out of my car in their high heels!

Once I was on campus and had to drop something off at the Bursar's Office. It was much too long of a walk from my own parking space, so I pulled into a handicap spot in the garage right next door to the office. I had been back in Tucson only a couple of weeks and still struggled, but seeing me from the chest up, no one would guess anything was wrong with me. Really, I looked perfectly normal, a little on the skinny side still, but unless you were to see the road map on my abdomen you would have no idea. Some guy pulled up next to me in a regular spot, looked over at me and mouthed, "You're in the handicap spot." Yes! I know! I did it on purpose! I'm sure that wasn't the only time people had that thought, but I couldn't worry about what others thought of me. One of my therapists had mentioned something about that, and it had started to sink in at the perfect time. She told me that some people would judge me and get under my skin. I learned those people just weren't worth my worry.

I knew I still was suppressing certain thoughts and emotions. I believed they eventually would surface but was able to ignore them for now. I had found a place where I was happy and didn't want to let that go, so I unknowingly suppressed a lot. Returning to Tucson had been the best decision, but I knew the high I was on soon would dissolve. Then where would I be? How would I feel? What was my next step?

May 2009 rolled around and school ended for the semester. Both of my roommates had decided they were going back home for the summer. There was no way I was staying by myself, so I planned to return to Colorado until fall. We intended to move into a new apartment that August for the next school year, so we packed up all of our stuff to move. My dad came down to move all of the heavy belongings, while Sarah and I carried the bedding and pillows. Poor dad! Fortunately, Jake let us take our stuff to his place so we didn't have to try and haul it all home. Girls tend to have lots of stuff, and ours filled a room or two at his house for the summer.

I enrolled in online summer school classes so I could continue to catch up as much as possible. Physically I felt I had stopped progressing. I continued to gain stamina, but I still had problems with everything I ate. I was always sick to my stomach. I saw Dr. Brown and he sent me to a gastroenterologist. Thus began a long line of tests. That messed with my head. My emotions were up and down, up and down. Most Americans tend to believe the busier we are, the better. I followed that line of reasoning and kept myself occupied.

The time to return to school came closer and closer. Again I was asked, "Are you sure you want to go back?" over and over. I always replied with a positive answer. I remembered how happy I had been when I returned to Tucson, and now it was my senior year – or what should have been. I wanted to go back and attempt to finish, or at least be with my class for the last time. I thought once I returned to the business of school and life there all my feelings of doubt and anger would dissipate.

Toward the end of the summer, a test finally showed a major problem with my gallbladder. Doctors said that could be a big part of my problems with digesting properly. They suggested surgery. With my previous medical history, the doctors in Colorado wouldn't perform surgery. That was perfectly fine with me. To be honest, I didn't want anyone touching me except the doctors in Tucson.

Mom and I headed back to Tucson at the beginning of August

for another surgery. I was disappointed, but my life had started to revolve around what I could and could not eat, spending days to sick to get moving, and I wanted it fixed. I had been through so many surgeries at that point I didn't really care. As long as it helped I was willing to put in the extra effort it would take to recover. Our new apartment wasn't quite ready for us to move into, but we were allowed to stay at the Ronald McDonald House again because I still was twenty-one. We celebrated my mom's birthday there, and a few days later, went out to celebrate my twenty-second birthday with other dancers. Two days later I went in for surgery.

Surgeons removed my gallbladder and revised my exit wound. It now looked so much better! Dr. Wynne told me they also removed pieces of rib that were poking into my liver. Most patients can have their gallbladder removed by laparoscopy; unfortunately, I could not. I had another nine inch incision.

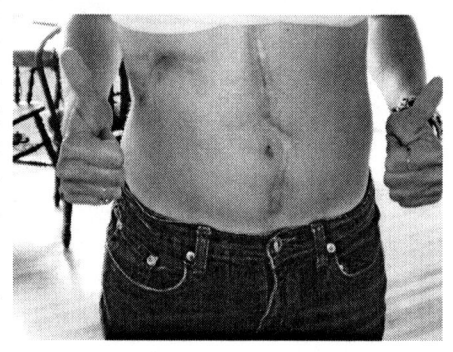

I had two exciting visitors during my stay that time. One was Chaplin Dave, who I hadn't seen in more than a year. The one who had come to visit nearly every day he was working. The other visitor was the man who had wheeled me in from the car the night I was shot. I had remembered a lot of faces and even names, but his was one I just didn't remember.

He came up and said, "Do you remember me? I was the one who rushed you inside. I remember thinking that there was no way you were going to make it. You were completely gray." Then he told me how much better I looked. Well, I hope so! Although I didn't really enjoy the hospital, I loved getting to see all my doctors and nurses again.

During my five-day stay in the hospital, my mom and two friends moved all of our stuff from Jake's house to our new apartment, which was on the third floor of the building. And it was 105 degree weather! Now, that's how you get out of moving. My friend

Jess courteously came to the hospital and napped with me, while her boyfriend, Tory, helped my mom move everything. Thanks Jess! And… thanks Tory!

When I finally left the hospital, my mom and Susan helped me unpack everything and put away all my clothes. I spent the next few days resting as much as I could. Three days after I left the hospital Sarah and Moira arrived. Here we go again!

Two days after that, just ten days after my surgery, I started back to school. I finally returned to the classroom in the hot August weather. I was on Percocet and had twenty-eight staples in my abdomen, but I was good and ready to go!

Chapter Ten

For nothing is impossible with God. – Luke 1:37

I RETURNED TO MY STUDIES WITH HIGH hopes that I would graduate, but in all honesty, I had no idea if I could. I had my work cut out for me!

Graduating later, with any other class, wouldn't hold the same value to me as if I were graduating with the class I had come in with. My class. It wasn't just about walking across the stage with them or even about receiving a Bachelor of Fine Arts in Dance, which had been my dream and aspiration my entire life. Instead, my focus was all that my class represented to me – everything we had been through, all we continued to grapple with. My struggles were not just mine, they were ours, but we already had found some measure of victory. It meant the world to me just to be back in school with them. If I could graduate with my class, I knew it would be one of the finest moments in my entire life, perhaps my crowning achievement.

As a dance major I knew UofA required a certain amount of both ensemble and technique credits to graduate. Ensemble credits mainly are hours spent in rehearsal for performances, but technique classes also are required to be able to participate in those concerts. In dance, just like in any type of athletics, you have to practice if you want to play. Technique classes teach you the skill and technicality of movement as well as help you build strength and stamina. You also learn how to correctly take care of your body, including proper alignment to help prevent injury. We spend countless hours rehearsing, and minutes on stage. That is why the performing part is always, in my opinion the most rewarding part of it.

Three years earlier, when I was a freshman, I had received advice to get all of my academic classes out of the way. Seniors need time away from the classroom to audition, and academics are harder to catch up on than dance techniques classes. This is only because dance professors also understood the need to be away from class. You can't just send in a resume and expect to get the job, you have to go in person and audition. All the professors knew and understood the importance of that. Being the planner that I am, I wanted to be able to immerse myself only in dance classes in my last semester at the university. According to my four-year plan, that fall I signed up for as many academics as I could and started working in the dance office again on a regular basis. I was healing from yet another major surgery, but I was in school. I knew that come spring I would be staring at a slate full of dance classes. Would I be ready? I fervently hoped and prayed that I would.

My advisor and Ballet Professor, Melissa Lowe, met with me several times to review my schedule and plan my senior year. She worked through my abnormal situation, trying to make my schedule the best is could be. She said, "Let's just assume that next semester you will dance. Let's try to do whatever we can now." She made phone calls to Dean Humphrey and others trying to pull strings for me. I was not trying to get out of doing any work. I knew I would have to work twice as hard. Some required classes weren't offered every year, and I had missed a few of those. I would have to do independent studies or replace them with a similar class. Melissa did her level best to give me the possibility of graduating with my class on time.

I wasn't dancing yet, but I was able to sit in and help with auditions that fall. The room was always buzzing with excited dancers at the beginning of each new school year. I loved seeing that, and once again being a part of it. Each year starts off with a meeting just before the first audition. All the freshmen and staff introduce themselves, and Susan always told everybody to "buddy up," meaning don't go anywhere without someone else. Ever. This year that warning held special meaning for me. When she said that, many heads turned toward me. While most students traditionally ignore that warning – I know I had – this year I would not. Everyone who had been there the year before shook their heads and said, "Yes. Be careful. Don't be walking around campus or anywhere by yourself." I was glad to see so many people stepped up and backed up Susan's talk. Despite what the incoming freshmen might have thought, it was vital information.

Returning to the dance world seemed a little easier this time. Although I did just have another surgery, it wasn't such a dramatic change for me that fall. I again was living with Sarah and Moira, this time in a new apartment. We were thrilled to be back together and knew it probably was the last time we would live together. We always were able to pick right back up where we had left off, so things were back to normal – except for the fact I still  wasn't dancing. My new "normal" continued to change every day. I tried to figure out how to live with the new adjustments that now were a part of my life.

I found myself connecting easily with all of my fellow dancers. Life started to fall back into place, maybe not all of it, but I started to feel like myself again in Arizona. One of the first weekends back, Sarah, Moira and I decided that we wanted to have a night that we would go out with all of the Senior girls. As we got farther into the year we knew it would be nearly impossible to get all the girls together in one place. We managed to do it. All of us went out dancing, and then we came back to our apartment for a sleepover.

A great start to the year!

The weather in Tucson during the beginning of that fall semester was incredibly hot. I walked around campus with my backpack on my back and staples in my abdomen. Probably not a smart idea, but I did have to get around! A little over a week into school I returned to the hospital to have my staples removed. I asked Sarah to come with me. Wow! My abdomen looked so much better, although the scar was now about eight inches long across the right side of my body. My exit wound no longer looked like a major indentation. It now was just a very long line.

The doctor saw my backpack and asked, "Have you been carrying that around with those staples in?" She picked it up to see how heavy it was.

"Yes," I said.

She shook her head and said I shouldn't be carrying that much weight around.

"Well, it's not that bad," I said. "And what should I do? I have to get around from class to class."

Luckily, Sarah and I had a couple of classes together for the next few weeks, so she took her books and I shared with her. This lightened my load a little. When I called home that night I told my mom that the doctor had said. Mom said, only half joking, "You could get a rolling backpack." Thanks for the suggestion mom, but I was not going to get a backpack with wheels!

The doctor who examined me that day was not someone I knew, so Sarah and I decided to walk around the hospital and greet the familiar faces we could find. We found some of my usual doctors who said, "If you dance again, or are in any shows, you make sure to let us know!" I told them I definitely would. I also looked for my nurses. I waved and said "Hi" to some people I had seen almost every day in the hospital, and they had no idea who I was. Others recognized me right away, making comments about how healthy I looked.

One of the nurses said, "You cut all your hair off!" She looked disappointed, remembering how hard everyone had worked to keep it healthy.

I quickly said, "I know! It kept falling out, so I had to cut it off."

They all told me it was very rewarding to see a patient return, especially one who looked as healthy as I did. In return, it was rewarding for me to hear.

One of the nurses I was able to visit was Joel, my first nurse at the hospital. He had taken care of me at my worst times. He was, by far, one of the kindest nurses I had. The night of the shooting he had talked to my mom when she was frantically trying to get any information about my condition. She clearly remembers what he said to her when he got on the phone.

"Don't you worry," he said. "I am going to take great care of your daughter."

My parents said those words were the most comforting they could have heard, so going back to see him was very gratifying for me.

Another of my nurses, Buck, said, "It's pretty cool if you think about it. You two are best friends, and you were hit with the same bullet."

Sarah and I started laughing and said, "Oh, we know!"

We all knew it wasn't a laughing matter, but now I was out of the woods. Sometimes you have to make light of the situation or it will eat you up inside. Life can become too serious, and we didn't want that to happen. My family, friends and I finally had found a place where we could crack jokes. When I was back home over the summer, we started to joke about how skinny I was. My girlfriends started to call it "The Alicia Brady Diet." While it certainly was an extreme diet, it came with guaranteed results!

I became very aware of the simple statements in life that many people often say. One, "Oh, I just wanted to shoot myself," found me chiming in with a sarcastic voice. "Trust me; you don't want to do that!" Sometimes people didn't know how to take my humor.

I also told many family and friends, "You know the saying that I would take a bullet for you? Well, that has a whole new meaning for me. I love you, but I'm not sure I would be willing to do that again." We all knew how unlikely it was for something like this to happen. Even today, I can't believe I was shot. Joking allowed us to slide the tension down a notch.

My family all became immune to saying the words, "When Alicia was shot." People often remarked, "You say it so calmly and casually." It does just roll off the tongue. That doesn't mean it has sunk in; it just has become easier to talk about.

I think my favorite question I was ever asked about the shooting, and I am continually asked on a regular basis is, "Did it hurt?"

I usually smile.

"Well, I was shot with an AK-47 through the liver. Yes it hurt!" Adding in a little sarcasm while it slips out of my mouth.

ملم

Toward the end of September the detectives called me and asked where I was living, in Colorado or Arizona. When I told them I was back in school in Tucson they asked me to come in and meet with them to discuss the case. When I arrived they escorted me to a private room to talk. They were kind and supportive, telling me how much better I looked and asking about my health and how I was handling things. They had seen all the pictures my mom had taken of my wounds, because they were part of the evidence. "Just seeing those pictures and seeing you now, it's unbelievable that you have come this far," they said. They asked about Sarah and Moira, and I told them we were still living together. Then they inquired about Jake, Nilo, and Danielle. I discussed how we had become friends and said we got together whenever we could. The detectives told me my friends were heroic. They said it was extremely unlikely anyone would have been able to react the way they did that night in that awful situation.

"Alicia, after we went through all the evidence of that night, and after the police came back to report what they had seen, we don't know how Jake was even able to make his way out of there," one detective said. I knew it was chaotic while we were there but became even more so after we fled to the hospital. "You are one lucky girl," they said. "You're lucky that those people were in the car with you and that you have the friends and family that you have." Of course I agreed. They continued and said, "Did you know that 18 rounds were fired that night?" I had no idea. I knew it had been bad, but 18 rounds? The next words out of the detectives' mouths stopped me dead in my tracks.

"We are closing the case," they said. "It is final today."

Time stood still. I was not prepared for this and had no idea what to say. They reminded me that the evidence pointed to a specific seventeen-year-old gang member. They had interviewed a rival gang member who had been across the street that night. He was the one the shooter was aiming at. He had actually been shot in the foot. The young fifteen year old still would not talk. Since it was gang related no one would speak up. Whether on the street or in prison, a gang member who snitches faces certain death, so no one would testify against him. The detectives continued to tell me it was dark out that night, so a positive identification was difficult. They said the evidence just wasn't strong enough. They continued to believe they had identified the shooter but didn't want to put the wrong person behind bars. Soon after they released the seventeen-year-old from custody he was shot in the leg, giving them even more reason to believe he was the shooter. He probably was shot by his own gang members because he had brought unwanted attention. A gunshot wound to the leg certainly would bring him pain, but wouldn't necessarily kill him.

"Yeah, I understand," I said. "But I didn't think my case would be closed this quickly." The detectives asked if I had questions. When I returned home I thought of a million things I should have asked, but at that moment, I quietly replied, "No." I couldn't think straight.

While I certainly was grateful for the work the police department had done, I left there wondering if they had put their best foot forward. If I had been someone else would the case be closed? What if I was the daughter of a politician, a judge, a famous coach? It was a disturbing thought. Regardless, the decision to close my case was out of my hands. I left the police station angry, bitter, and with a huge hole in my heart. I hated the person who had pulled the trigger.

I returned to our apartment, and the girls asked what had happened. I lost control and sobbed, "I can't believe this!" I was yelling now. "How could this happen already? If I were someone who was well known the case would not be closed." I continued in my frantic state of mind. "He tried to kill someone and I was in the way. The case is closed. Because he wasn't successful at killing me, he will not be punished!" Sarah and Moira tried to calm me, but I was too agitated.

I wondered how I could continue to live knowing he was still out there, knowing he could do this again to someone else. The next victim might not be so fortunate. I was still trying to figure out how to get on with my life. I didn't want to hate him forever, and I knew I probably never would come face to face with him. *How do I forgive this?* I wondered. *How do I even begin to think about that?* Forgiveness was much too big a task for me then. I knew it did me no good to hate him, but I didn't care. At that time I thought I never would be able to let go. I thought I never would forgive. Eventually I discovered it was another piece of my life that needed mending back together. I didn't realize at that time how big a piece it was.

ﻋﻠﻰ

Life, as always, kept moving full speed ahead. My anger and hatred started to fade away. I continued the task of everyday life.

When October rolled around the emotions started to come in waves. The three of us knew it had been close to a year from the shooting, and we struggled with what to say to one another. I couldn't forget that a year ago at this exact moment I was shot, or I was in the hospital. I relived every detail, all the memories of that time. For some reason I never replayed the good memories. I asked one of my therapists about this one time. I didn't understand why I thought about the shooting and its aftermath all the time. I also didn't mind, even though it brought up all those old emotions, explaining to others in detail what had happened. My therapist said many times, when we experience something so traumatic and dehumanizing, we have to say it out loud and hear it in order to grasp it.

I knew I couldn't change the past, but I also couldn't help but wonder what life would be like now if I had never been shot. I just couldn't seem to fold my thoughts around the fact that a year ago I was shot and almost died.

My mom knew I was caught up in a constant struggle. While the actual shooting itself was unimaginable, that was only a small part of the trauma. My hospital stay wasn't time spent resting in a bed while making a steady recovery. The other crashes my body suffered were just as traumatic as being shot. Not once or twice, but I crashed three more times before I would see light at the end of the tunnel. I had taken the bullet more than once. I told my parents, "I am hurting. I don't know what to think or how to feel. I don't know how to react." I thought there was an appropriate way to handle all of this, and I wanted someone to tell me what to do. I didn't understand that everyone grieves in their own way, and no one could do that for me. My parents told people at church and in the community that I was depleted and really could use some encouragement. Dozens of people wrote letters and sent me e-mails. It always helped me to be reminded that people continued to think of and pray for me.

My dad sent me a simple card during that time that reminded me how much he loved me, and how blessed I am to be his daughter.

Alicia, I remember the day you were born as if it were yesterday. What a joy then and now. Hope and pray this year is wonderful. You are my love. Love, Dad.

The weekend of October 11th and 12th marked the one-year anniversary of the shooting. It happened to be the same weekend as Jazz Dance Showcase. Sarah, Moira and I always talk about how some of us thought the anniversary itself was the 11th, because that was when we left the house, but to others it was the 12th. That was the day my parents received that fateful phone call.

Instead of staying in Tucson that weekend, the three of us and Jess decided we wanted to get away. We did not want to be surrounded by constant reminders of what had happened. We wanted to be in solitude and take some time together to step back from our busy lives and unwind. Moira's family had a timeshare in Palm Springs, California. It was an easy decision to make when Moira mentioned it, and we all agreed it would be the perfect place to get away. We thought we owed it to ourselves! We made plans for the weekend and a few extra days, and hit the road for the five-hour drive from Tucson.

It was twice as hot in Palm Springs as it was in Tucson, so we spent most of our time by the pool, reading and soaking in the sun. We went out to dinner, watched movies, and ate frozen yogurt every day. We did some shopping with the tiny amount of money we had. We took out the golf cart a couple of times to look at the beautiful scenery and pretend like we were part of the golf scene. It took our minds off what seemed to be haunting everyone for the past few weeks. The day of October 12th dawned, and many people called and texted me to say they were thinking of me. I talked to almost every family member on the phone that day. I think our little trip was the perfect way to spend the weekend. We were together but creating new memories. The shooting itself, as well as the following months, had been emotionally draining for all of us.

I slowly started to peel back the layers of Sarah and Moira's recovery. Sarah told me, "I didn't know what to do. You were the one I did everything with. I went to school with you, had classes with you. Then came home and had dinner with you every night. I sat and watched our shows together with you. And then, you weren't there."

She continued to tell me that she was so lost and confused. Just like me, people were telling her to just move on with life. Just like me, she was completely lost and didn't know what to think. So many people thought they had the right answer when they told us to move on, get over it, it's in the past. But if we asked them, "Okay, how do I do that?" they wouldn't have the slightest clue what to say.

As I came to the realization that my best friends had been struggling severely too, and because I had sought out wise counsel, I started to become a bit more content with what I had and where I was. I still didn't want to accept it, but I slowly realized I didn't have to listen to those who said, "Just move on with your life." I had to do it in my own time.

This journal entry was on the one-year anniversary of the shooting:

It's been a year since everything happened. It's so strange how my body knows the exact dates of the shooting and all the crashes that followed. I went into a zone for a few days, feeling as though I wasn't even present. Sometimes I feel like I can't stop the tears, and other times I don't feel anything at all. Thinking about it has made me sick to my stomach lately. My body is getting those heat flashes again. Along with that comes the claustrophobic feeling. I don't know what I want people to feel towards me. Some days I really don't care, and other days I want to scream at people for not understanding me. Especially when they act like they do understand me. The thing is I don't want people to feel sorry for me. I want people to understand me. I don't think anyone will ever be able to do that.

When I read this now, I remember how far I have come. Seeing progress from day to day was discouraging, but knowing how far I had come from October 2008 to October 2009 was inspiring to me. While I knew I had come a long way, you still can see how much I was battling within myself.

My body instinctively knew the dates that I had been rushed back into life-saving emergency surgery. I wouldn't try to anticipate those anniversaries, because it caused unbearable fear and anxiety. Nevertheless, many times I woke up in the morning after suffering another gut-wrenching nightmare. I would look at the calendar and realize, "Oh, wow, this is the day my diaphragm ruptured." Or, "This is the day I had a ruptured aneurism." The dream I had on the one-year anniversary date of my ruptured aneurism was one I will never forget.

I dreamed Sarah, Moira and I were leaving our house to meet up with friends. It was dark outside. For some reason we were somewhere in the Colorado woods. Soon we were being chased down by a gunman. I was running as fast as I could. We all split up. All of a sudden I found myself crawling through a maze, which slowed me down, and the gunman got closer and closer. The maze I was crawling through was made of body parts. I found myself on the ground crawling through ribs. There were rows of human rib cages, but only the right side, the side where I had been shot. Suddenly, I was in a lab talking with someone, and I realized I was a scientist. The other person had come to look at a body that was in a huge vat. I realized it was my body, but I continued to talk and show him around the lab. Then I pointed up to my other body, my body in the vat. I told the other person that when I clicked the button I held in my hand, my body standing here, with you, will pass away. But I will jump into the body in the vat, and that body will wake up. And when I went to click the button, knowing I would die, I woke up. I had escaped death yet again.

Now, people ask me all the time if I had bad dreams. Yes I did. My body obviously remembered all the trauma it had been through.

December 2009 rolled around, and the girls and I spent hours decorating our apartment for the holidays. We made our own snowflakes and put lights up. We loved to do these things together. I remember one friend called us on a Friday night as we were decorating and asked if we wanted to go out somewhere. "Nope! Sorry! We are cutting out snowflakes for our apartment!" Once our home was decorated we decided to have a Christmas party. We had a blast!

Around this time of year is when we signed up for classes for the next semester. I took a deep breath and signed myself up for a slew of dance classes including the higher-level classes. I had no idea what I would physically be able to do. It wasn't as though I could ask a professor for an opinion on how long it might take me to come back. I had been shot a little over a year ago. This was not your typical dance injury. No one had any idea how long it would take for me to step back into class, including myself. I hadn't stepped into a single dance class since then, but figured I had nothing to lose. It was worth the try. All of my professors were very supportive and wanted to help me as much as they could. So I signed up, not knowing if I could come back and take them or not. I had 4 hours of incomplete classes to finish from the time of the shooting. In addition, I signed up for 24 more credits. Crazy!!

I returned to Colorado for Christmas. It was a wonderful holiday with the entire family together. It's not often all of my siblings are in one place! Kendra was home from Missouri, and both my brothers were able to get enough time off from work to spend a few days at home. I also spent a lot of time with little Emma and my parents. Next to Emma, I am the runt of the family. I enjoyed getting to poke at and pick on my other siblings, knowing they would do nothing in return because they were afraid of hurting me. If someone tried to tackle me I would yell, "Don't hurt me!" and they quickly backed off. It doesn't work today as well as it did then, but it was fun while it lasted.

During break I let my mind and body relax as much as possible. I was thinking and preparing myself for what was coming the next semester. I still had academics to finish up and many dance classes to tackle. I headed back to school in January.

The first day of my final semester of college, I stepped back into a dance class for the first time since the shooting. I chose a modern class to begin, and I don't think there could have been a better place to reacquaint myself with the love of my life, dancing. I hadn't spent much time training in modern dance growing up, but I quickly had come to love it at the UofA. My dance professors made it easy – each of them was very unique in style, but all were equally brilliant. This particular class was taught by Amy Earnst, whose method of teaching and style suited me wonderfully. I knew I would have a limited range of motion in the beginning, but I also thought I might be able to emulate her movements with my body. She is very conscious of ensuring her dancers warm up properly. She also watches us carefully for correct alignment. the very basics that make you excel as a dancer. The very basics that I needed. This class was full of graduating seniors, and dancing with my peers was the perfect way for me to begin again.

Amy also took the time in her class to focus on abdominal work, which was the foundation of what I needed as a dancer. No doubt, my body was weak, but I was moving! I did the very best I could. As class went on and we started to move more I knew that my muscle memory still was there. My body remembered, "You're a dancer! You've been through a lot of trauma, but you remember this." Even before stepping foot into class I knew technique would be slow to return. It would take a lot of work to get strong, to regain the balance, the turnout, the fast muscle twitch. Modern dance is very grounded, so we do a lot of floor work. I had a hard time getting myself up off the floor, because the strength – especially in my hips – just wasn't there. The same went for jumping exercises, which were very challenging for me. I had considered myself a leaper all my life. Jumping had always come easy for me, and now I had to haul myself into the air. But, wow! I was in class! Right away I became very aware of how fit my body had been before I was shot. I also realized the strength I had built up over the years as a dancer had a great deal to do with my very survival.

Thread

Dance studio 301 was right above the Stevie Eller theatre. Sunshine always streams through its big glass windows to brighten the room. I remember standing by those windows, as I waited for my turn to do the combination across the floor, looking out, and thinking to myself, *This is where I belong. I'm here.*

Along with the modern class I also signed up for Ballet and Jazz. Ballet isn't movement the human body was built for to begin with, and now it was overly demanding and difficult on my body. With all my abdominal surgeries the movement seemed almost impossible for me – especially things such as an arabesque or a cambre back, which require a lot of extension from the torso. My torso didn't want to have anything to do with arching or extending back, so I just did the best I could.

One day during my first week back I had to step out of class for a moment. A big chunk of skin had torn away from the bottom of my foot and it was bleeding. Believe it or not, I was unusually excited to see this! I missed going home at night so sore I could barely move; going home with bruises all over from floor work. I had even missed seeing blisters form on the soles of my feet.

Jazz dance had been my first love as a child and I was thrilled to be back in that class with Michael Williams, my professor. While it wasn't as hard for me as ballet, the first class taught me the movement would be harder for my newly-structured body to work with. Even after an entire lifetime of dancing, I had forgotten that you have to engage a specific part of your brain when learning a new combination. I discovered it wasn't just the physical aspect of dance I would have to work on, but it was the mental portion, too. It took skill and years of practice to not only maintain the information given to you, but to dance it with proper technique, with energy, and with heart.

Returning to dance class reaffirmed just how much I had missed it. This sent me down another path of my recovery, as I was able to take hold of something I thought I might never get to enjoy again. Although I had a long way to go, I also knew that with perseverance I could do it!

Now that I had returned to dance classes, we all seemed to be in continual motion. I was pleasantly surprised at just how well I could move. My last performance opportunity had been in October

2008, and it now was January 2010. Fifteen months had slipped by. Physically I wasn't ready to perform and thought it might take me a year or more to be fully prepared.

When I was in the hospital Susan had told me, "When you dance again, since you didn't get to perform in the last piece, I'll put you in one of my new pieces."

I had just replied, "Okay, thanks."

I didn't really believe, at the time, that I ever would have the opportunity to do that. But now, opportunity was knocking. At the end of that first week I thought, *I can do this. I might have to fake a few movements, but I'll pull it off.*

So I found Susan and said, "Remember how you told me, if I thought I was ready, I could dance in your new piece?"

She said, "Really? Yeah! We just started and are not very far along on it. We will put you in it."

I let her know I was moving much better than I thought I would and I really wanted the opportunity to perform again. So, I was at the next rehearsal.

All of my fellow dancers supported me in this effort. Susan's choreography is very fast, demanding, and impulsive – basically everything my body had a hard time with. But I loved it! I thrived on being able to work up the stamina and the strength that allowed me to move like that again. I was bound and determined to make it happen. I was too excited to be frustrated over minor issues; instead, those challenges just made me want to work harder.

Many times Susan asked me, "Can you do this? Do I need to adjust it a little bit, so it will feel more comfortable on your body?"

I always told her, "No. You don't need to change anything for me. I'll find a way to make it work."

That night I called home. "Hey, Mom, guess what? I am going to be in the next show!"

She started crying tears of joy and asked when it would be. It was scheduled for the following month. That February, part of our show series was called Premium Blend. I was able to once again take the stage. Many people back in Colorado had asked to let them know if I was able to perform again, but it was such short notice and so far away, my mom was the only one able to come to the show. But I had several other special guests in the audience that weekend – the doctors who had said if I performed they would come to see me. They all did! Dr. Rhee, Dr. Wynne, Dr. Friese, and Dr. Amini all came to the show, along with Dean Humphrey. They all came to support me in my victorious return to the stage. Their presence was a gift to me.

Opening night I was given a special award on stage. My fellow students had nominated me for the "Ralphie Spirit Award," named after a UofA dancer who had been killed. Ralphie had been full of compassion for others and never spoke a negative word. The award was created to pay tribute to him and all he stood for. I was honored that not only did I receive the award but that my friends had nominated me for it.

Director of the School of Dance and Dean of Fine Arts, Jory Hancock, went above and beyond to make this night extra special for me. When he called me on stage, UofA President Robert Shelton came out to present the award. They also recognized my mom, who was sitting in the audience. All this happened before I even had the opportunity to perform. It was an emotionally-charged night! It was hard to imagine my return to dance could possibly get any better, but it was about to.

I stepped behind the curtain and took my spot on stage. Adrenaline pumped through my body. An enormous smile spread across my face. "Thank you, Lord," I whispered. "Thank you for allowing me to do what I love again." The lights came up, and I started to dance.

When I came off the stage Sarah, Moira, and Jess were waiting for me. They threw their arms around me in a victory hug. I started to cry, thinking only about how blessed I was. No, I couldn't move like I did before, but I did have the full use of my arms, legs, everything I needed. I wasn't broken, just a bit more fragile than I used to be. Jake, Nilo, and Danielle also had come to see the show. Since the performances didn't work with their schedules they came to watch one of our rehearsals. It meant a lot to me to have them there.

After the show I went to the lobby and found my mom, all my doctors, the Dean and the President of the School. We all took pictures together. Dr. Friese joked, "You know, if you come back in to complain about anything we are going to have a hard time believing you after seeing how well you danced!"

My first performance after the shooting now was in the books. We all returned to everyday life, hectic life. I continued to work hard in school, still hoping that I would be able to graduate on time. I spent most of my time with the girls. We had made a "to do" list; and extremely long list of all the things we wanted to do or see while we were in Tucson. Most of the things on the list had something to do with food. Although we all are very studious, we occasionally took a day off to spend it together, usually by the pool or on the couch watching our favorite shows. We were living!

One day the girls came home laughing so hard. "Alicia, we were walking to the dance building together today," they said. "We heard this really loud noise. Both of us hit the ground." They kept laughing. They finally figured out it was a car backfiring. They both fell to the safety of the ground while everyone around them watched, not knowing what to think. The picture formed in my head, and I started laughing. This was now a natural reaction for us.

The Student Spotlight show was coming up quickly. Students choreograph the pieces for this show, and then audition our choreography in front of all our dance professors and staff. They select a few to be performed in the show. Sarah, Moira, Jess, and I had worked on a piece of choreography for one of our classes. We spent many hours outside of the class finishing the collaboration. It is difficult to take four different sets of ideas and bring them all together to create one piece of moving art. But we did it because we wanted to audition it for the show. The piece was modern-based movement called The Meadow. It reflected our spirit and resilience with one another, that we were there together, and we were going to love and embrace the time we had left. It was quickly coming to an end.

We auditioned and then held our breath, waiting for the results.

When they sent out the cast list that night we all crowded around the computer to read it. We were in! We saw our number and started jumping up and down, screaming, overjoyed!

I also have a childhood friend named Victor, who had danced and trained with me at Zetta's. Although we both attended UofA, one day we realized we had not collaborated since we had been at college. We knew the showings were in a week, but we decided to create a piece for the student audition, as well. In just two rehearsals we choreographed a duet called Vodka Martini. Don't read too much into that title, it was the name of the song! Susan had given us some random music to listen to, and that was the one we both liked. Only Victor and I could have pulled that off together. We had danced together for so long that we moved very similarly and worked comfortably and efficiently together. The movement came out swiftly. We auditioned Vodka Martini, and it was put in the show, too!

Once more I got to call my family and tell them I had the chance to perform again. Not only is it a honor to be at UofA, but it is a privilege to perform. This time many family members were able to make the trip. When the weekend of the show came, my mom, dad, Grandma Brady, Grandma Ely, Emma, and cousin Keith all drove to see me! That is a long drive for anyone, but it was extra long when the car was fully packed and the passenger list included children, ages four and five. Both grandmothers told me the story of Keith and Emma trying to watch a movie on a DVD player in the car. The little ones were in the very back, and the DVD player was up between the driver and passenger seats. "Grandma, I can't see. Your head's in the way," they kept saying. "Grandma, your hair is in the way. Grandma, move your head." I know it wasn't a relaxing drive, but I was glad they were here.

Both of my grandmas came in to watch my Modern and Jazz classes. They sat next to each other in the front of the room. A friend came up to me and asked, "Are those your grandmas?" I told her yes. She asked me if they were friends, and again I said yes. She was so amazed by that, because her grandmothers don't even speak to one another. In many cases, what we went through would tear a family apart. We still had our hard times, but in the end it has only tied us closer together. For that, I am forever grateful.

It was show time. Not only was even more of my family in attendance, but my wish was coming true – I was getting to dance on stage with my closest friends! I had prayed about this. It was happening! Before we went on stage for the first performance we stood backstage in a circle holding hands. We had all worked so hard to be there. We relished the moment and took the stage together. It was captivating. And dancing with Victor in the same show was the cherry on top. We had danced together since we were twelve years old. Having the opportunity to do it once again in this special place was not only exciting, but it was heartwarming for me.

The weekend of the show my family pretty much had taken over our entire apartment. Of course the girls were always there to welcome them. Sarah and Moira had met Emma several times before, so Emma always loved to see them and play with them. Emma, being the sweet but rather bossy little girl that she is, made them play Cinderella with her. She always made them be the Prince! She would drop her shoe, make one of them pick it up, put it on her foot, and then dance with her. The girls happily played along.

I was getting ready for one of the matinee shows and heard a knock at the door. I had left my door unlocked so my family could just walk in, so I didn't know who it was. I went to open it and found my sister Kendra! I was astonished. I had no idea she was flying in. It was only going to be for the day, but she flew in to see my show! While Kendra and I are alike in many ways, our packing skills are completely opposite. She brought a single backpack with everything she needed, including clothes, homework, and books. She had flown in for a quick trip from Missouri. It was such a pleasant surprise.

A few weeks after that show, somewhere around the end of March, I found the courage to sit down with my advisor, Melissa. I asked, "Am I going to be able to graduate on time? Or at least walk with my class?" I hadn't asked the question out loud before, because I was afraid to hear the answer. As far as I knew most of the class was graduating and then moving out of Tucson. While I loved all the dancers, I didn't think I would thrive there after all of my closest friends had left. Melissa had been doing everything she could to facilitate this happening. Not all of my credits were in yet, some were almost finished.

Finally she told me, "It looks like you are going to be able to walk with your class in May!" I wouldn't technically have my degree until August, because I still had about six credit hours to finish up. But I was going to be able to walk with my class! A year and a half ago, this had been an impossible feat. That last month of college was a whirlwind between finishing up classes, dancing, performing, and making a big effort to spend as much time with everyone as possible.

Once we knew I could graduate, people started asking about my plans afterward. I had no idea. My sights were set on graduation. That was my ultimate goal, so I hadn't given much thought to what might happen afterward. I had no idea what my future held. Meanwhile everyone around me already had jobs awaiting, some were planning on attending Graduate school. Most of them had auditioned and received dance positions. At that time it didn't bother me to know I had nothing planned after graduation. I just wanted to finish school and earn that degree. I still had days when I had to sit and watch class because I ached or was too swollen to participate. If I was being paid to dance, I didn't have the option to sit out a day. I doubted I could get a job dancing, at least not right after graduation.

The last day of dance class was held as usual, in Studio 301, my favorite room that overlooked the campus. We had been working on one of Amy's pieces, in groups of two. Sarah and I had paired up together. That last day we all sat down in front of the big windows and applauded one another, as we took turns on the floor, dancing for each other. While I sat next to Sarah and watched the rest of the class take their turns I thought, "I have been coming to this place since I was nine years old. Not only am I graduating, but on time, even after everything that I have been through." I had nothing to complain about. I simply couldn't ask for more.

Sarah was leaving town with her family early the morning after graduation, and Moira planned to depart a few days later. Most of my friends were headed back to their homes soon after graduation. They all were going to be gone in the blink of an eye.

Once again my family drove to Tucson. This group included mom, dad, Emma, Grandma and Grandpa Brady, and Grandma and Grandpa Ely.

The morning of graduation I received a phone call from a reporter at Fox 11 News. She had heard my story through Ed Flores, the photographer for the dancers and performances at the UofA. She called and said, "We would like to run a story on you and your graduation today." Of course, I said yes!

Later that day, when we were at lunch, I started crying. Just out of the blue. Everyone looked at me franticly asking if I was okay. I said "Yes," in a voice of pure bliss. "I am so proud of myself." Then I chuckled a little and said, "I can't believe that I am here, that I have made it this far. I am graduating!" Smiles came at me from every direction.

When we returned to the house the news crew came in. They interviewed my parents and me on film. Then Sarah, Moira, and I put on our caps and gowns and headed to graduation. The crew was going to meet us there along with our families. They rolled film as our class walked into the auditorium. Our class sat together, and when it was the UofA School of Dance's turn to walk, we all stood up and waited in line to step on stage.

Most of us had done this a thousand times. We had stepped onto stages throughout our entire lives, but this time was different.  When they called my name I walked to Jory. He stood looking at me, continuing to clap. Then he gave me a big hug, and I slowly made my way down the stage hugging the rest of my professors. They all told me how proud they were. I was proud to be standing there with them.

When they called my name no one mentioned what had taken place over the last year and a half. I walked across the stage just like everyone else. I had thought the shooting would take away everything I had reached for. But, at that moment, nothing separated me from my lifelong dreams.

Chapter Eleven

We are pressed on every side, but not crushed, perplexed, but not in despair, persecuted but not abandoned; struck down but not destroyed. – 2 Corinthians 4:8

AFTER GRADUATION, EVERYTHING SEEMED TO DISAPPEAR AS quickly as it had come. Another change was approaching, and this time it was a switch I didn't want. I had graduated, but since I had missed a year of school I still felt that I was lagging behind. I had no idea what I would be doing. I toyed with the idea of staying in Tucson awhile, but I didn't want to stay in Tucson without my closest friends surrounding me.

Almost all my classmates left within a few days after graduation. Sarah, Moira, and I spent our last night together staying up all night. Sarah left early that morning, around 3 a.m. Her family came to put all her things in the car. Man! I did not want to say goodbye! So we didn't. Instead we all stood in the kitchen bawling. We had endured a long road together and knew we would never truly be torn apart. None of us really knew what waited in our future. We each had different ideas of the directions we wanted to take. We knew we needed to part ways and hoped one day we would all be able to come back together again. But for now, it was time to say goodbye.

My family and Moira stayed around the next few days. When

they left, I went from never having a moment alone to dreading the deadly silence in my apartment. I ended up staying in Tucson for the summer to finish up those last few credits. Luckily, my friend Jess was able to stay in town for most of the summer, too.

I had managed to graduate by working purely off of adrenaline. I pushed through and finished school. Once I had met that goal, I didn't know where to set my focus. My life felt like it stopped. I had made it to the top of my biggest hill and didn't know how to proceed from there. I slowly started to feel I was taking one small step at a time... backward. I spent a very slow summer in Tucson, not knowing where that next step might be.

Most people asked, "Why don't you get a dancing job?" Naturally, I wanted nothing more than to be a professional dancer. But like everything else, there is a time and a season. Auditions are not always year round, and missing them meant you might have to wait another full year. I had been dancing again for just five months, and my body was nowhere near strong enough to dance five or seven days a week as a full-time job. I also knew I did not have the mental capacity to handle that yet.

I had a grandfather who lived a few hours from me in Chandler, Arizona. He was my mom's biological father. Growing up, I didn't spend much time with him, because he always lived in another state. Toward the end of my senior year in college he had a heart attack. He pulled through but had several complications. My mom had visited him in the spring when I graduated, but hadn't had another chance to see him since then. That summer he became very ill once again. I visited him for a day while he was in the hospital. I was really the only one in the family close enough to drive a few hours to see him. I kissed him goodbye and told him I would be back in a week or so. But one morning we all received a text message from his stepdaughter, my aunt. She sent out a mass message, so I got it the same time my mom and everyone else did. Sarah Ary had been out the last few days visiting me, and I had just dropped her off at the airport. Now I was alone in my apartment and horrified to read, *Dad's dead, he shot himself in the head.* It was a distressing way to find out, but she was frantic and didn't have the time to get on the phone to call everyone. I understood completely. I called my parents right away and could tell dad was trying to comfort my mom, but what could he say? I asked my mom if she was okay, and she said, "I will be."

My mind raced. *I don't know how much more of this our family can take. My family is still hurting, and I am not the only one with health problems.* It just seemed like it was one thing after another. But that's life. It wasn't something any of us could understand, yet I knew we were tightly knit, and we would pull through. God would continue to hold us up.

My mom, Aunt Beth, and Cousin Austin came out shortly afterward for the funeral. My mom is rock solid, because her faith in the Lord is sure. I remember thinking to myself, *If she falls apart, then so will everyone else.* But she never did. Together, we survived one more family crisis.

Sarah, Moira, and I had planned a little reunion, which came at the perfect time. Moira was back living in California, and Sarah had flown into that state for an audition. We all decided to meet in Palm Springs again. We enjoyed another weekend together, doing what we do best. We bathed in the sun, watched movies, went dancing, and ate. Although we hadn't been apart a long time, we still had a lot of catching up to do. It was the perfect mini-vacation. Being around them always lifted my spirits and brightened my smile!

I had come a long way over the past year, working hard to get my strength back. I danced almost every day, did cardio, lifted weights, and did Pilates on top of that. Now, my biggest problem was digestion. I had to cut a lot out of my diet, trying to avoid everything that made me sick. I still had those days that my abdomen swelled so much I had a hard time functioning, even after that last surgery. I didn't really expect things to go back to normal. I mean, I had been shot in the gut! But still, I was so careful about what I put in my mouth; I had no idea what was causing this.

My apartment lease in Tucson almost was up, and I soon would be heading back to Colorado. I finally went to the doctors to have them check out my digestion problems. I had planned on going earlier in the summer to have it taken care of, but I just didn't. I always thought I didn't want to be that patient that always complains about something. I certainly did want the pain and discomfort gone but didn't want to be seen as a hypochondriac. I wanted to continue progressing and hoped to avoid another surgery at all costs! So, of course I waited until the last minute to go in to see the doctor.

I saw Dr. Friese and Dr. Rhee. They thought it might be a hernia by the swelling, which was odd, because I don't swell where the average person might. I swell on the right side of my ribcage. They also told me the way my nerves and muscles had been cut, and the way bits and pieces of my ribs were missing, they didn't know for sure. My body isn't going to look or react like someone else might, because my body is not normal anymore!

They said they could do exploratory surgery to see what was going on. At the same time they could do some scar revision, which would help with mobility. I said yes. "If I am looking at another surgery, I would rather get it done now," I said, "instead of waiting a few years down the road and being knocked down again."

My apartment lease was up, so we had to move everything out. Luckily I had a second cousin, Gary, there in Tucson who helped mom and me with most of it. We drove back to Colorado, stayed a week, and then turned around to return to Tucson for another surgery. This time we stayed with my dance professors Susan and Michael.

I knew I probably could have had something done in Colorado, which certainly would have been easier on everyone. But I still only felt comfortable with my Tucson surgeons. My parents felt the same way. Better safe than sorry! I never had any fear going back into surgery at UMC, because I knew I was in good hands. It would take a lot to take me down after all I had been through.

Dr. Friese headed up this surgery, which ended up being just a scar revision. There was no hernia, which was good. I had no stitches this time, and I didn't even stay a night in the hospital. We just stayed with Susan and Michael for a week. It was only a week away from UofA classes starting again, so I had several visitors while I was there. They were all back for the school year. Soon we were headed back to Colorado.

Unfortunately, my recovery was very slow this time. Just a few months ago I had been at one of the highest peaks in my life, and now I was coming to my lowest valley. I knew I wanted to dance but didn't know how I could make that happen. I had no motivation.

My classmates and best friends now were dancing across the United States and the world. I had friends in Japan, Italy, Australia... everywhere. And here I was living back in Cañon City, the small town of my childhood, where I didn't even have the option to dance and train with a quality company that would allow me to work back where I needed to be. I hoped to audition for a professional job one day. Cañon City was not the place to do that. That is why I had trained outside of our town when I was younger, and it was no different now. After graduation you go off to do bigger and better things. I returned home.

Don't get me wrong. I was so appreciative that I had and always will have a home to return to, but that didn't make it any easier. I still dreamed of dancing professionally. I had hoped to move back home one day to settle down, long after my dancing career had ended. Yet here I was, back at the starting line again, with no direction or inspiration. I was drained. I knew I wanted to dance, but life was now so different. The surgery had been so simple, but it had sucked me back into depression again. It felt very similar to the first time I had come home.

I knew my mental state could go a long way toward determining my physical state. This time I wasn't prepared with a plan. I just floated along, thinking, "I'll get back up on my feet when I do. I have nothing to push myself toward, so I'll take my time." It was apparent there was nothing beckoning me forward, because I put forth very little effort. I had nothing to look forward to. I knew I had to heal physically, which would take time. I had to take it one day at a time, and I am not a patient person. I couldn't yet see God's perfect timing, although I know that His timing throughout my life has been exactly right. Even today I work on my patience level, which hasn't improved much, but I know things work out when they are supposed to and not one second before!

Physical distress and mental trauma go hand in hand, but I learned it is impossible to fully recover without spiritual healing. I could not move forward and be content without all three aspects – physical, mental, and spiritual – coming together in my life.

By now I had seen my scars in the mirror nearly every day, but I saw them as a hindrance. My reflection only brought thoughts of the suffering I had endured and continued to bear. Instead of remembering I had survived, I thought only of horror, insecurity, and anguish. I was in the depths of despair. I knew I couldn't live under my parents' roof for the rest of my life. I needed to hold a job, but I couldn't. I needed to start making and saving money. I had a college degree that I had worked very hard for and wanted to use.

So finally I started working on getting as healthy as I could. I continued to eat healthy, worked out, and started back to dance classes. I believed that would take all of my problems away! Dancing! *Everything will flee away from me*, I thought. *Mentally, physically, and spiritually I will be healed, because dancing is what I love to do. It is what brings me joy.* Dancing always has been my entire world. That was all I knew.

I had to work a lot harder after other surgeries than I did with this one, but I simply had no incentive. As time went on my body did progress physically and mentally. It just happened naturally. I wasn't pushing myself like I had all the other times, or pushing myself like I should have been. I was so out of shape!

I was stuck in a rut and confused. At least I wasn't going backward anymore, but I had absolutely no progress forward. I began to realize maybe it wasn't so much about my mental and physical progress this time, but instead my spiritual progress. That was an issue I had been avoiding for far too long.

Although I was healing physically I began to think I wasn't going to make it through all this. I didn't know if the weight would ever be lifted off me. I'd had all that I could take. I slowly started to lose sight of my dreams, thinking that losing dancing would be the end of me.

I still questioned why. I always had a deep throb of pain and sorrow. I held hatred toward a person I didn't even know. I didn't understand how anything good could come out of such circumstances. I decided it was time to face these difficult questions.

I knew I hadn't pulled myself out of the muck. Others had prayed that my family and I would be given the strength to pull through, and we did. I was well aware of that. Others continued to pray for me. Even today people come up to me to say, "I still keep you in my prayers." The battle I currently fought was not the same as fighting for every breath. The battle I now was fighting was a bigger and if possible even more overpowering fight than anything I had faced in my entire life. It was a spiritual battle I had to face.

A year ago I was back at school, busy, caught up in the chaos of life, which I loved. I remember thinking, *At least I am living a life right now. I'm at school with friends. I think I can get through this.* But I also knew there soon would come a point where I was going to collapse and tumble. I thought, *I know that it's coming. This is not normal. I am dealing with this way too well.* I was approaching that breaking point.

Now I had days when someone would try to hug me, or sit and talk with me. I pushed them away, saying, "Don't hug me. Don't touch me." I didn't want to be embraced or to talk about anything that had happened. I started to push away any comfort or help that was offered to me. Many times others asked what was wrong. I shook my head back and forth, NO NO NO! "I don't know what to think or how to feel anymore. I don't know what I want. But I can't stay in this place. I'm stuck. I can't seem to move my feet."

When I did explain this to my family and friends they were all very supportive. They told me no one expected me to have it all together. But while they supported and loved me, none of them felt they were in a position to give me the advice and help that I needed at that time. How could I deal with this? Life was too overwhelming for me. I didn't want to go through the rest of my life with a heavy heart. I had a crushed spirit, and I wanted to change that. I wanted to be lighthearted and not take everything so seriously. I wanted to enjoy life again, but I didn't know how.

One Sunday in the autumn of 2010 my mom was at church talking to a friend who mentioned the Ranch of Hope, a nearby counseling facility that her son had attended. The ranch provides five days of Christian-based intensive counseling in the beautiful Sangre de Cristo mountains, near where my family used to ranch. The program involves four or five hours of daily counseling. My mom mentioned it to me and I said, "Yes I think that is something I would want to do." I was afraid to go, but that fear made me realize I needed this. It scared me, yet I knew it was another piece of the puzzle of my recovery that needed my active participation. Some pieces fall into place, others have to be picked up.

In mid-October I went to the Westcliffe and Rosita area of

Colorado for almost a week at the Ranch of Hope. Every day I talked through the past two years. I poured out my heart and spoke of the smallest details – how it happened, how I felt, how others felt. I roomed alone, so I spent my evenings reflecting on everything that I had processed that day. I went on walks. I read and I wrote. I finally began to understand why I felt the way I did, and I slowly discovered the process of working through it.

In the cool, crisp air of the Sangre de Cristos, I finally started to make the connection between my mental, physical, emotional, and spiritual hurt and healing. Not only did I have a broken heart, but I was grieving. My feelings bubbled up, no longer willing to be pushed beneath the surface. My emotions were unavoidable! I had to experience them and go through them, just like the motions of everyday life. Continuing to suppress those feelings was only going to hinder me and slow me down. I learned there is no right or wrong way to feel. I acknowledged my emotions, and owed an explanation to no one. There was a time and a place for each of those complicated feelings, and I had to let myself fully experience all of them. I also learned it was best to express those feelings, most of which were dark and angry, to someone I held to the highest standards of trust and value, because I knew that person would not judge me.

Since the shooting, many different people had tried to impose their wisdom upon me in some way. This happened every day. While I was grateful they cared enough to try to help, their advice wasn't always the best for me at that time. My time at the ranch gave me the professional help I so desperately needed. As humans we are not meant to cope with some of the tragedies in life. That is what others are for!

My counselor believed I was going through a grieving process; I was mourning the life that I had lost. I appreciated his viewpoint and agreed. Indeed, I was grieving. We discussed the five stages of grief, which are denial, anger, bargaining, depression, and finally acceptance. We also talked about where I was in that process. Most days I was in the depression stage, but occasionally I skipped to an angry or bargaining day. Never had I found the point of acceptance.

What makes us adults? He said that eighty percent of who we

are is created internally before we become adults. Many people had told me I was mature for my age, but I thought it came by necessity and not by choice. I had to grow up during the last couple of years, and quickly. I learned lessons in a few years that most people take a lifetime to learn.

I realize that I could have turned to drugs and alcohol, which seemed the easy way out. But I didn't. There were several other paths I wanted to take. But I didn't. I could have refused to take the step toward counseling. But I didn't. I knew it would have been much harder on my family if I had died. But I didn't. It would have been a lot easier on me if that bullet had instantaneously killed me. But it didn't.

I knew my God loved me and had kept me here on Earth for a reason. I still didn't understand how He could allow something like this to happen. I wrote in my journal:

Humbly obey God regardless of present circumstances and in His good time either in this life or the next, He will lift you up.

I finally learned that now I had a heart that wouldn't trust or love – and I can't do one successfully or fully without the other. I knew I would have to learn to let my guard down again. I had to realize that not everyone was out to get me, that people sincerely loved me and cared what happened to me. With my experience over the past two years, that was difficult to believe.

Each separate piece of me had to be restored and bound back together. My wounded spirit left my healing incomplete. This was something the doctors couldn't work on with their hands – there was only one who could fill that empty space.

I would never come to a place of restoration without that missing piece. Finally recognizing that was a shift in direction for my life. I may not have acted on or remembered that each day, but just understanding it gave me back a little hope for my future.

Everyone who surrounded me had different but equally important jobs. My task was of the greatest importance, because I knew my body better than anyone. Was I crazy to think that way? No. I wasn't. I still needed to be persistent in my healing, whatever that meant. I needed to pay attention and listen to what my body was telling me. I finally knew that didn't just mean the physical part of my healing, but the spiritual side, as well. I knew how to seek out help, but the rest of it was new to me.

While at the Ranch of Hope, I read the book, *When You're Ill or Incapacitated* by James E. Miller. I discovered that during the times I couldn't move, couldn't dance, I still had the ability and capacity to grow. I needed to take time to be less concerned about doing and be more open to just being. "Find the joy in everything. Laugh. Take yourself lightly," he wrote. "You are not alone, but upheld. While you know fear, also know courage. I know doubt, but also know faith. I wonder, but can also hope. Make as much out of this time. Feed your soul."

As I sit today and write this book, I realize my life was heavy and sorrowful at that time. I needed someone to give me permission to smile, to tell me, "It's okay to be happy, Alicia." My family, friends and I can all have a good laugh now about all that has happened, or at least find the light in certain moments. Back then my joy was only momentary.

After reading for hours each day and meeting with my counselor, I left the ranch, wondering, *What can I make with this time of my life? What are my priorities now? Are they in order? Will I take this time to grow in wisdom, compassion, and courage?*

I knew that others could not do this for me. Only I could make that change. Only I could persevere. All that had been broken down had to be built back up. Only I could heal, but I would have to allow the Lord to help me. I knew I wasn't where I wanted to be physically, but I also knew that didn't have to hold me back. I still could grow as a human being. I could gain more than I had lost.

When I left the Ranch of Hope I didn't apply what I had learned every single day. It had just begun to seep in. The new knowledge was in my head, not in my heart. But the light was beginning to shine through. The door was cracked. I wasn't ready to push it open the rest of the way. I knew that I could have a future, but I still wasn't sure how.

Later that month I made the decision and moved to Colorado Springs, about an hour north of my hometown, to continue my dance training. I returned to my childhood dance studio and teacher, because Cañon City didn't have an suitable place for me to continue training. I wanted to be in a comfortable environment, a place where I could come and go as much as my body would allow me to do, but a place that would push me and encourage me. Zetta, my dance instructor from the age of six to eighteen, had the utmost confidence in me. She knew all of my strengths and weaknesses and could push me to be the best that I possibly could be.

It was important to train and work with someone who understood my physical limitations. On the days when I awoke too sick to make it into class I didn't want to explain my situation to someone new. Even today, I hate having that conversation with anyone. It's awkward explaining to a complete stranger that I had been shot; it makes the average person uncomfortable. This wasn't like my need to talk about the shooting to my parents, friends, roommates, doctors, physical therapists, or someone at church.

"I don't know if I am ready to go to a place where people don't know what happened to me," I told my parents. It seems strange now, but I was either complaining that there were too many people who knew everything about me, or that I wanted more people to understand me. At that time it was healthy for me to talk about the shooting and its aftermath. I wasn't ready to step away from that. Yet I didn't feel the need to start those conversations with new people in my life, so I returned to my familiar dance studio, where I was welcomed with open arms.

I started taking dance classes just a few days each week. It was difficult to step back into that studio, not only for the underlying reasons but because it had become a different place than it had been during my childhood. New people and a new building greeted me. I hadn't expected it to be exactly the same – after all, I had been gone for five years. I still loved it there, but it was no longer the dance environment I now was used to. Just as in any work place or home atmosphere, our surroundings have a lot to do with how well we progress and thrive. I just hoped I could succeed there.

I was willing to work myself up to a demanding and grueling schedule. But I could not escape the question, *Why am I working so hard?* I was used to dancing at a highly-ranked college. Zetta is an excellent teacher, no doubt, but it was tough for me to see past the fact that I was starting all over again. I never have, and never will, step into a dance class and give only half my effort. It's all or nothing. While I was growing up and attending college, I never second guessed my passion for class. Rarely did I have to give myself an extra push, only if I was overly tired that day. But I always enjoyed every single second of class. It was still my passion, but I wasn't enjoying class quite like I had last May at the university. There was no one to blame for that. I was a different person now. Many things still seemed hopeless to me. Although I had many little glimmers of hope, my fears and uncertainties took over.

I hoped that my dancing would once again restore me, that it would bring me the happiness and fulfillment I thought my life was missing. I thought stepping back into class would allow the other parts of my healing to come together, and everything finally would fall into place.

I worked diligently and strove to find some semblance of the dancer I once had been. My body was weak, and my anatomy was not the same. I had to find new ways to balance, to distribute my weight, to stretch, to move bigger and faster. I certainly wasn't the dancer I used to be. I still was learning about my newly shaped body, which seemed to be constantly changing. It was frustrating at times! Everything used to come so easily. I had to step back occasionally and remind myself just how blessed I really was.

I started back into my jazz classes. There is nothing like working so hard through a class that you can't breathe when it's over, working your legs so hard they feel as though they will fall off. It took all the willpower I had to move my body that fast, but I did it.

Returning to dance this time did not fill the void. There seemed to be something missing. I no longer had the flutters of excitement that I used to. Perhaps I had idolized dancing my entire life, and now it wasn't living up to my expectations. That feeling was completely unexpected and uncomfortable.

Soon I was stuck in limbo. I danced and taught classes everyday. Yet I began to think, *What else is there for me? Where is the thrill?* My life felt like a meaningless dead end.

I had let a lot of wise counsel sink in at the Ranch of Hope, but was still dealing with depression and had not yet accepted my life now. Still spiritually wounded, I was not ready to talk about or come to terms with the hurt placed upon me. The hurt that the Lord had allowed. I didn't even want to understand it. Yet life went on.

A few months later, in January 2011, I signed into my e-mail account with the University of Arizona. I receive direct information about important news around campus, and this day I received an e-mail that the UofA basketball game had been cancelled. What? Basketball is an incredibly popular sport at the university! One that I supported. Then I saw the game was cancelled because of a nearby shooting. My first thought was, *How horrible, but I'm not surprised.* Then I continued to read and discovered former United States Representative Gabrielle Giffords and at least eighteen others were shot. Six of the victims already had died. As more articles and news emerged about the mass shooting, I learned one of Gabrielle Giffords' leading surgeons was Dr. Rhee, the Trauma Division Chief who had saved my life so many times.

Memories came rushing back. I began to receive text messages and phone calls from family and friends who said they were thinking about me. I thought about the victims and their families, knowing exactly what they were going through. It was heartbreaking, another senseless act of violence that had taken more than one innocent life. As a victim, I learned that violence doesn't change just the one who takes the bullet – it changes everyone who surrounds you.

Another thought crossed my mind as I watched Dr. Rhee and Gabrielle Giffords' neurosurgeons on television. *She is in good hands.* I knew that from experience. While no one wants to be in that situation, I know today that my survival was a miracle. Those doctors had been strategically placed for me at every single moment, just like they now were for the victims of the most recent shooting.

Around the first anniversary of my shooting, my brother Sean sent me a card. He wrote: *It is difficult to understand your tragedy, but I fully understand your miracle. You know, people are saying you will do great things, but I say you have already done great things. Love, Sean.*

I truly understood those words when that shooting spree

occurred in that Tucson shopping center. It's hard to understand the tragedy, but over time, a lot easier to understand the miracle.

A few months later, sometime that April, my mom received a phone call from the University Medical Center in Arizona. The Friends of the UMC Trauma Center were planning a luncheon to launch their new support program. They called to ask if either my mom or I could come as a guest speaker to share our story as a trauma patient at the University Medical Center. No one in Tucson was certain where I was at that time. Last I had spoken with any of the doctors I had planned to travel some, to audition overseas, so they were uncertain if I was even in the country. I was still here. In that moment I was glad that I was so close to Arizona and not overseas somewhere. I was very excited about this opportunity. My mom had given them my telephone number, so I eagerly awaited the call.

Friends of the UMC Trauma Center was a project in the making for several years. The organization was formed by a small group to support the Trauma Division and allow it room to work and grow. Its members supported the level-one trauma unit. After the shooting involving Gabrielle Giffords and so many others, the popularity of the hospital and trauma center skyrocketed. They decided to launch the new Friends program sooner, rather than later, and worked hard to get everything in place.

I did not hesitate when they called to ask me to speak at the launch for the Friends group. "Yes!" I said. There was no question. I wanted to participate, especially considering the most recent shooting. Many people had lost their voice, but mine was loud and strong. I was elated to be asked to share my story, to get the opportunity to see everyone again. Unfortunately, I had to tell them I had no money to do that right now. "I have only been working part time," I said. "It would be impossible for me to do this right now."

Kari said, "Well, let's see what we can do, and we will call you back." She returned the call the next day and said, "Dr. Rhee said that he would make sure that everything was taken care of." They offered to pay for my flight, hotel, and transportation.

The very next week I was off to Tucson! This would be a special occasion, a completely different reason than I had ever imagined. I had been asked many times, "Aren't you scared to go back there?

Why would you ever want to go?" My reply always has been no. It always will be no. Yes, something tragic that completely changed my life happened there, but my good memories far outweigh the bad. I was so privileged to meet the people during some of those horrible circumstances and I never would take any of it back.

Susan picked me up at the airport and took me straight to campus, so I could say hi to all of the dancers and professors. There was a show that weekend, so I was able to stick around and watch some of the dress rehearsal. Then she dropped me off at my hotel. The luncheon was scheduled the next day.

I walked in for the event and was fortunate to meet all of the "behind the scenes" men and women that I had never had the opportunity to meet before – the founding members of the Friends, the doctors' wives and secretaries, and program coordinator. These were the people who worked behind the scenes to put everything into place. I saw Doctors Rhee, Wynne, Friese, and O'Keeffe, and met several others for the first time.

We were seated for lunch and I was surprised and honored to find myself next to Richard Carmona, who had served as Surgeon General of the United States from 2002 to 2006. I had the opportunity to speak with one of Gabrielle Giffords' staff members, who also had suffered a bullet wound. I remember telling her, "I never have met anyone else who has been shot before." It was humbling for me, and although it sounds strange, exciting at the same time. I was with another survivor.

To be in a room with all of my doctors as a healthy being, socializing as a friend and not as a patient, was an elevating moment for me. I was honored to not only share the narrative of how I had been shot, but the story of my experience with the doctors, nurses, and the entire hospital. I also spoke of how, in the very worst of circumstances, my family and I were able to find some peace of mind. (Part of me wanted to add that maybe I could give a seminar on how to escape death. After all, I did have nine lives. I decided to leave that part out.)

We honored these special people who take on the important job of saving lives every single day, a job they do with grace and poise. I am proud to be one of their patients. I was flattered to be able to help recognize each of them with the honor that was well deserved but far overdue. I believe the Lord was working through their hands to save my life, but without the hands of these physicians, I would not be alive. Nor would many other patients.

How do you tell someone, "Thank you for saving my life?" They had rescued me, not just once, but over and over again. I tried that day. I spoke from my heart and did the very best that I could do. After the luncheon I was on Cloud Nine. I honestly had hoped and prayed for an opportunity just like this to come along. I finally had the chance to recognize and thank them in a very public forum. Not only did they deserve it, but others needed to hear it.

When I returned back to Colorado, I found myself thinking that maybe this is another place in my life where I can be used. I can tell my story. I had found something that brought me joy, and like dancing, was comforting to me. Every time I was able to share my story, another small piece of me mended. It was not only healing, but rewarding for me. I started to see that maybe the plans I had formed as a nine-year-old girl weren't the only thing the Lord had intended for me.

Sharing the personal side of my story with the people who helped save my life, with my family, friends, and even acquaintances, gave me a new energy. For the first time in a long time, I felt a potent strength that gave me a push in the right direction. It wasn't an easy one, but it was the one that would lead me to rest in peace. That direction signaled to me, *You are going to be okay*.

About that time I wrote this in my journal:

When things seem all wrong look for growth opportunities. Be on the lookout for what the Lord is doing in my life and stop trying to carry out my intentions while the Lord is leading me in another direction.

I thought maybe I had found that new life path.

Soon after I returned from Tucson I was able to perform in Cañon City. Mr. A had invited me to come back and be a part of a big show. This was the stage where I had performed countless times throughout my life. It was the same stage where my big benefit concert had taken place. For the first time in many years I was able to step onto that stage as a performer, as a dancer. This show was in my hometown, in the community that had supported my family and me over the past few years. It was nothing short of exhilarating to be performing for them once again.

There was no way I could ever adequately say thank you for what my community had done for me, but this was an opportunity to lift them up. Many people had said to me, "I can't wait to see you dance again." I knew that was the only payment any of them ever hoped for. They certainly did not expect to receive anything in return for their generosity and kindness, but now I had the chance to pay them back with dance. Just dance! I felt the joy I always had when I stepped onto the stage. That was an incredibly special night, a chance to share the love and support from my community.

My heart began to change. I had idolized dance my entire life, but once I returned from Tucson, I began to realize dancing wasn't going to fix all my problems, as much as I wanted it to. My heart for dance never changed – it still lifts my spirits and makes me happy. But like others who have addictions or idols, I had latched onto something in the hope it would solve all my issues. I began to acknowledge the only thing that truly could bring the joy back into my life was peace, and that would only come through acceptance. I started to think, *Okay, I really need to pay attention to other things going on around me, and make a change.*

My family, friends and I always joke that I "dated" dance when I was growing up. I did. That was the only thing that interested me the most. I was in love with dance, and spent all of my time with it. Nothing was going to come between me and my dancing. Growing up, I thought dancing was the only thing that could bring me happiness. I slowly recognized that dancing always had been only a small part of my life. It took more than twenty-three years for me to come to this realization, and it took the thing I loved the most almost completely out of my grasp to understand dancing does not define me. Yes, it is a part of what I do and always will be. But I finally discovered that who I am is of much greater importance than anything I ever will do.

That comprehension startled me. I had believed the exact opposite my entire life, thinking if dance is taken away from me I don't know who I would become or what I would do. Dance was all I ever wanted to do. I thought without dance, I would be lost.

The visit to Tucson and the opportunity to dance for my community gave me the dawning knowledge that finally and truthfully, I was going to be okay. But "okay" is a common word we use all the time. Okay? No, I never was going to live the same, dance the same, or feel the same, but I knew that and recognized it. I was at peace with that. I thought I could someday accept where I was at, because it was where God wanted me to be, but I still hadn't reached that point in my life. I needed to follow where I was lead, not always do what I wanted to do. Maybe that no longer meant dancing all the time like I had my entire life, but I knew God had given me this gift of dance. He had kept me around for a reason. There was a reason I still could dance. He clearly has not taken that away for a reason. Maybe He knew I couldn't handle dancing as much as I used to, but I was going to listen and follow through with the other parts of my life I was being called to, even though it was difficult. I loosened the grip on something I had been in love with my entire life. I understood the dancing would come in His perfect timing.

For the first time, I felt new opportunities were knocking. I was willing to open up to these opportunities to see what they were. Before the shooting I never would have given anything but dance a second glance, but now I was opening up to new possibilities.

When we do God's will, I wrote in my journal, *we will find it easier to be joyful and thankful.*

My days were becoming more joyous.

Unfortunately, throughout 2011 I had been having a lot of issues with my ribs. When I was shot most of the ribs on the right side of my body were shattered. Originally my doctors planned to secure those ribs with mesh to help with the healing, but with all the other medical problems I had, my ribs were the last thing they worried about. I had a few ribs that continuously gave me problems. There wasn't much to hold them up any more, so they constantly poked me and were in the way when I danced and worked out. They popped over other things inside my body. Simply put, they were painful and kept me from moving my body as freely as I would have liked.

I went to see a thoracic surgeon in Colorado. He quickly decided he could do a rib resection if I wanted. What? Another surgery! I still had not made it a full year since the shooting without a surgery of some sort. But again, I didn't want to be years down the road and then need this done, so I said yes, thinking, *Let's just get this all out of the way now.*

Don't submit to circumstances, I had written in my journal, but to the Lord who controls circumstances.

That philosophy now was being put to the test.

I had never been so scared going into surgery. I thought this doctor didn't know me or my body the way the others did. What if something happened? My family did their best to keep me calm. The surgery was very successful, and I was very pleased with my decision. I had been told I would have a four-inch incision, but it ended up being about ten inches long and featured another twenty-eight staples. By then I didn't care how long my scars were or where they were for that matter, as long as the job was done and I was safe. It was also nice to look twice as skinny on the right side of my body. After several ribs were taken out it took off an inch or two. I can't complain about that!

I knew this was going to be a hard recovery, but I had a fresh spike of enthusiasm and felt driven to come out of it as swiftly as I could. I was ready. I was mentally strong and ready to get back on my feet. And, I did.

Chapter Twelve

I remember my affliction and my wandering, the bitterness and the gall. I well remember them, and my soul is downcast within me. Yet this I call to mind and therefore I have hope. Because of the Lord's great love we are not consumed.
– Lamentations 3:19-

I HAD ENDURED TEN SURGERIES AND RECEIVED 24 units of blood and 13 of plasma. I had battle wounds that covered most of my abdomen. I had been through countless hours of physical therapy. I'd lost track of the number of doctor visits, appointments, procedures, X-rays, MRIs, blood draws, staples, stitches, CAT scans, hospital beds, psychologists, and psychiatrists. I'd had countless ups and downs, meltdowns, flashbacks, and nightmares. I had mourned and grieved. I had hated, been easily angered, and fallen out of trusting anyone. But by the grace of God, and with the help of others, I had managed to pick myself back up.

The three-year mark of the shooting was approaching. While I still remembered the events vividly those moments now didn't affect me as much as they once had. Slowly, the trauma was starting to loosen its grip on me. While the events and aftereffects of the past three years had changed my life and shaped the person I have become, the bad memories started to fade as I realized they did not have to define me. They no longer identified my life as they had almost three years ago.

No, my life was not what I had expected. But then again, whose is? All along my plan had been to graduate from the UofA and then immediately head off to dance professionally in another state or out of the country. There would be no stopping me! I would stay on my feet and continue to dance until I physically dropped. I would go wherever it took me. Or so I had thought.

My life had changed quickly. I no longer lived like most girls my age; my body felt at least three times that age. My purse contents were even distinctive. Like most women my age, I carried a little wallet, lip gloss, maybe a little makeup. But then I also carried pepper spray, a Taser (yes, indeed, I do have a Taser), and on most occasions you could catch me with digestive enzymes, Gas-X, and some type of over the counter pain pills. If I run out of pills, I can always count on a grandma to have some of those around!

I had to plan out everything I ate so I wouldn't get sick. On many occasions I found myself telling my friends, "I'm so sorry, I can't do anything tonight. I need my sleep." I had a new way of living, a different way of thinking. I had to adjust to that. In the beginning I pushed it away, because I didn't want to live like that. But wisdom and understanding finally began to find their way into my life along with all the other changes. This was now who I was, where I was. I wasn't going to compromise that – I wanted to be the person I had been created to be.

Even with our limitations in life, we can accept its challenges. We can dare ourselves to do better, to be better, to be the best we were meant to be. But we will fail if we constantly fight with the choices we make in our lives, the geographical locations and places we find ourselves. I fought too hard for too long. But now, after three long years, I realized I could no longer fight. I did not need to. I was right where I needed to be.

One day I sat with my daily devotional and read Proverbs 19:21. *Many are the plans in a man's heart, but it is the Lord's purpose that prevails.* I realized then nothing had turned out like I thought it would. This was not where I thought I would be at this stage of my life. But I knew if my goals fit into God's plan, he would help me reach those goals. If not, He would gradually change the desires of my heart. I was starting to learn the difference between what I wanted and what I needed. Sometimes these moments of understanding have to smack you right in the face. This verse provided that moment for me. Oddly enough, it was just a day or two before the third anniversary of the shooting.

The morning of October 12 dawned a crisp, sunny, fall day. I went out into the bright Colorado sunshine for a walk, and the moment the warm rays hit my face, release flooded through my entire body. My face warmed as the sun seemed to send a special surge of heat through me. I smiled. I felt everything had been reopened to me, and everything in life was new again. I knew in that very moment that I was going to be all right. I was capable of pulling the pieces together. I was on my feet and moving forward. The light was with me, and I was perfectly fine with where I was. This was where the Lord had put me, where I was supposed to be. And with that, I achieved the moment of pure acceptance I needed. It had taken me three full years, but I finally accepted my life and everything it held.

I started to feel complete again. The moment I was shot my life had disintegrated. I had felt lost for a very long time. I slowly had been pulling it all back together. I now was getting to the final pieces, the ones that matter the most. Everyone who struggles with loss, tragedy, or change needs time to be rescued from the muck. It takes time to learn the value your life and your identity, which is not determined by your work, biography, agent, or any award. Being a child of God, I don't have to be defined by anything but that. Nothing big or small, no person or circumstance can hold me back.

This was God's plan for my life. He knew what He was doing. Everything had been in God's perfect timing. I looked back on my life with renewed vision and saw everything, from the time I was a little girl to this very moment, unfold in His perfect timing. Everything had been set up according to His plan, and everyone who had been woven into my life had been in the right place at the right time.

First and foremost, my God had placed me in a family of faith, great faith. At least one of us at all times was looking up toward Him, and because of that, we were able to work through this difficult time in our lives and come out intact. I was able to stay strong and draw strength from my incredibly loving family. My poised parents, who continuously hurt and ached, were able to lean on one another. They were sustained by many others. I had loving brothers and sisters who became even closer to me. My extended family came nearer to my side. Together, they always were there for me and built me up. My strong backbone came from my family, and we stayed connected because we had faith.

I had a family member sleep by my side every single night I was hospitalized. Much of my stay was spent on the cancer patient floor, where I noticed the other patients while I took my short walks. They were of all different ages. Many of them were alone. Most of them probably stayed there longer than I did. I remember thinking, *There is no possible way I could do this alone.* I had the luxury of family by my side, but I knew others patients didn't have the same comfort. I always had believed I was a very independent person and thought I was old enough to handle most things on my own. I learned age doesn't matter. The human being wasn't built to handle something like this alone. Even when we try, we fail.

It would have been impossible to recover from this without my family, faith, and without my belief there is a God who is not only in control, but who had planned everything out to make my life even better than I could ever have imagined.

I had spent a lifetime in dance, training since I was six years old. That intensive training came to my aid when I was shot. Yes, I know how harsh that sounds. I don't think that is the only reason I am a dancer, but I know my training had significant impact on my survival. I had spent years learning how to stay focused under pressure, how to be persistent, and how to breathe and work through physically demanding situations. My body was strong from years and years of countless hours spent building up muscle and stamina. If I hadn't been a dancer, my reaction would have been different. My recovery would have been different. My entire outcome would have been 100 percent different.

The University of Arizona was the only school I had applied to. I had set my path to that exact spot when I was just nine years old. I was meant to be there. The friends I made at the UofA, despite all that took place, gave me a reason to go back there and finish what

I had started.

One of the hardest moments to consider and embrace was the exact moment I was shot. Of all the people in Tucson, of all the people out that night, I happened to be the one person in the direct path of that bullet the moment the trigger was pulled, the moment the first bullet was fired. The chances that I, someone who has no association with gangs whatsoever, would be in a drive-by shooting were extremely low. Yet I was in front of that bullet. I now joke that I took one for the team that day. While most of us, including me, looked at the situation and believed "wrong place at the wrong time," I can't help but change my way of thinking now. My new perception and outlook on life allow me to believe, *Maybe I was in the right place at the right time.* Perhaps my injury allowed someone else to survive. It certainly allowed me to live and grow in ways I never had imagined.

The bullet hit my liver, the only organ in the body that regenerates itself, before it exploded out my side. More than a year after the shooting one of my doctors told my mom something he never would have said while I was still so ill. "The initial gunshot wound to the liver gave her less than a one percent chance of survival," he said. That did not include everything else that happened after that night. According to statistics I should not be alive today. Clearly, I am that one percent.

Some of the most incredible moments of divine intervention took place the instant I was shot. There is no question that being shot in the liver is deadly, but sometimes whether a shooting is lethal depends not only upon the location of the wound but the speed of medical attention. I was in the car with two strangers who were able to react in a way that was nearly impossible. Jake, who happened to be the driver, knew exactly where to go. And Danielle, who happened to be sitting close to me, knew to apply lifesaving pressure to my wound. Jake got me to the trauma center in record time, but without Danielle's hand upon me, I would have surely died.

And then there were all those people who came in contact with me in the hospital. Every single one of them, from the moment I was thrown on the table, was important to my survival. Chaplain Dave called my parents that night while he stood by my side.

He continued to stay there night after night. From day one, my nurses comforted my family and me every hour of every day. There was no doubt that every nurse and every physician was perfectly placed during my stay at UMC. All the events that happened after my initial gunshot wound were mind-boggling but they happened in the perfect order to safe my life.

I did have many complications after the initial gunshot; however all of those complications were sequenced in a way to keep me alive. After my first surgery, when they cut me from right underneath my sternum to my pubic bone, they closed my incision. A week later I suffered a massive infection and they had to go in again, leaving my incision open to close on its own. Soon after, my diaphragm ruptured. During that surgery, they operated through my exit wound and made it larger than it originally was. It also was left open to close on its own. When I had the ruptured aneurism they were able to plug it and stop the bleeding, only because they previously had created a bigger hole in the side of my body. Not only that, but if I had been completely sewn up, I would have suffered internal bleeding that would have killed me within seconds.

God's timing is perfect. Every doctor had been at the right place at the right time. The way it worked out was not coincidence. While at that time I would never have believed it, I am saying it now: Every setback was perfection in timing and what I, as a small human being, could handle. After my last big crash at the hospital, I knew I could fight no longer. I knew the next major emergency would be it. I had borne all I could, and rested in the knowledge that I was ready to let go and slide away if another big battle came my way. But the Lord knew my strength and my weakness, and He gave me just what I could handle.

I was able to go back to school and graduate on time and with my class. I now hold a Bachelor's of Fine Arts in Dance from the school of my dreams. This is where I was meant to be. While I don't always like God's timing, and I sometimes think mine would be better, there had been perfect timing and a reason for all of the madness. There is a reason I am still alive.

My understanding of all these elements emerged in a rush of acceptance. Not only had I finally accepted where I was, I was now learning to appreciate His perfect timing. In addition, I continued to see what I believe is a powerful message in this story, and that is the power of prayer.

Prayer has been so prevalent throughout this journey. Many from my community have shared some of their stories with me and told me of their countless hours spent in prayer, night after night. One good family friend, Peggy Gair, told me this: "I prayed so many arrow prayers up during the day while you were in the hospital, I believe the clouds were perforated. I was on my knees many times begging for your life. I remember praying that if your sister needed to get home from the Philippines to see you 'one last time,' that Christ would make that happen." Many others told me I had been added to prayer lists that stretched around the world. Peggy was one of those who said her own mom and her mother's church had added me to their prayer list as well. This is how Peggy explained this effect. "I have always had this vision I call the 'cheerleader' effect of prayer. Jesus listens to every prayer, but when you get a whole stadium praying for one person, it has to be an awesome sound to His ears!"

We are told to be joyful in hope, patient in affliction, and faithful in prayer. And so the cheerleader effect had taken place. Prayer increases our faith, and it provides a place for us to unload and unwind. Perhaps most important of all, the prayer of a righteous man is powerful and effective.

James 5:15 says, *And the prayer 'offered in faith' will make the sick person well, and the Lord will raise him up.* This prayer offered in faith most certainly was not from me. Not during my stay in the hospital or even afterward. It came from my family, friends, community, and strangers. Strong faith had helped me see through the darkness. We still have to remember it is not a strong faith that does the healing, but God. Our prayers are simply a part of His healing. Sometimes He just might wait for those prayers before He intervenes. However, in my case, I think he stepped in right away, just maybe not in a way that was obvious to the casual observer.

God continuously speaks to us. It may not always be through an audible whisper. Prayers may not be answered right away, but He always will work things out in His timing and according to His plan. Everyone had prayed for healing, and it came. It didn't come right away, but it did come.

My family always had someone to lean on. My church family was a big part of that. Their faithful and fervent prayers had brought healing. Many battled with their own issues, but continued to keep us in the forefront of their prayers. We all should be able to lean on one another for support and prayer during times like this. So many people constantly asked what they could do for our family, when they already were doing it. There is no better way to help than to ask the One who is all powerful for His hand to heal and to help.

God hears prayer; He heard mine. I learned that holding onto my burdens simply weighed me down. I had done that for too long. Only when I was able to cast all my cares upon him was I sustained and I found rest for my soul.

Why am I suffering? I don't understand this. I don't want to be in this position. Please take this pain and sorrow from me. This was my plea at the beginning, but then I remembered that His grace is enough, and I am blessed beyond anything I could ever ask for.

God didn't necessarily take away all my physical affliction, but His power was displayed through my frail human body. His power was made perfect in my weakness.

I've enjoyed long talks with my grandma about how this entire ordeal served to make our faith more abundant. Often people look at my situation and say, "How could you possibly believe in a God who would let you get shot?" But I just say, "How could I not believe in a God who has saved me, lifted me up, and held me throughout this ordeal? How could I not believe in a God who gave me a better life because of this?"

Blessings now overflowed for my family and me. Our family's financial needs being met was nothing short of a miracle. Most importantly, my life today, a life that I never would have planned for myself but is better because of the tragedy, is another miracle. All these blessings had come from the most evil, bloodcurdling moments in my life.

I finally was coming to a place of spiritual healing. It never was my intent to separate the physical, mental, emotional, and spiritual, but I believe they had been separated the moment I took the bullet. My body fell apart in every aspect. Many people understand we can't split the physical from the spiritual. It took me a long time to recognize that and come to terms with it. It took years to make the connection between the two again, and to remember that Christ is the Lord over both body and spirit. There is absolutely nothing that can separate us from Him. I acknowledged that I had fallen and stumbled. I was bruised and hurt, but never broken. I was not built to break.

All of my relationships had changed. Every single one of them. My relationships with my parents, my family, and my friends could have dissipated, but they all stuck with me. I know there were many times when I was a whole lot to handle. I am still a lot to handle! In the beginning I had no idea how to cope or deal with these emotions, so they came out in anger, in tears, and in bitterness. But we worked through them together. Thankfully, I had loved ones who stood by me, and now we enjoy better relationships because of it.

My relationship with myself even changed. It had to. You have to have a relationship with yourself. You can never get away from yourself. You take that with you everywhere you go. That is why valuing yourself and accepting where you are and who you are – limitations and all – is so important.

I have become aware of how powerless I was before I leaned on the Lord and put all my trust in Him. I had awakened to a greater presence. It was not in vain but for the sake of something greater. I learned not to lean on my own understanding, but to lean on someone who always has the truth.

I asked close friends and family to write of their experiences during the shooting. My eyes were opened wide! I thought it would be a nice way for people to express what they had felt, a sort of healing process for all involved. I knew I was not the only one who had lived in a dark place during that time. I was not the only one who had suffered. I was incredibly touched and overwhelmed by the love and compassion they all expressed.

There had been things that upset me for a long time. Certain people hadn't visited me as often as others. No one cried when I did. But after reading what everyone wrote, I realized it had nothing to do with loving me less or downplaying the situation. I learned most people prayed faithfully for me every night. When they woke up they looked at the day and tackled anything in their way as if they were doing it for me. Most knew I would not want their pity, so what did they do? They all knew there was very little they could do to help me, but if there was one thing they could do, it was dance! So they danced.

I have many friends who still apologize to me because they were unable to be there at that time, but I now know they were thinking of me. They were the ones who were on their knees begging for my life every single night. Those friends had done everything they could, and more!

I understand we are all created differently. Some people aren't bothered a bit to come into the hospital, while others can't make it past the front doors without fainting. That's what makes us unique and human. That is why we have dancers, and then we have doctors. People were afraid of how they might react to seeing me. They were scared they might say the wrong thing. This wasn't like visiting an elderly sick relative. I was a friend who was young and still had her whole life ahead of her. It was a rude awakening for every person who stepped in to see me.

God knew I couldn't do any of this on my own. That's why He put everyone in my path for a specific reason and a specific purpose. Like everyone else, I have my moments of pride. But if those who helped me would not have been there, if I had not allowed them to help me, if God would not have put them in my path, I never would have returned to school. I might have left the hospital in a body bag. Yet God gave me the strength to ask for help. He gave me the strength to never give up, even when I wanted to.

Humility does not come naturally to most of us, especially in this day and age. Humility means proper respect for God and what He has put in our paths. Even when I hate those obstacles at times. It is not intended to place self criticism upon ourselves, but it does mean that the wall of pride must come down. We must allow ourselves the help that we need and recognize with humility that we cannot do anything on our own. I have learned the lower I bow down, the higher I will be lifted up!

I will be the first to say that it is, indeed, tough to ask for help, even when we need it the most. But many times, we can't progress and grow in the ways we should, because we allow our pride to stand in the way. That is when we need a helping hand to reach out. Take my advice. Take that hand.

At times I still hear, *What happened to you is not fair, Alicia.* I agree wholeheartedly. No, it wasn't fair, but life isn't fair. And that's okay. If I cling to the belief that life should be fair, but my circumstances are unfair, it will destroy me. I have to let grace conquer whatever has been unfair to me. I choose to let it go. I don't have to talk down what happened. I don't pretend it didn't happen or I wasn't hurt by it, but I will never again let it control me.

For the first time in many years I was content. I had accepted where I was. I was ready to share the most important part of my journey, and that was the spiritual side. I was learning to rejoice in what was happening in my life now, even if it was all beyond my understanding. I might never truly comprehend what had happened.

The timing was right, and I finally was truly ready to once again step back into dance class. I was ready to go somewhere no one knew me or what had happened to me. I didn't feel the need to step into class and discuss my wounds or my limitations. I wanted to be critiqued for what I could do as a dancer, not as a handicapped dancer. I started dance class where no one knew anything about me, except that I was a fellow dancer.

The trauma had changed me. Now, my inner attitude did not have to reflect my outward circumstances. It did not have to control me, and I would not allow it to. I had learned to be grateful for where I was and what I had. I had learned not to compare situations, because there is a reason we all live different lives. We are built to handle things uniquely. God creates us to handle what we can, to be pushed so far, but never to our breaking point. We are allowed to lean on and count on one another, to pass our blessings on to each other.

This isn't to say others aren't born into harsh circumstances. I know that I am privileged. I am a well-educated, white woman living in America. Life doesn't get much easier than that, yet I have struggled. Finally, instead of dwelling on my problems, I try to be thankful for the life that I have and pass the blessings on to others. "Peace is not the absence of pain. Peace is not the absence of pressure. Peace is confidence that God knows what he is doing. It's confidence in God's competence." (Richard D. Emmons)

It now was hard to believe I had ever been so low. It also was difficult to believe where I was now. I didn't need to compare my life to others. Sure, I still had moments of disappointment, but my parents encouraged me, "Alicia, look how far you have come," they said. "There is no other place for you to go but up!" I knew that God would show me my way. He always had.

My broken heart was transformed. I finally had reached a point that I didn't need to talk about the shooting every day. Yes, someone had pulled the trigger and God had allowed it to happen. But my wounds didn't have the final say. I trust God, who is much wiser than I am, who can heal me. I allow His grace to do what I cannot. Only He has the ability to overcome evil.

Chapter Thirteen

When I said my foot is slipping, your unfailing love, oh lord, supported me. When anxiety was great within me, your consolation brought me joy. – Psalm 94:18-19

PEACE FILLED ME NOW, AN ATTAINMENT THAT once had seemed far out of my reach. Many of my daily activities were different than what they had been before the shooting, but my entire life no longer revolved around that moment. The daily lives of my family, friends and me no longer centered on my wounds.

One day I sat down with my parents and told them I felt ready to share my story in a different capacity. I had shared it many times before and even in front of large crowds. But this time I wanted to share it with my church family, the people who had known me since I was born. The people who had prayed unceasingly. The people who loved and lifted my family up in the worst moments of our lives. Most hadn't seen the entire picture of my journey. They had seen only bits and pieces. I wanted to share my experiences with them and tell them what they had meant to us. Most of all, I wanted to reveal the work Christ was doing in my life. I felt it was important that this message come from me, not from my sibling or cousin or through the grapevine.

It was time to step out of my comfort zone. While my faith always had been a part of my story, I had not yet been able to share it in front of my church. I was ready to stand in front of all the believers who had prayed me back to health. I was ready to testify openly and honestly about God's eternal grace and endless miracles.

Strangely enough, a few weeks before the shooting, Moira and I were sitting in my room talking about our lives. I shared with her that I didn't feel I had a very inspiring testimony because my life had been uneventful and easy. Now here I was with this testimony. Truth is, everybody's testimony is significant and can inspire others.

I went to Pastor Jim and shared what was on my heart. He was happy to let me speak and believed most of the congregation also would be grateful to hear my story, from me. Our church was enjoying a series on "Blessings," which was a natural fit for my narrative. Sunday, October 30, 2011, the topic was "Blessings that Come through Suffering." It was a perfect match.

My message was prepared. My heart was ready, but this was one of the hardest things I ever had done. I was no stranger to performing. Put me in front of a thousand people to dance, and all my anxiety turns into energy. This was not technically performing, but it was standing on a stage in front of a crowd. It had been easy in Tucson to tell my story to a crowd of mostly unfamiliar faces. I looked them in the eye and while my emotions surfaced I managed to keep most of them from rolling down my face. I had spent years holding in my emotions, not letting people see how I felt or understand the weight I tried to carry. Now I stood before the people who cared about me the very most, prepared to share my innermost thoughts and struggles.

Pastor Jim introduced me as I sat with my family in the

congregation, my heart pounding. It beat even faster when he called me to the stage. I looked out at so many familiar faces and tried to figure out how I could get through this intact. I couldn't figure out where to focus as I talked.

Tears welled in my eyes before I even began to speak. I saw the tears and felt the heavy hearts of so many in the congregation. I realized I wasn't the only one in the room who had suffered, or was suffering from tragedy, heartache, or illness.

My mom's brother had been killed in a trucking accident before I was born. My Grandma Ely told me that a parent never gets over losing a son or daughter. "No parent should have to bury their child," she had said. It doesn't matter if your child is a one year old or 50 years old, it hurts you just the same. My parents are so grateful they did not have to face that. Even today, my mom or dad will say to me, "We are so blessed that you are still here. We are so grateful and thankful that the Lord allowed us to keep you." This was the message, the greatest testimony I could give. I am still here! I was the one percent who survived. I had a voice, and I was ready to use it.

This was the first time I had been so open and honest. Although my body literally shook, I continued to keep a steady voice as I went through my testimony.

I spoke of how I had been raised in a God-fearing, Christian home. My parents always were present and involved in my life, supporting and encouraging me in everything I did. They guided me steadily through childhood and my teenage years. Coming from this home that was so rich in love and faith, I had no complaints, or at least not any more than the usual teenager!

I told the congregation I had dreamed of being a professional dancer since I was a little girl. The Lord seemed to be helping me reach those dreams, because He allowed me to attend the only university I had applied to. I was living and loving life. But one night, it all changed. I believed everything had been taken from me and I never would get it back. I didn't believe I could pull myself back together. I thought I was damaged goods. In that split second, I shattered into a million little pieces physically, mentally, emotionally, and spiritually. I spent the next few years of my life picking up those pieces slowly and with a grave and heavy heart.

I spoke of the night I had the aneurism and told them that was the moment I finally surrendered to the Lord. I realized I wasn't the one in control. That was night I had heard God, the night His presence was so tangible to me. He was so close, as if I could have reached out my hands and touched his face. That night I literally knocked on heaven's door. It was the night that changed everything. I surrendered and finally started to rest in the comfort of His arms. Had I never surrendered I would not be standing in front of them sharing my story.

Perhaps as much as anyone, I understand that it's easier to give up than to hold on during times of great despair, but giving up means giving up on God and giving in to despair. Life isn't fair or easy. I'm so glad that I fought for life. Without giving in to the Lord I never would have survived.

I spoke of not just the physical struggle, when I was fighting for each breath, but of the spiritual aspect as well. I talked of the times I was ashamed of myself and fearful of those around me. I had lost touch with who I was.

The great orator and statesman Winston Churchill once said, "Never give in. Never, never, never, never, in nothing great or small, large or petty, never give in except to convictions of honor and good sense. Never yield to force; never yield to the apparently overwhelming might of the enemy." I had not given in. I had endured. Pressing on is all part of life. There are times when we have to choose whether we want the pain of pressing on or the pain of giving up.

Life became a roller coaster after the shooting. I was moving blindly around every corner, being thrashed around, and thrown up and down. My life seemed out of control, and continued to wind and twist in ways I never saw coming. My life had changed. I didn't like that at first.

The day my mom unknowingly helped me realize I was living in self pity, was the day I began to see things differently. She had told me exactly what I needed to hear. I now know there is a time to grieve. But I also had to be aware and guard myself against prolonged self pity and bitterness. That had dug me a well of solitary confinement, a hole that was so deep I couldn't climb out.

I had not, and never will, set aside the moments in life that have changed who I am. We all experience those times in life – the moment that takes away a loved one, or destroys the desire of your heart. We don't have to set those aside and ignore them, but those moments sometimes require a change in attitude and a change in heart. As an adult, I had to recognize that I needed my sovereign God. Like most people, I thought I could handle anything and everything on my own. I couldn't. As a child I had someone I trusted to look after me and take care of me. As I grew up, life came at me, and it came at me hard. I needed to learn to trust again. I needed to place that trust solely in God.

Coming to the Lord means believing in and committing to His guidance. I had to learn to live above my circumstances, to see life from God's point of view. He gave me the strength to face the endless problems that streamed into my life, with good cheer. Gaining His perspective, which is a much wiser and understanding viewpoint, helped me to distinguish between what was important in life and what was not. Life slowly started to be less overwhelming. I stopped falling into my circumstances and tried my best to live above them. When I started to do this, the shattered pieces of my life started to fall back into place.

We all encounter problems that seem to have no immediate solution. Even if they seem petty to others, they are our personal trials and are significant to us. These problems can make us bitter or better. We have a choice! We can feel sorry for ourselves or let such problems be a stepping stone for us. Let it enable us to rise up and live above them. The view from above gives the perspective to see that the obstacle is only a temporary problem.

This world is a needy place, one that does not offer solutions in this life. Instead, turn to God, who remains perfect and unchanging, unlike humans. I know this is so easy to say. I found it to be true in other situations but just didn't see how it could be true in mine. I had a need to understand why things happened the way they did. I finally realized that need was distracting me, and I had to let it go. Most of the time, the consuming desire to understand will fail you.

Why me? I wanted to know that. That question may never be answered, at least not in this lifetime. Why does God heal some believers and not others? Why did my parents get to keep their child when others lose theirs? We, as humans, have no answers. I do know that God has chosen me according to His divine purpose. I believe the Lord allowed this to happen to me. However, I do not think He orchestrated it. He gives us free will. We were created to think for ourselves. I believe my shooter had the choice to pull the trigger.

Just because He works good out of extraordinarily bad situations, doesn't mean that He designs them. He doesn't have to use these moments for His glory, but He does. God's grace does not depend on suffering to exist, but where there is suffering, there also is grace. In times we don't understand, but desperately seek enlightenment, we must ask ourselves: Will we allow God to be God without His explaining it to us?

Yes, it is hard for me to grasp and impossible to understand the hurt I have suffered. But I believe this is His plan for me. I must allow Him to shape and mold me into who I was meant to be, who He wants me to be. I discovered that sometimes molding starts with suffering.

Our afflictions come for different reasons. Some misery simply is the result of our own foolishness, yet some is because we live in a fallen world. Christ never sinned, and yet He still suffered. In this life, we will have trials and tribulations, we will be persecuted, and we will be victimized. All who follow Christ must be prepared for this.

Trusting in God does not mean we will escape loss and suffering. We can't avoid strife in this world, it is inevitable. But we must remember we are never alone. Although there are times we may feel deserted, times we believe we are stepping forward by ourselves, the Lord never leaves our side. We are never abandoned.

We all know "life happens," yet we still try to escape or avoid our difficulties and afflictions, especially while in the midst of them. Our goal should not be to avoid, but to face suffering with patience, confidence, and calmness. We should ask for help to get through such times victoriously, to face our trials with courage. We must seek opportunities to grow. While fear is a natural part of life, it does not have to take over. Gods gives us the power to face our fears with bravery.

Suffering affords us the opportunity to endure and be made

mature and complete. In fact, many spiritual blessings are packaged as trials. We must not retreat from our afflictions, because they often are some of the most precious gifts we ever will receive. Sometimes He tells us to wait. When we do, He will make it worth every moment. Sometimes God wants us to take the path less traveled for His purpose. We don't grow during the steady and easy times. We grow when life seems almost unbearable. When we allow the Lord to work in us, we emerge as better people.

There are moments in life when we must be confident to stand on our own. We will be misunderstood, feel lonely, or be set apart. Standing on our own, hand-in-hand with the Lord, will allow us to reach just a little higher. Life is difficult, and it drains us at times, but there is a purpose to this. There is a purpose in suffering. Suffering is never good in and of itself, but when it is in the hands of God, it produces more than just the pain of simply trying to make it through each day.

I now understand that suffering can produce joy, because He has chosen someone like me, someone who is weak, to accomplish His purposes. For when I am weak, then I am strong. My weakness is designed to permit me to see the Lord's power when he allows difficulties to come into my life. Some see God as a crutch, something to temporarily lean on. But we are far too weak to face our trials on our own, to face life alone. He does not want us to remain weak, but to be strengthened during this time. Depending on the Lord is not weakness, it is acknowledging His strength. Our world might see dependence as immaturity, but in God's kingdom, dependence is a sign of notable maturity.

God will fully equip us to handle whatever comes our way. He will bring us through our trials and enable us to accept life as it is. We can accept where we are without worrying about our limitations, our disappointments, our lack of perfection, our frailties or failures. When we focus on what we do not have in life, we spend our time and energy on situations that make us unhappy and cloud our minds. When we don't focus on our imperfections we can learn to accept life as it is.

It may take weeks, months, or even years to come to a place of acceptance. It took me years to accept. I had to accept that my way of thinking, even my way of living had changed. Life had changed.

Now I can look at my scars and say, "These are my battle wounds. They are a gift, and I am proud of them."

This is no easy task, but we were not promised an easy road. At times it takes sheer will to overcome adversity. We have to be led by hope. When we hope in the Lord, we have renewed strength.

Without acceptance, there is no peace. No peace of mind, no rest. Peace is a gift, independent of circumstances. We can find peace in turmoil. The peace we receive from the Lord will transcend our understanding. This is the peace that will guard your heart. We don't have to follow the same route every single day, the route that we blindly maintain. Instead, follow the Lord's way. When we can learn to trust that His way is perfect, even in the midst of our messy lives, His light and presence will shine on us.

It may seem impossible to get through our problems at all, so how do we get through them with grace? Even with joy? The best way is to befriend a problem. We can accomplish that by being thankful for everything. It may not be easy, but we must embrace what it is and where we are. Most importantly, we must give it over to God. He will not fail us in whatever we commit to Him.

There may be conditions in our lives that require us to remain still. Many suffer from being bedridden, some of the Lord's most cherished children are shut away in prison cells. We shouldn't wish these moments away, because they can be the times to search for His will. Resistance and resentment only weakens us. When we have a thankful and grateful attitude we can see our time of stillness as an opportunity to grow. Even if we are outwardly wasting away, inwardly we can be renewed and transformed day by day.

We don't have to pretend that we are happy while in times of trouble. I can truthfully say that most of my hospital stay was without a smile on my face. But we must have a positive outlook. When we look at life this way we can begin to see the transformation these trials can produce. Thanking the Lord and being grateful for what might seem to be an awful situation may be a bit uncomfortable at first. If we are persistent, the words we have prayed eventually will make a difference in our hearts. Our thoughts are powerful and easily overshadow our earthly problems.

I think we have all been in a place where we felt like Atlas, kneeling with the world on his shoulders. Oftentimes we miss what's in store for us because we are carrying the weight of the world. Remember, we don't have to!

I don't know anyone who truly likes to suffer. Human flesh is brittle and weak. But some of our greatest blessings come through our suffering when we allow God to do His will. He can and will bring good out of any circumstance if we allow Him to. He can heal the brokenhearted and bind up our wounds. He can give rest to the weary and give hope to the hopeless. He will meet us wherever we are. These troubles should only make us affirm in a loud and strong voice that our Creator is all-powerful, all-knowing, and all-present. While bad things are not good in and of themselves, God has a purpose for letting them into our lives.

Chinese pastor Li De Xian, who has been repeatedly imprisoned for preaching the Gospel of Jesus Christ, said, "Humanly speaking, we know that no one likes to suffer physically, but I know that if God leads me into it, He will give me the strength to survive it."

God will weave and thread our lives according to His plan.

There may be times when we cry out, pleading for the pain and sorrow to stop. When it doesn't end and He tells us no, then His grace is enough. Believe that His grace is sufficient. We will find strength at that time that we never knew we had, because He didn't fix it right away.

I remember one of my counselors telling me that God is good, but that doesn't mean He is safe. One day after this counseling session, shortly after I had arrived back home for the first time, my dad came to pick me up. I told him what Amanda and I had talked about that day. "God is good, but that doesn't mean He is safe," I said.

Dad replied, "I have really struggled with that. As your dad I have always wanted to protect you. And since you were a little girl I have always prayed for your protection. I always trusted that God would take care of you, and then this happened." Just that single sentence helped us both to realize that I can't protect myself, my dad can't protect me. There is truly only one who can. And He still had protected me, just maybe not in the way my dad or I would have thought in my best interests.

In all honesty, I can tell you that I never rejoiced in my suffering. At first I certainly did not see all of this as a gift for me, a gift that came in an unusual package. It was a gift I never would have asked for, but it was a gift that had forever changed me. It was the gift at another chance at life, a chance to share my story, to dance again, to love others – even my enemies – unconditionally. It is a gift that I will not refuse. While I have had some adjusting to do, I also have learned to embrace it.

Strong character is not the only thing the Lord builds within us. He also brings the ability to empathize with others, to have compassion. He gives us the capacity to relate to others, which is something every human – especially those who are suffering – looks for. Empathy comes from the actual experience, without it our ability to relate doesn't begin to compare.

I joyously speak for those who cannot speak for themselves. "Never even in these times, underestimate what you as a person can do. God will work through anyone who has submitted to him of any age, to accomplish His will on Earth. If any man or woman is willing to obey Him, it can change the destiny of millions." (The Voice of the Martyrs)

We must let no one or nothing determine our values and standards in life. It is easy to give in when we are in a vulnerable place. Instead, commit to be the person that God has created us to be. Whatever you do in life, do with all your heart. We must love one another, because hatred does nothing but harm us and keep us from being the best that we can be.

We all have times of complete despair, when we feel that no one understands. We have to remember there is someone who does. Jesus Christ knows exactly what it means to be human, to be in the flesh, to be tempted. I take great comfort in knowing there is someone who understands me and understands me completely. That was a huge part of the struggle for me. How could I let others in? How could I trust others? Love others? Forgive others? If I had no one to understand me, to help me see that the sun always rises, I could not have endured.

While some of us are liberated from pain in this life, others are not. Either way, we are set free. Either way, it is victory. The hurt that we all face will not last forever. Suffering produces perseverance, perseverance produces character, and character produces hope!

Death casts a shadow over all of us; we are helpless in its presence. We cannot overcome it no matter the size and strength of our courage. Death seems to have the final say. But there is one who can walk with us through that dark side and bring us to the other side.

This is our ultimate hope, that there is life after death. No matter what happens here, we have the assurance of eternal life. We will be in a place where all suffering will end and sorrow will flee away!

Everything we endure can be put to good use by allowing God to teach us to trust Him more fully. Our task is to faithfully pray, trust, and believe. And remember that nothing can separate us from His love. Even when we feel like we are in a million little pieces, He can mend us back together. He doesn't just walk with us, He goes before us. He upholds us. Although there were times when I felt alone and was barely hanging on, I know at the moment I was shot the Lord had His hands upon me. His perfect timing and amazing grace saved my life.

Before I was shot, everything in my life had gone according to my plan. I thought the Lord was giving me the desire of my heart by allowing me to dance. I always believed dancing was a gift from God. Now, it is a gift given to me once again. This time around, I will use it for His glory, something I didn't do well before the shooting.

Dancing does not define who I am. I know who I am. I still dance, but now I don't have to in order to be happy. My passion for it isn't any less than it was before I was shot. The joy I receive from dancing is also no less. But God has set plans for my life that involve much more than just dance. He has plans that will lead me to prosper in my life, plans that are much bigger and better than anything I could ever have imagined. He has plans to make me more, not less. I will be more, because I have suffered.

Chapter Fourteen

You gain strength, experience and confidence by every experience where you really stop to look fear in the face. You must do the thing you think you cannot. – Eleanor Roosevelt

I HAD MADE A BUCKET LIST FOR myself shortly after I had arrived back in Colorado in December of 2008. It was a list of some of the things I wanted to do in my lifetime. Some of the items were activities I had done when I was a little girl. Things I had taken for granted. Now I didn't know if I ever would be able to do those endeavors again. A lot on the list included fun activities I used to enjoy like horseback riding and skiing. Others were those things I always had wanted to do but never had the opportunity – graduating college, dancing professionally, skydiving, traveling around Europe, swimming with dolphins. I always had wanted to do that! There were many ideas on that list, both big and small.

My list also included one thing I never imagined I could conquer. Forgive my shooter. I had it written in my journal as though it was an event I could plan for and lead up to. It was a moment I wanted to happen, but truthfully, I never believed I would get there. I figured that writing it down was good enough for me.

Forgiveness was something everyone surrounding me had to grapple with. Kendra had left for Manila just a few weeks before to work in a children's home for three months. A few days before the shooting she had flown to Malaybalay, Mindanao, where she was able to connect to the Internet. She felt pulled to get online and check her e-mail. From seven thousand miles away, she read the horrifying truth from my oldest brother, Sean.

> Kendra, I'm not sure how best to write this, but you need to know. I'm going to head over to mom and dad's house in a few to try to reach you on Skype. First of all, she is currently stable, but Alicia was shot last night in Arizona. She and a few friends were driving and heard gunshots. Alicia was shot in the abdomen, and her friend was shot in the leg. Alicia is currently in surgery. Mom and dad are on their way to the airport right now. Alicia will be in surgery for a few more hours. Mom's last update by the nurse was that she is critical, but stable, and that ALL of her vitals are stable. They are in the process of repairing her stomach. She is probably going to make it! I know this isn't the way that you would want to find out, but you need to know so you can pray for her. If it's possible for you to try to stay awake for a few more hours, I'm going to try to contact you on Skype. I love you!!! And keep praying! I'll try to contact you again in about 20 minutes.

The handful of friends Kendra had there were people she had known for only a few weeks. Not knowing how to comfort her in a situation like that, she said she felt completely alone. But even in that time she knew she wasn't truly alone, that God was teaching her to rely solely on Him. He was the one who wasn't going to leave her side.

The World Racers, were another missionary group that had been in Malaybalay working with Kids International Ministries. The night after Kendra found out about the shooting she went out to dinner with them. After dinner they all gathered around her to pray. They prayed for me and for our family, but they also prayed for the shooter. They prayed for his heart and his life. I remember she told me that she was angry at first, thinking, *How can you pray for him? He almost killed my sister.*

Just like me, it was hard for Kendra to hear. Why would you pray for that person? Even so, the message did not fall on deaf ears. Kendra was reminded that we are all sinners and we all deserve the love of God. Unfortunately, I was not as swift to come to this same belief.

From the moment I was shot I had seen the gunman as a person who was not worthy of a simple prayer or forgiveness.

I had been wronged by someone, a person I didn't even know and probably never would. I had clung to that thought for several years now without realizing I was the only one being damaged by the grip that lack of forgiveness had on my life. As that pain continued to destroy and hinder my heart, it was not touching him. I thought justice for me would be for him to rot in prison for the rest of his life, to feel the pain I felt, for his loved ones to feel the hurt that my loved ones felt. But we are not to seek revenge against those who treat us unfairly, even when that goes against every fiber of our being.

While I finally had reached a place of acceptance and healing, there still was a piece of me that stewed in bitterness. Most of the pieces of my life had mended back together. I had enjoyed a great deal of spiritual healing that allowed me to regain a sense of self and self-worth, but this was a heavy burden upon my heart. It clung tightly to me. Rather, I clung tightly to it. I had acquired the ability to dismiss the shooting as an act of violence and think of it as an accident, which allowed the gunman to be distant and imaginary making it separated from the rest of my life. I didn't know if it was bitterness or if I just was not willing to let go. Like the other broken pieces, I knew it eventually would catch up to me.

Like I've said, sometimes things have to hit us smack in the face to make us understand. I received that wallop when I was reading. "Who are we to judge?" I read. "Who am I to judge, and to not forgive?" I realized that when I don't forgive others I am denying my common ground as a sinner in need of grace and forgiveness. Indeed, that was exactly what I was doing.

Again, I was stuck. Stuck from not letting go, stuck from thinking the shooter got away with this, stuck believing there was no justice. How could I deal with this? How could I put this behind me? I knew my experiences had shaped my life and would continue to do so. Somehow the Lord had given me spiritual, mental, emotional, and physical healing throughout this ordeal. But I still had no closure in this. The young man who had chosen to pull the trigger and changed my life forever had gotten away with it! I didn't have a face to put a name to. I did not see a solution or pathway to lead me to forgiveness.

I realized I continued to refer to the shooting as an accident. It was not an accident. True, he wasn't aiming at me, but he pointed the gun at someone and pulled the trigger with the intent to kill. When the case had been closed I was disillusioned, disheartened, and felt let down. Just because he wasn't successful in killing me didn't make it any less of a crime. In reality, it would have been a lot easier for me if I had just died.

I knew, if nothing else, he would be judged in the next lifetime. But I wanted to see justice for myself. Truthfully, I wanted to forgive but believed it was a conscious decision I would have to make. That meant a change in attitude. It meant action. I didn't want to say the words out loud if I didn't believe wholeheartedly that I had forgiven him. When I finally said that I forgive, I wanted it to mean something.

Forgiveness often seems to be the last thing we do, when it needs to be the first. I had suppressed clemency for so long it now created a massive gap in my life. Knowing he still was out there was almost unbearable. I couldn't stand the thought he was living the same life he always had.

When I first returned to college my prayer was to catch him and bring justice to his actions. Over the years, though, my prayer started to change. I started to pray that a door would open to show me where my heart should be, to guide me and lead me to take baby steps toward compassion. This was around the time in my life when I finally found peace, so I thought I might be able to take that first step. So I started to pray that I would be allowed the kindness, compassion and grace to forgive, because I knew at that time I didn't have that empathy and mercy.

I had to remember to trust in God. That meant every piece of me, every piece of my life. I had to trust the offender to the God of grace, the God of mercy, and the God of justice. When I finally chose to obey that command, something extraordinary happened.

It was around Christmas time. I remember that because I was sitting next to Kendra in church, and she was home only for the holidays. As I was reading the bulletin I came across something about prison ministry and an upcoming seminar. Ironically, I grew up in a county with thirteen prisons, both federal and state. If I ever wanted to get involved in something like prison ministry, this would be the place to do it! I never had thought of volunteering with a program like that, but for some reason it stuck with me. I looked at my sister and said, "I wonder who is in charge of that?" Kendra said, "It's probably the Gotts," who are members of our church.

I let the thought sit for a few days. The next week I called our church secretary to get the Gotts' number, thinking I was volunteering for the women's jail. I didn't think I would be a good fit for the men's prison, and I have to admit, the thought of stepping inside a men's prison almost made me pee my pants. But when I called, I discovered the seminar was for one of the men's correctional facilities.

Dick and Carol Gott were ecstatic that I had called. I told them I never would have thought I would talk to them – or anyone – about this, but there I was. I felt I was being called to do so.

I had been so frightened by the shooting that I could not even look anyone in the eye when I first returned to Colorado. I still was afraid, so I knew stepping into a prison would be a challenge for me. I knew I would have to keep my head held high. I also knew the person behind that bullet was not here, but he was my only thought when I considered the inmates behind these bars.

My perception of the human race had become distorted and twisted. I had these feelings about the one person who had shot me, but I allowed those emotions to multiply to every person who had committed any type of crime. I now saw inmates as subhuman, unworthy of forgiveness. I hated seeing others this way. I knew I was wrong, and I didn't want to continue to feel like that. I was being called to take the steps necessary to change that.

The Gotts told me about the seminar that was coming up over a long weekend. We would go into the prison once on Friday night, twice on Saturday, and again on Sunday. This would be a good way to decide if it was a good fit for me. They told me I could try it, see how I felt, and then go from there. I greatly value my parents opinions, so I told them about my decision and asked them what they thought about me stepping into prison. They were a little taken back but also commended me for even trying to do this. As always, they fully supported me.

I met with the Dick and Carol a couple of weeks before the seminar to talk about my expectations and the realities. We discussed appropriate attire and behavior, time and length of our visits, what I could take inside, things like that. I remember telling Dick, "I am really scared to go in, but that is why I think I need to do it." He reminded me that most of the men we would see also were believers. They were hungry for the Word. It was a privilege for them to meet with us, and they would do nothing that might take that opportunity away.

Then he reminded me that I would be lifted up in prayer. That rang a bell for me. I knew that was true! Another good thing I discovered was there would be many volunteers over the seminar weekend, not the usual group of eight volunteers during the typical weekdays. While I still was nervous, I left there a bit more at ease. Excitement started to fill me for what was to come.

The week of the seminar happened to be an incredibly busy time for me, which ended up being helpful on my nerves. I didn't have time to dwell on the weekend ahead of me. When at last the day came and I knew I would be inside a prison that evening, I thought to myself, *Maybe this isn't the best fit for me. Maybe this isn't the best decision for me. Maybe I shouldn't go.* I knew it was nerves and fear, but I prayed all day, *Lord, please keep my nerves calm. Please keep me calm.* And I trusted the spirit within me would help me to show the love for those who I may not have felt love toward.

Those I would have considered to be my enemies became friends, and the impossible seemed to happen. The people who I judged and turned away from were the people God called me toward; people who would forever change my heart. Together we were being renewed and set free! God continued to use any and every unusual circumstance to bring about his purpose in life, as I was about to be reminded.

Volunteers met at the church to circle up and pray. We hopped into cars and were on our way. As we drove past the security gate I didn't seem to have any anxiety. I had lived only ten minutes from all of these correctional facilities for most of my life and had never set foot in one, which is a good thing! I also realized I never would have thought twice about volunteering there, or anywhere else, unless I had been shot. It makes me sad to think what it took to make me reach out to help others. But hey! I finally was here.

I considered the fact I live in an area with all these prisons and now had an invitation to enter them. I thought about the wonderful couple who performs this remarkable prison ministry and just happens to attend my church. It speaks volumes to the Lord's timing and to me being exactly where I am. I didn't even have to drive an hour to get there. I drove a few minutes. It's not exactly a luxury I thought I would look forward to one day, but now I do. So we drove up to the correctional facility on the outskirts of Cañon City that night.

We went through the front doors, and I was surprised at how calm I was. We started through security as more volunteers showed up. My mind continued to ease as I saw more familiar faces. I became more and more eager to get inside. The first set of gates opened and I stayed calm, but a spark of nerves ran through my body soon after. The doors closed behind me, and the loud thud startled me – maybe because I have had heightened senses, especially hearing, since the sound of that fateful gunshot. The doors slammed shut and locked behind me. I'm sure that sound is a common one for the officers and inmates, but it shocked me. I realized I couldn't get in or out without someone opening the doors for me. I took a deep breath and found the courage to continue on. We walked through hallways and more barred doors to find the prison chapel.

I was surprised to see some of the inmates setting up for the evening. In fact, they even had their own worship team along with a few sound men. That shocked me! Most people on the outside, people like me, are so naïve to what life is like inside a prison. These men had worked for their sound equipment, guitars, and synthesizer, and had purchased them with their money.

We helped set up what we could and then circled up again for prayer before the men started to come in. The inmates arrived quickly. Most of the volunteers that accompanied me were seasoned. I'm sure I looked new, and the expression on my face must have been priceless. All the volunteers lined the middle aisle, and I made sure I had someone right at my side the entire time. Everyone knew this was a bit unnerving for me, and they tried to help take the pressure off.

Dick had informed me the men like to walk down the middle aisle and shake the hands of all the volunteers to greet us. "They just like to tell you thank you for coming," he said. But he also told me I didn't have to shake anyone's hand if I didn't want to. As the inmates started to make their way down the aisle, I moved back further from the line of volunteers and stood behind them. It had never been more apparent to me that they were the inmates and I was the volunteer. In my mind it was black and white, just like I had seen my shooter – completely different from me, with no connection whatsoever. They all wore the same color, forest green, and I did not. I was very aware of where all the other volunteers stood. I kept an eye on who was close to me and who was not. Some of the inmates saw me "hiding" and came over to me to extend a hand. I took the hand of the first man. He looked me right in the eye and said, with pure sincerity, "Thank you so much for being here. God bless you." I was taken aback by that. I don't know what I was expecting, but certainly not that.

More men continued to spill into the room. They all had huge smiles on their faces. They continued to take my hand and tell me how grateful they were that I was there, that we all were there. It wasn't an act. It was honesty. This was a special time and place for them, and I could tell they cherished every moment of it. The more hands I shook the more the ice began to thaw.

I had forgotten they were human. I don't have to hate them, or the person who shot me, but that doesn't mean that I agree with or like their actions or some of the choices they have made. I haven't been proud of every decision that I have made in my life either. Maybe these people had not made the best choices in life, but I realized I was a hypocrite when I said I love the Lord while I hated others. I'm not saying I hated these men, but I can say there was one person who I had no tolerance for and did not ever want to have.

After everyone had settled in, Dick went to the front and welcomed everyone. He introduced some of the new volunteers. I was sitting in the second row and stood when he called my name, but never turned around to look at the full room behind me. Then the worship team went to the front of the room to start the service. They began to sing, and I did not expect to hear what I did.

I have never heard anything like the joyous sound of those men worshipping. They held nothing back, and their loud voices echoed blissfully off the walls. Their hands and heads held high. Smiles spread across their faces as they shouted and sang to the Lord. I had a hard time focusing on my own worship, because I was so intrigued and in awe of the way they all worshipped. There is nothing like that sound!

After the first line of that first song a huge smile swept across my face. I knew I was being told, "Alicia, listen to this. Listen. I have you here for a reason." Once again I was completely taken aback. They worshipped with dancing and singing, and it was so apparent they love God. I didn't know why they had been incarcerated, but I did know I saw the love of God shining through them.

That first night we did not have much time to break into small discussion groups. I thought that was good for me. I was being eased into this one small step at a time. As we checked out and left, I wasn't fearful like I had been. My heart slowly was starting to soften, something that it badly needed to do.

I read something early the next morning before we returned to the prison. It set my pace for this day and certainly opened my eyes for what was about to happen. "No longer must we be held captive by resentment towards others when they hurt us. When we are resting in God's strength nothing can shake us." Although I have to admit at times I have, and I think we all have, we must never underestimate the power of Jesus to forgive and mend us back together.

We went back in early that morning. The men greeted us in much the same manner as the night before, but I felt completely different this time. Instead of hiding behind the other volunteers I made the effort to extend my hand in friendship. "Thank you for having me here," I told them. I was happy and grateful to be there. It was a privilege for me. I found myself thinking, "Thank you for leading me here, Lord."

Our morning worship began with "Amazing Grace." It was a reminder of what I had read earlier that day. Nothing has to hold me back. We are freed from anything that enslaves us, anything that has its grip on us. We are freed from evil. This truth sets us free and allows us to be all that we were created to be.

Soon after worship, we split into small discussion groups to reflect on the passages that Dick had read and preached on. There were between eighty and one hundred men there, so we split into groups of around twelve. There were between fifteen and twenty volunteers there. I was leading a group with another volunteer, John Sporleder, who is another member of E-Free. He also was my middle school principal. We picked a random spot in the room and sat down, and the men closest to us came in to join us in a small circle. Little did I know that the Lord was making sure everything fell into place just the way He wanted it to be.

I thought about the fact that a year ago, no, not even a few months ago, I would never have stepped into a prison. The night before I probably had been too scared to sit down in a circle with these men, but today I was perfectly comfortable. There I was.

We started into the study and asked, "Do you see yourself as a new creation? Do you see yourself as God's creation?" Every man in the group opened up, sharing his heart. I knew it was nice for them to sit and talk with two people who weren't their cell mates or someone who worked there, but every story that I heard left tears in my eyes. They shared openheartedly, with a stranger, about what their lives had been before they had come to know the Lord. It was apparent many of them did not have the upbringing I was blessed to have. They hadn't known the Lord. They hadn't been shown what true love was.

One man shared, "I don't have any skills. I have been a professional criminal my entire life. This is what I have always known." He continued to tell us how he had just happened to come in one day when John was giving the message, and it spoke to him. I smiled when he went on to say he used to make fun of people like us, people who are believers. "But now here I am," he said. "I am a new creation. I have a new life."

Stories like this continued to pour out. These men weren't looking for someone to pity them, because they know why they are inside. But they serve their time with changed hearts. As I heard more and more I was graciously reminded that we all do suffer in life. I think there is comfort in knowing that, and even greater comfort in knowing God is there to encourage and carry the load.

None of them could talk about their families without tears in their eyes. Many of them have lost their families because of the choices they have made, the poor choices. But now many have made the choice to follow Christ and because of that, they have slowly started to gain back what was lost. They had started to receive blessings.

The man sitting next to me shared that his father was a minister who preached the Word of God to everyone else every week. "But, when he came home, he beat us," he said. "I never knew what true love was. (realize how important that choice is. It is not your parents choice, or your brothers or sisters, or spouses, only you can make that choice) It took something as drastic as coming to prison to understand what that is." He said many people look at us in the "here and now," with no idea of where we have come from. "I'm not making excuses for the choices I have made," he said. "But no one has any idea of what brought us to certain points in our lives."

I couldn't help but think of my shooter. I knew he came from a gang background. He probably didn't have his parents around much. I'm sure he wasn't a believer. But what had brought him to that point in his life? What made him open fire with an AK-47 into a crowd of people? He had never known God's love.

Time was up and we had to leave while the men headed off for count and lunch. Most of us volunteers went to lunch together, sharing stories of our groups. I started to see that stepping alongside others to help, or even to be an ear for listening, made my own problems begin to fade.

Time went quickly and we soon returned for our afternoon session. We had another time of worship and then split back into our small groups. This time we started with the question, "How do you relate to the Lord in His suffering?" Many shared that they could relate to the thief on the cross.

One man named Greg hadn't spoken up much earlier, but I had noticed him because of his tattoos. He had three dots on the side of his eye, and I knew they meant "Mi vida loca," or "my crazy life." That was usually gang related, so naturally it caught my eye. I had started to pay attention to things like that now, although I wouldn't have noticed it just a few years ago.

He started to speak and openly talked about his time "gang banging," a term that made my mind freeze and my body stiffen. Greg had a big smile on his face and seemed to be very in tune with what was going on. I kept thinking, "I can't believe I am sitting here having a cordial conversation with him, with all of these men."

Shortly after we had moved into our small groups again John had to leave. He asked if I was okay by myself. I told him I thought I would be, and he agreed. He left, and I found myself sitting alone in a group of twelve men. Twelve inmates. Unthinkable just a few short days ago.

We continued to talk about our suffering in the Lord. As conversation started to die down, and with perfect timing, Dick stepped in. We had discussed whether or not I would share my testimony with these men, and I had just said I would see how I felt. If it felt right, I would.

Oddly enough, I was at ease by then. My testimony isn't a story I share lightly. Sitting here with these men was uplifting to me. It was God continuing to heal my wounds. Now, their forest green colors faded and I no longer sat next to an inmate. I sat next to a brother in Christ.

I turned to Dick and said, "I think I'm at ease enough to share a little of my testimony." Then I turned back around to face the circle. The man sitting next to me asked, "Just curious. You are very young. What made you interested in wanting to come in here?" I thought that was the perfect opportunity for me to share some of my story. I told them why I thought I had been called to be there. I probably told the shortest version I ever have told, but still was overwhelmed with tears. These tears weren't the hot, bitter tears of an angry young woman in pain. Instead, they were happy tears of the joy and grace that had been placed upon my heart in just the two short days I had been there.

"I grew up in Colorado," I told them, "in a Christian family. I probably grew up very different than most of you did." I told them of leaving for college in Arizona. "While I was there I was in a drive-by shooting. I was shot through the liver with an AK-47." At that moment they all sat back in their chairs with their heads dropped.

I told them it was a gang-related shooting. For some reason, I naturally looked at Greg when I said that. I told them I had spent a lot of time in the hospital and had just had my last surgery six months ago. I told them I had a lot of healing in my life during the past few years, but since the person who shot me never was caught, I never faced it. I didn't know how to deal with it. I told them I wanted to move on with my life and I wanted to forgive, but I had no idea how to do that. Coming there was the first step for me. I was brutally honest.

"I saw most of you as people who didn't deserve forgiveness," I said. "But I have been so humbled and touched by all of you here today. I have been so blessed, because now I know that isn't true." All eyes were on me as one of them said they appreciated my honesty. I saw their heavy hearts, and I started to cry tears of joy and tears for the release that was being given, that I had so longed for. One of them reached out and handed me a tissue. He asked, "Have you forgiven your shooter?" I said, "I haven't, but I am working on it. After coming here I know that I can forgive."

Dick had been standing there the whole time, which was one of the reasons I felt it was a perfect time to tell my testimony. He now stepped in and said, "You know, Alicia's story is the other part we don't often see. You all have victims, and I know we have prayed for them many, many times." I am sure that many of their victims seemed distant and far off, just like my shooter did to me. Yet it still carried such a mighty force over me, over us. Dick continued by saying it was just as important to pray for their forgiveness as it is to forgive yourself.

Another man said, "Forgiving myself is the biggest and probably the hardest thing to do, but when you can do that, it is like taking a hook out of your heart." They struggled with forgiveness just like I did. Forgiveness has the same meaning, and is just as necessary whether it is forgiving yourself or someone else.

Time was once again coming to an end. We all circled up and prayed together.

Justice must be satisfied, yet by God's grace it is not done out of poison and bitterness, but it is done in the context of love. What I witnessed that day, what I heard, and what I was about to hear was rectitude for me. It was done in the most unusual way, in the most extraordinary circumstances. It was not how I or the world would see justice for me as a victim, but it was true justice by His unending love and mercy.

After Dick lead the closing prayer many of the guys in my group came up to me and thanked me for sharing. I turned it around and told them, "Thank you for sharing." I don't know if any of them had an idea of the impact they had on me. How much, in just the few hours we had spent together, my heart had softened. I had found a compassion I never thought I could have.

One person waited for me until all the rest of the men around me had cleared. It was the man with the dot tattoos, Greg. "Your story really touched me," he told me. "It really hit home." He had to stop, because his voice started to shake and tears began to well in his eyes. "I am here for shooting someone when I was seventeen years old." I started to cry. He continued to look me straight in the eye.

"I never got to say I'm sorry to my victim," he told me. He paused. "So, I want to tell you, I'm sorry." The very words he, as a perpetrator, was compelled to say were the same words I, as a victim, needed to hear. The moment swept us both clean.

What was meant to harm me has been used for good. When we love and pray for those who have wronged us, evil will be overcome by good. The evil that had been planned out for me to be a victim has turned into the Lord's victory. My life has changed, utterly and profoundly. I once believed that dancing was my entire life. I lost that life in a moment of sheer violence and thought I never would get it back. My life now is fuller and richer than I ever could have imagined.

That profound moment taught me that the night I was shot I did not lose my purpose in life. Instead, I found my purpose in God.

A message from the Authors

IF THIS STORY HAS TOUCHED YOUR HEART and you feel led to lay down your old life and become a new person in Christ Jesus, we would encourage you to do that right now. We are all incapable of saving ourselves. We are all sinners; however, there is one who can save us! God sent His Son, Jesus Christ, to die on a cross, paying the penalty for our sin. Jesus came to this earth in human flesh; he understands us; he died for us; then, he rose from the grave. If you believe and trust what God has done for you, we would encourage you to pray this prayer. "Lord Jesus, I trust in you and believe that you are the son of God. I believe that you came to this earth to die for my sins. I accept you as my Savior and ask you to fill me with your love. I pray that you would help me live my life in a way that is pleasing and glorifying to you."

Alicia Brady was born and raised in Cañon City, Colorado, and is the third of five children. She has attended the Evangelical Free Church her entire life. When Alicia was six years old she began dancing and absolutely fell in love with it. By the time she was nine, she knew that's what she wanted to do when she grew up. Dance! She was passionate, determined and diligent in the pursuit of her dreams. When it came time to go off to college, Alicia was accepted the prestigious School of Dance at the University of Arizona.

Alicia was advancing towards her dream and loving life in Tucson, when during her junior year of college, her aspirations were destroyed by a sudden burst of violence. One night, while out with her friends, Alicia was a victim of a drive-by shooting. She was shot in the abdomen with an AK-47. Alicia spent the next couple of months in the hospital, fighting to stay alive as one medical disaster followed another. Initially, she had less than a one-percent chance of survival, but she did survive.

Although Alicia's body doesn't move like it used to, she is still dancing. This is just one of the countless miracles that God has performed in her life. Alicia believes that the Lord will use her story for His glory, and that she can be a voice of encouragement for those who are hurting.

Alicia says, "We all have struggles in life, and at times, heavy burdens to carry. Often, we have no control over our circumstances; however, we do have control over our reactions to those circumstances. When you look to the Lord, he carries you through your struggles with grace, strength, and perseverance."

Debbie Bell, a native of Colorado, is an avid lifelong reader and writer. She is married and has three adult children, two grown stepchildren, two grandchildren, and two dogs. She also finds time to enjoy local politics and is actively involved in her community through numerous agencies, organizations and associations.

Debbie has known Alicia and the Brady family for years. In fact, one of Debbie's daughters took dance classes and danced with Alicia in high school. A faithful member of the First United Methodist Church of Cañon City, Debbie also is a born-again Christian who believes all things are possible through God and His son, Jesus Christ.

photo courtesy of ed flores

CPSIA information can be obtained at www.ICGtesting.com
Printed in the USA
BVOW08s0928130913

331117BV00003B/10/P